GOD'S COVENANT PARTNERS

Dick Bernal walks what he talks, and he'll talk to anyone. Whether you're a debauched existentialist, a religious legalist or that person in the middle of the road of life struggling to hold on to God in a crazy world, Dick Bernal can reach any heart.

JUDGE REINHOLD
Actor

I have always found Dick Bernal's actions to be consistent with his promises. He manifests a childlike devotion and trust that is not only refreshing but also healthy in covenant relationships. Few men can maintain wholesome relationships as long as Dick Bernal has, and his witness proves what he has written. He will not only teach you how to fulfill God's promises in your life on this earth but will also lead you to enter into a special relationship with God. The one person that God called His friend was Abraham, because he simply followed whatever instructions God gave him. For the same reason, I believe Dick Bernal to be a friend of God's; therefore, whatever God shares with him, I want to know about. That's why this book holds keys to truths that will give you far greater insight into God's plan for your life.

KIM CLEMENT
Prophetic Image Expressions

Real friendship is a relationship made of mutual love, understanding, concern and trust. Real friendship is being able to, without fear of negative consequences, disagree without disconnecting; to share your deepest self without being judged. Real friendship is thinking of what you can add to a relationship rather than what you can take from it; what you can learn as well as what you can teach. Real friendship is knowing that you can count on someone to share warmth and closeness, whether or not you see or talk to them all the time. You can make or receive a call that says, "I love you," without wanting anything in return. Pastor Dick and I have real friendship—we have a covenant with each other. I commend his efforts in putting together this exposition of God's covenant with man.

SMOKEY ROBINSON
American music icon

Dick Bernal makes an important statement with this book. He reveals a misunderstood truth not obvious to the Body of Christ: God's blood covenant with us in exchange for a small commitment from us. It is encouraging that God's covenant relationship applies to all vocations and not just ministry. This book is deep but enjoyable reading. If taken to heart, it will have an enormous impact on any believer.

KEN ELDRED
Businessman and Author of *God Is at Work: Transforming People and Nations Through Business*

GOD'S COVENANT PARTNERS

BY DICK BERNAL

WORD & SPIRIT
PUBLISHING

Published by Word and Spirit Publishing
P.O. Box 701403
Tulsa, OK 74170
WordAndSpiritPublishing.com

Scripture quotations in this book are taken from the following:
AMP—Scripture taken from THE AMPLIFIED BIBLE, Old Testament copyright © 1965, 1987 by the Zondervan Corporation. The Amplified New Testament copyright © 1958, 1987 by The Lockman Foundation. Used by permission.
ASV—The American Standard Version, Thomas Nelson and Sons, first published in 1901.
CEV—Contemporary English Version. Copyright © American Bible Society, 1995.
CJB—The Complete Jewish Bible. Scripture quotations are taken from the *Complete Jewish Bible*, copyright © 1998 by David H. Stern. Published by Jewish New Testament Publications, Inc. www.messianicjewish.net/jntp. Distributed by Messianic Jewish Resources. www.messianicjewish.net. All rights reserved. Used by permission.
CSB—Holman Christian Standard Bible. © 2001, Broadman and Holman Publishers, Lifeway Christian Resources, 127 Ninth Avenue North, Nashville, TN 37234.
ESV—Scripture taken from the *English Standard Version*, Copyright © 2001. The *ESV* and *English Standard Version* are trademarks of Good News Publishers.
GNB—Scripture taken from the *Good News Translation*, Second Edition, Copyright 1992 by American Bible Society. Used by Permission.
KJV—King James Version. Authorized King James Version.
THE MESSAGE—Scripture taken from THE MESSAGE. Copyright © by Eugene H. Peterson, 1993, 1994, 1995. Used by permission of NavPress Publishing Group.
NASB—Scripture taken from the *New American Standard Bible*, © 1960, 1962, 1963, 1968, 1971, 1972, 1973, 1975, 1977, 1995 by The Lockman Foundation. Used by permission.
NCV—Scriptures quoted from *The Holy Bible, New Century Version*, copyright " 1987, 1988, 1991 by Word Publishing, Nashville, Tennessee. Used by permission.
NIV—Scripture taken from the *Holy Bible, New International Version®*. Copyright © 1973, 1978, 1984 by International Bible Society. Used by permission of Zondervan Publishing House. All rights reserved.
NKJV—Scripture taken from the *New King James Version*. Copyright © 1979, 1980, 1982 by Thomas Nelson, Inc. Used by permission. All rights reserved.
NLT—Scripture quotations marked *NLT* are taken from the *Holy Bible, New Living Translation*, copyright © 1996. Used by permission of Tyndale House Publishers, Inc., Wheaton, Illinois 60189. All rights reserved.
NLV—Scripture taken from the *New Life Version*, © Christian Literature International.
NRSV—The Scripture quotations contained herein are from the *New Revised Standard Version Bible*, copyright 1989, by the Division of Christian Education of the National Council of the Churches of Christ in the U.S.A. Used by permission. All rights reserved.
RSV—From the *Revised Standard Version* of the Bible, copyright 1946, 1952, and 1971 by the Division of Christian Education of the National Council of the Churches of Christ in the U.S.A. Used by permission.
WEB—The World English Bible, Rainbow Missions, Inc., Mesa, CO 81643-0275.

God's Covenant Partners
Copyright © 2022 by Dick Bernal
ISBN: 978-1-949106-81-7

Printed in the United States of America. All rights reserved under International Copyright Law. Content and/or cover may not be reproduced in whole or in part in any form without the expressed written consent of the Publisher.

*To the original covenant maker—God, whose
unending love for me has transformed my life and
brought me into an unimaginable covenant partnership
with the creator of heaven and earth.*

*To my wife, lover, friend and the woman for whom
I have the highest spiritual admiration.
She introduced me to the Lord, the church world and
what it is to be in agreement with the calling on our lives.
Without Carla, I would not be where I am today.*

*This book is dedicated to you. God longs for you
to discover the life He destined for you to live—here on earth,
and forever in eternity.*

CONTENTS

Foreword by Jim Brown 8
A Note on Bible Translations 10
Introduction 11

1. Covenant Introduced 14
2. Covenant with Adam: The First Family 28
3. Covenant with Noah 40
4. Covenant with Abraham 50
5. Covenant with Jacob 70
6. Covenant with Joseph 88
7. Covenant with Moses 101
8. Covenant with David—Part 1: Inward Development 112
9. Covenant with David—Part 2: A Time of Transition 130
10. Covenant with Isaiah 151
11. Covenant of Redemption 165
12. Covenant Sealed with the Spirit 208
13. Covenant of Prayer 222
14. Covenant of Wealth 234
15. Covenant Calling 255

Acknowledgments 268
Endnotes 269

Foreword

For years I have worked to stop gang violence in this country. Why? Because gangs kill innocent people, and gang members kill each other. They engage in all types of criminal activity. They negatively affect every aspect of community life. So why isn't society more involved doing the same? I wondered, *Where is the outcry? Where is concerned society?* Most of all, *Where is the church?*

To me, the church is the most powerful force in the earth. It spiritually affects millions of people daily. So I reached out and met with ministers around the country in search of a solution. I quickly realized that those I contacted were not going to address this issue. The reasons were very complex, and I came away understanding that they declined to work in "the belly of the beast" because it was dangerous. There was no promise of financial gain or glory. Sadly, I concluded that society-at-large had given up on these misguided young people a long time ago.

Then I met a man. Pastor Dick Bernal of Jubilee Christian Center. This man was the first minister to say, "Jim Brown, I understand, and I will help you in every way that I can." In spirit, he became my partner. He raised money for Amer-I-Can, an organization I founded to combat the growing violence and tension that continues to plague this nation. He also utilized our life skills curriculum among Jubilee's members and helped us institute that curriculum all over Northern California.

Violent gang members whose lives were beginning to change were invited into the Jubilee family. Pastor Dick not only opened up his church, but he also opened up his home and invited our young people to be a part of his home life, and to get acquainted with his family. He also introduced us to his philanthropic friends who stepped up and joined forces with the Amer-I-Can effort.

Many other ministries, following Pastor Dick's great example, have now started to work with Amer-I-Can. Pastor Dick Bernal is a man of God who shares his life with people, regardless of their race, color or creed. And he continues to impact the lives of young people daily all over this country.

I know this book is about God's covenant promises to man. Yet I can say that Dick Bernal's promises to me have never been broken. In fact, he has done much more than he promised.

Jim Brown
NFL Legend

A Note on Bible Translations

Because translations have their limitations, comparing and selecting specific translations was important in order to provide you with a broader understanding and perhaps a slightly different angle than you might be used to. When you have memorized or studied the Bible from one particular version, there is a tendency to become too familiar with Scripture. The Bible may lose its effectiveness and its message may become predictable. Please note that in places where the Scripture is listed without a particular Bible version identified, I paraphrased the content of the passage to make it appropriate to the story line, being careful not to change its intended meaning.

Introduction

There are millions of us around the world who are professing Christians. We rise early on Sunday morning and make our way to the house of God, where we usually begin our church services singing songs to or about God. Then we give our monetary offerings to God before the man (or woman) of God opens the Bible and tells us what he or she believes God wants us to hear. At the conclusion of the service, some respond to the call of God by going to the altar, and we all recite a closing prayer to God. We then leave church with the people of God and proceed to lunch—where we, of course, pray to God to bless our meal before we dig in.

We are the faithful . . . the devoted . . . the born again. But how much do we know *about* God? The prophet Isaiah declared, "My thoughts are completely different from yours. . . . And my ways are far beyond anything you could imagine. For just as the heavens are higher than the earth, so are my ways higher than your ways, and my thoughts higher than your thoughts" (Isa. 55:8-9, *NLT*).

Does that mean that we're supposed to worship God without knowing Him?

Being mindful of this admonition in Isaiah, I was baffled by the instruction found in the same chapter. Here Isaiah says, "Seek the Lord while He may be found, call upon Him while He is near" (Isa. 55:6, *NKJV*). Sounds confusing. The truth is, the Bible is not a mysterious book reserved for a select few scholars to understand. I believe that God wants to be known. And He wants to be known as our Father. Yet how does God, who cannot be seen with the natural eye, relate to man?

After nearly 30 years of teaching the Bible, I've found that a little research—together with conventional wisdom—brings tremendous revelation. Isaiah's often-quoted passage of Scripture has convinced perhaps millions of people over the years that it's futile to try to understand God. So their faith is reduced to "blind" faith: keep a stiff upper lip and press on; "*Que sera, sera*"; God's will be done!

"Do two walk together unless they have agreed to do so?" (Amos 3:3, *NIV*). God has chosen a term called "covenant" to restore relationship with His creation and to guarantee eternal life to those who call upon Him. In order for man to partake of this covenant, the New Testament records the ultimate sacrifice of God's only Son offered to redeem mankind in order to consummate the covenant.

Yet, when I think of covenant—the bond between two parties—I return to Genesis, the book of beginnings, where it all started. Here is the first time we observe God act or respond a certain way, setting up laws that will govern His dealings with man. The book of Genesis is essential for us to grasp because it sets the foundation for covenant.

In this book, with Genesis as my starting point, I will create a vivid portrait of God's redemptive plan for man by examining covenant as it unfolded through biblical history. I will include thumbnail sketches of individuals God chose to play significant, and perhaps not so significant, roles to illustrate the power represented in covenant.

Abraham, Isaac, Jacob and other patriarchs of the covenant were mere men who sought to understand and know God, even as I have. And in my own quest for God, I can relate to and appreciate the faith of these men. In their struggles, their mistakes and salient weaknesses, they wrestled with the reality of living their lives in covenant with the Almighty. Rather than viewing these individuals as stereotypical "saints," I discovered that they were just like you and me. Though they are a part of our spiritual heritage, their fascinating and inspiring stories reveal a message for us today—that we are well able to walk in the same covenant as they did.

My approach to life has always been very practical, down to earth and nonlegalistic. Therefore, I have sought to reach those who have had a hard time relating to "church" and to God and who are yet searching for truth. Pastoring is a people business, and I've discovered over the years while ministering to people of every walk of life that those who understand covenant possess strong faith. Those who struggle in their faith remain frustrated and waffle between the opinions of others, wishful thinking, and hoping and praying.

As you read through this book, take time to consider what you read. The books that have enriched my life are the ones I have personally embraced and not simply read and put on a shelf. At the end of each chapter is a section called "Life Lines," where you will find nuggets of truth that summarize the subject matter presented. I have also included questions and comments to assist you in reflecting on the personal implications of each chapter.

As a father, I certainly do not want my children to be insecure about their dad. Likewise, I believe our heavenly Father does not want us to constantly wonder where we stand in our relationship with Him. My desire for you is that as you read through this book and ponder its message, any doubt or uncertainty you may have had in your relationship with God will be replaced with a resounding affirmation of your rightful position in Christ on earth as it is in heaven.

Pastor Dick

Chapter One

Covenant Introduced

*I will not violate my covenant, or alter the word
that went forth from my lips.*
Psalm 89:34, RSV

Christianity must begin with the reality that God is good and that He wants you to know Him.

God certainly doesn't expect you to understand everything He says or does. (I don't know everything about my wife, but I know enough to have a meaningful relationship with her.) Yet God continues to reach out to man for fellowship, for relationship, for covenant. You can never have a close relationship with a God you can't relate to. Attending church once a week won't do it either. Our relationship with Him must be carried out in daily interaction with Him, allowing Him to be at the center of our life. Experiencing life with our Creator is the destined purpose for every human being.

Understanding that my heavenly Father was interested in a personal relationship with me was the beginning of my relationship with Him. Frankly, I wasn't sure why God would be interested in me, but I was willing to give Him a try. My impressions of God weren't exactly accurate when I first started this journey, yet I was willing to dispel the distant feelings I once had about Him. My search began by digging into the Bible to find telltale signs of God's past dealings with man.

The Bible is referred to as a book of covenants. It contains two great covenants: the second covenant completing the first. These covenants are referred to as the Old and New Covenants, or Old and

New Testaments, which form the text of the Bible. "Testament" is a weakened version of "covenant." *Berith* in Hebrew and *diatheke* in Greek both mean "covenant." *Berith* also means "to choose, select, nurture, to sacrifice for." "Covenant" also means "to cut where blood flows."

Studying the Covenants revealed many virtues of God's character in practically every encounter He had with man. "He made known His ways to Moses, His acts to the children of Israel" (Ps. 103:7, *NKJV*). That means that God did not (and does not) want to remain distant with His creation.

It is appropriate to mention at the outset that within the two great Covenants we will examine, there were different types of covenants entered into that are important to explore in order to broaden your understanding of this complex subject. All covenants were legally binding as God was solemnly invoked as a witness.

The principles required to operate in covenant will be illustrated throughout this book in no particular order. However, a believer's knowledge of covenant is without significance if he isn't able to embrace a meaningful relationship with the Author of his covenant.

The instruction and motivation needed to have the kind of relationship with God that connects you to covenant is why I have written this book. If you never get past the practical knowledge of most everything written in the Word of God, you cannot walk in the benefits or promises contained therein. Simply stated, knowledge translates into wisdom only after it has been put to practical use.

"The friendship of the Lord is for those who fear Him, and he makes known to them his covenant" (Ps. 25:14, *ESV*).

COVENANT LINGO

A first necessary principle to covenant is communication—the means of conveying thought and exchanging ideas and information with a sense of mutual understanding. I'll refer to this communication as "covenant lingo." In covenant relationship, one person cannot form a covenant any more than one person can form a friendship. Covenant requires a reciprocal interchange between partners. With time and patience, that divine interaction grows and forms a healthy relationship needed for a fruitful life. Let patience have its perfect work in you so that you may be established and strengthened in your faith (see Jas. 1:4). Without this foundational truth, your relationship with God will falter and become mechanical.

By definition, "lingo" is a specialized set of terms that must be learned to effectively communicate—like learning a language. *Webster's Dictionary* also defines "lingo" as the special vocabulary of a particular field of interest. The Bible conveys the concept of covenant in every book, theme and message—from Genesis to Revelation. Therefore, if we are ignorant of God's covenant lingo, we will view the Bible as quaint and irrelevant and, perhaps, neglect the value of covenant altogether.

What kind of lingo does God speak? It is the lingo or language of faith. What is faith? "Faith is the substance of things hoped for, the evidence of things not seen" (Heb. 11:1, *NKJV*). It is how the world was formed. Then God said, " 'Let there be light'; and there was light" (Gen. 1:3, *NKJV*). You see, God creates by the words He speaks. God looks into the future but declares it in the present, as though it already exists. "But without faith no one can please God. We must believe that God is real and that he rewards everyone who searches for him" (Heb. 11:6, *CEV*).

David of old was called by God in his youth, while he was still tending sheep. Divinely summoned into the presence of the prophet Samuel, David was utterly dumbfounded to hear the words, "Behold the king." But David did not immediately become king. Instead, those words would be tried and tested by David and prove to be true only after much training and experience. Yet, by faith, David was king the moment the word was spoken over him.

Gideon is another example to consider here.

God spoke words of faith into his life that at first Gideon wasn't ready to believe. To appreciate and perhaps relate to who this ordinary man was, eavesdropping on Gideon's conversation with the Angel of the Lord will provide clues. While he was hiding in a cave, threshing wheat in a winepress, the Angel of the Lord appeared to Gideon and said, "The LORD is with you, you mighty man of valor! . . . You shall save Israel from the hand of the Midianites. Have I not sent you?" (Judg. 6:12,14, *NKJV*). Gideon's cynicism is first seen in his natural reaction to the circumstances. "If God was with Israel, why were the Midianites oppressing us?" Continuing his dialogue, a more fearful Gideon emerges. "How and with what could I ever save Israel? Look at me. My clan's the weakest in Manasseh and I'm the runt of the litter" (Judg. 6:15, *THE MESSAGE*).

Ever feel like Gideon—small, insignificant and powerless when you were asked to do something for God? Excuses abound in the heart of the fearful. "Dick, I want you to build me a sanctuary, a lighthouse in the Silicon Valley" was the command I heard from the Lord back in 1993. With the economy on a downturn, and the price of real estate soaring, how in the world would this ever come to pass? It would have been easier for me to sit in my comfortable chair at home watching sports, reading the newspaper and living an otherwise uneventful existence, watching life pass me by. Would I be willing to pay the price to make a difference?

I didn't realize that my faith would be tested to the degree it was when I stepped out to obey God. Battling the Sierra Club, bad press and the U.S. Army Corps of Engineers, who wanted to turn our building site into a marsh for ducks, we faced many challenges on the road to fulfillment of the word from the Lord I received by faith. My journey was long and arduous, but the outcome was extraordinary. (You can read about it in my autobiography, *My Father Doesn't Own a Gas Station*.)

How could Gideon believe God's declaration to him, knowing full well that he was too young, too fearful and the least in his father's house? Nevertheless, God commanded Gideon to take the lead in defeating the Midianite raiders who swept into Israel's territory each year at harvest time, impoverishing God's people. God has a way of contending with those who contend with His own.

What was God going to do with a man who wasn't fit for battle, much less qualified to lead an army? God took a heavenly glance into Gideon's future and declared the outcome to him as though it had already occurred. The law of faith was in operation—which is the key to open the door to God's covenant. When man understands this lingo, he has an advantage, because he is able to connect to God with greater effectiveness.

Gideon stepped out in faith and obeyed God and gathered this fearful yet committed army of 300. Incidentally, the enemies they were up against were described in the Bible as "a swarm of locusts . . . their camels were like grains of sand on the seashore—too many to count!" (Judg. 7:12, *NLT*).

Nonetheless, Gideon and his men were poised for battle. Aware of Gideon's state of mind in this divine assignment, God continued to encourage him that the battle was already won. "The evening before the attack, the Lord sent Gideon down to observe the enemy's camp. There he overheard a man telling of a symbolic dream in which Gideon crushed the Midianites. A confident Gideon then ordered the attack, telling his men to suddenly appear waving torches, blowing trumpets and shouting."[1]

Panic and confusion seized the sleeping Midianites so that few of them were actually killed by Gideon's army, but far more were killed by their allies. As the report of Gideon's victory reached the other Israelites, they grabbed their weapons, pursued the enemy and overtook them in a valley surrounded by deep ravines. God made sure that Gideon's ragtag army of 300 was not able to gain victory without Him. And, indeed, shouts of victory and celebration followed. Amazingly, after that decisive victory, Gideon served as judge over Israel and ruled for 40 years.

God knows the beginning from the end. He knows our future. God knew that Gideon would win the battle because God would intervene to make it possible. God will tell you what is ahead 10 years in the future but will declare it as though it is so today, because God is in covenant with you. From the cradle to the grave, God sees and knows everything in advance.

These examples demonstrate the reciprocal interchange between man and God in order to fulfill His purposes on earth. Relating to God in a relevant way is how we all learn to defy the limitations that are often commonplace in our lives.

"Relate," part of the word "relationship," means to have a friendly relationship with somebody based on an understanding of the person or on shared views or concerns. After all, healthy relationships are built on strong communication. You don't have to be a professional counselor to know that stress in relationships occurs when there is a breakdown in communication.

When we learn God's covenant lingo, believing what He has promised may be a challenge at first; but the more we declare the Word of God and rely on Him to fulfill His covenant, our uncertainty, doubt and unbelief will give way to the miraculous!

BLOOD COVENANT

The Bible is considered a blood-sworn oath between God and man. The covenant in the Old Testament, between God and man, was sealed with the blood of animals; whereas the covenant in the New Testament was sealed with the blood of the Son of God. In fulfilling this Old Testament rite, Jesus gave us the "cup of the new covenant" of His blood, which was shed for our sins (see Matt. 26:26-29; 1 Cor. 11:23-26). That is why blood sacrifice is no longer required to atone for (cover) sin.

The spilling of blood, even when commanded by God in the priestly sacrifices, in the Old Covenant carried with it a certain element of sin, for all life is holy and God-given. As a visible reminder of our mortality, blood has been used in sacred rituals and magic to purify, to curse and to protect. Throughout the world, blood has always been a powerful symbol of both life and death.

What does the earth say about the innocent blood of abortion victims? Unjust wars? Criminal violence? The earth is groaning.

Earth "hates" the shedding of innocent blood. Somehow earth is programmed to respond to both good and evil. When Cain, one of Adam and Eve's sons, presented an unacceptable offering to God, but his brother, Abel, presented an acceptable one, Cain murdered Abel, and the earth cried out to God from the ground (see Gen. 4:10).

Every civilization in recorded history since Adam and Eve has instituted some form of blood covenant. Even today you can go to the remotest areas of the Brazilian rain forest, Borneo or Africa and find people practicing blood covenant in their primitive cultures. I was watching a television program one day. A film crew was on location in Africa documenting a wedding ceremony. During the ceremony, a particular tribe stuck an arrow in a cow's neck, mixed the blood with wine, tied the man's and woman's hands together and they drank this mixture. Although they were making a blood covenant rite, they probably had never read the Bible and knew nothing about Jewish history.

In the nineteenth century, a newspaper reporter from the *New York Herald* went looking for the famous Dr. David Livingstone, who had been in Africa for many years as a medical missionary. While in Africa, Livingstone owned a goat for medicinal purposes; he had ulcers and needed to drink the goat's milk. Everywhere he went in Africa, he took his goat with him. One day, he and his interpreter made their way to see a chief who was well known throughout Africa. His interpreter exclaimed to Livingstone, "This is the greatest opportunity you have, because if we can make a covenant with him, no other tribes will hurt us. He's the most powerful man in the land. Do what he tells you." At their meeting, the chief gave Livingstone his staff—an old piece of wood with copper around it. In exchange, the chief wanted Livingstone's goat.

Aghast at the thought of letting go of the goat, Livingstone struggled with the exchange, telling his interpreter, "I have ulcers, and I need the goat's milk." His interpreter begged, "Give him the goat. Forget about your ulcers. This is the key to Africa." Livingstone didn't understand at first but reluctantly gave him the goat. From then on, everywhere they traveled throughout Africa they carried that staff with them. When other tribes threatened to do them harm, they saw the staff and said in fear, "No! He's in covenant with the big chief, and if we hurt him, the chief will kill us."

David Livingstone didn't realize how strong covenants were until this encounter.

A covenant is supremely sacred, perpetual and unbreakable. It's the basis of every primitive religion known to anthropology. The Aztecs and Mayans were some of the most bloodthirsty people that ever lived. It was common in their rituals to rip out the heart of an enemy soldier and offer it to Quetzalcoatl or some such other god. Blood sacrifice was required to appease their gods.

Teaching people in heathen countries on the subject of blood sacrifice and covenant isn't a problem. They are more attuned to and able to embrace it than Westerners.

Why blood? Because the life of the flesh is in the blood. Also, blood has two basic properties: It washes (or cleanses), and it empowers. Blood covenant is the foundation of all biblical truth.

THE PASSOVER

Blood covenant is the basis of the Jewish Passover—a historic event from Jewish antiquity that is still commemorated by Jews the world over. God's chosen people were enslaved in Egypt under the strong hand of Pharaoh. Obsessed with the afterlife and with building pyramids as eternal memorials, Egypt's Pharaoh worked the children of Israel into the ground. Their bondage brought desperate pleas of agony to God, who heard their groanings and remembered His covenant with Abraham, Isaac and Jacob. God instructed Moses to liberate His people from the jaws of their bloodthirsty enemy (see Exod. 4).

Pharaoh did not want to let go of his free labor force. So God brought judgment for justice to prevail. Part of God's judgment was to release ten plagues upon pagan Egypt. God's chosen people were exempt from the first nine, but not from the tenth plague. The tenth plague was the death of all firstborn, including the firstborn of Pharaoh. The Bible describes what would occur when this plague was released: "Widespread wailing will erupt all throughout the country, lament such as has never been and never will be again" (Exod. 11:6, *THE MESSAGE*).

However, God gave Moses the remedy to insulate the Israelites against the last judgment: the blood of slain lambs. "The blood will serve as a sign on the houses where you live. When I see the blood I will pass over you—no disaster will touch you when I strike the land of Egypt" (Exod. 12:13, *THE MESSAGE*). This deliverance was a prophetic picture of Christ the lamb that was slain for the whole world and whose blood was for the remission of our sins. This was also a type of beginning—new life after Passover.

COVENANT VERSUS CONTRACT

Our world today is vastly different from the world of antiquity. With the advent of the Internet in the twentieth century, and other global trends that influence our lives through media and technology, we live in a fast-paced society that is consumed with the need for progress. While success and progress are not sinful in and of themselves, from God's perspective, modernity can prove to be distracting.

For example, today we use legal instruments called contracts that outline the terms and conditions individuals agree to when negotiating business, commerce or any other transaction. Professional athletes sign contracts to get paid—but also to protect themselves. Amazingly, the handshake to seal an agreement is virtually nonexistent today.

Contracts were invented by man but originated from the idea of covenant. The biggest difference between a covenant and a contract is that a contract guards and protects your rights; whereas in covenant, the other person guards and protects your rights. In addition, contracts can and are often easily broken.

When attempting to embrace biblical concepts that don't exist in today's culture, a believer can underestimate the pervasive power that a modern worldview has over him. A person's worldview, his or her perceptions, colors every decision. If modern culture dictates a person's worldview without any influence of godly character, that person will be hindered from forming a meaningful relationship with God. On the other hand, biblical paradigms are not easily formed in a society given to greed, lust for power and worldly pursuits. So it's doubly important to know what God's

Word tells us about how to live in relationship with Him:

> Don't become so well-adjusted to your culture that you fit into it without even thinking. Instead, fix your attention to God. You'll be changed from the inside out. Readily recognize what He wants from you, and quickly respond to it. Unlike the culture around you, always dragging you down to its level of immaturity, God brings the best out of you, develops well-formed maturity in you (Rom. 12:2, *THE MESSAGE*).

When God initiated a covenant with man, the covenant contained His unalterable commitment to supply grace and faith to man. Because this covenant between God and man was a lifelong pledge and often included one's descendants, it was not made quickly or without formality. Indeed, this covenant was a legally binding relationship, which was the highest form of mutual commitment.

A COVENANT CEREMONY

In biblical times, covenants sometimes included conditions, warnings and promises. A breach of a covenant between the parties was regarded as a heinous sin that involved punitive damages. At times, covenants involved mutual bargaining between the two parties; but at other times, God sovereignly administered them, as in the case of Noah and the Flood. To give you an idea of how involved these covenants were, here is an example of a covenant ceremony between two parties:

1. *The terms of the covenant were negotiated.* The mutual bargaining in the covenant between two parties included their families, who bound themselves together in blood agreements in order to fill the gaps created by each other's weaknesses or needs. Where the first tribe was strong, the second tribe was weak. Where the second

tribe was strong, the first was weak. Together, they were both strong. After their loyalty was sworn to each other, the families joined their names together as a permanent sign that they had become one.

2. *The parties prepared the sacrifice.* As the parties prepared for the covenant ceremony, they chose representatives and a place to cut the covenant. At least three large animals were sacrificed. Their carcasses were split down the spine and the halves were placed on the ground opposite each other. The result was a trail of blood between the halves. The path was called "the way of blood."

3. *The parties exchanged their coats.* When the ceremony began, the representatives exchanged their coats. This signified the mutual exchange of authority. By this act the covenant representatives were saying, "All that I do and all that I have is now yours."

4. *The parties exchanged their weapons.* Through this gesture they were saying, "My strength is now your strength. Your enemies are now my enemies."

5. *The parties then walked through "the way of blood."* Twice the representatives walked through "the way of blood." Then they would stop in the center. There they pronounced pledges of loyalty, making promises to each other that could never be broken. This pronouncement or vow was called "the blessing of the covenant."

6. *A curse was also pronounced.* The curse was the penalty for breaking the terms of the agreement. They swore by their God, thereby making Him a third party to the covenant.

7. *They ate a covenant meal together.* The covenant meal consisted of bread and wine. The bread signified their

flesh, and the wine signified the blood. The covenant meal represented their willingness and commitment to lay down their lives for each other.

The covenant articles exchanged had eternal significance. They were visual aids that provided object lessons that were effective tools to the learning process. (Their greater significance is explained in later chapters.)

We cannot develop strong faith without understanding covenant—otherwise all of our actions are emotional, lacking the covenant paradigm to guide us. If we don't understand our covenant with God, we're not going to understand God, marriage, loyalty to a church or the Christian life.

If a self-made man is told that he must depend upon the sacrifice of another, that his salvation is a gift he does not earn, that his pride must give way and he must cry out for God's mercy, he revolts. This biblical concept of covenant is not found in the psyche of modern man—hence, the urgency to recapture it in our lives.

Dr. Jim Powers, a dentist who was visiting our church, fell in love with one of our members. He was a deist, maybe even slightly agnostic. He continued attending Jubilee reluctantly by the urging of his girlfriend. He was studying for the California Bar Exam to become a lawyer and was studying contracts. From the pulpit, I declared that until you look at the Bible the way a lawyer looks at a legal document, you'll never understand it, because the Bible is also a legal document, and it was signed, sealed and delivered by Jesus Christ our advocate. Therefore, your rights are steadfast. Astounded, Dr. Powers exclaimed, "I have never heard a preacher say this before!" After that sermon, he began to read the Bible as if God was saying what was going to come to pass, and he found that God's promises were unbreakable.

The greatest covenant that was ever initiated, fulfilling all other covenants, is the covenant relationship between the Father and the Son, the ultimate *blood covenant*. God did not covenant with a mere man as one limited in vision and weak in fulfillment of that covenant. In the New Testament, God covenanted with the

God-man: Jesus! Therefore, we are united with God through Christ's humanity; conversely, God the Father is united with us through Christ's divinity. In Jesus, God and man become *one in covenant*.

If God is in covenant with you, what is God getting out of it? He should be getting *you*! What are you getting out of it? God, and everything God is!

A biblical paradigm is certain to give you a proper perspective of the "system" of our society. This is a critical key in the believer's life; the forming of this biblical paradigm is known as "renewing the mind." It will take time to pinpoint the areas of your life that are not subject to the Word of God and to adjust your thinking, but it is worthwhile when you imagine the freedom that comes with living and abiding in covenant relationship with God.

Life Lines

- The sovereign protection that the Israelites experienced in Egypt when the death angel passed in the midst of them is still available to us today. If you will by faith apply the blood of Jesus to the doorpost of your heart, you, too, will experience that same supernatural protection. No weapon or demonic assignment that is formed against you will prosper. Trusting, believing and obeying the Word of God are important when facing uncertainty!

- Gideon's experience reminds us that God uses ordinary people to accomplish His purposes. One thing that distinguished Gideon was his willingness to risk obeying God. If you are having a hard time obeying God, fear not, He will never ask you to do something you can do on your own; otherwise, you have no need for faith. Do not worry about the future. One step at a time is enough for God, and for you.

- The fear factor was a reality in Gideon's life. Even though Gideon and his men were afraid, they still moved forward, and God won the battle for them. Are you in a battle? Let God do your fighting for you. Remember, God made sure Gideon couldn't win the battle on his own.

- Gideon needed heavenly intervention, as we all do. Surrender your need to be in control to fight your battles alone.

- "Courage is reckoned the greatest of all virtues; because, unless a man has that virtue, he has no security for preserving any other."[2]

- The words "fear not" and "do not fear" appear 350 times in various forms in the Bible. Fear may cause you to question God in a matter, but the Word of God and prayer will help anchor you while you are waiting for God to intervene.

- Our society is alienated from the concept of covenant, yet we are called to live a covenant life before God and the world. Has the "world system" affected your perception of covenant? You may need a paradigm shift.

- When a believer is in covenant with God, he or she can cease striving and enter into a place of rest regarding God's plan for his or her life.

CHAPTER TWO

Covenant with Adam: The First Family

So God created human beings in His image. In the image of God He created them. He created them male and female.
Genesis 1:27, NCV

In Genesis, we are introduced to God's creation. God created the heavens and the earth; another name for these two is "universe," "uni" meaning one. The first chapter of Genesis provides the framework within which we understand the universe and man's place in it.

The earth was not designed by God to be fragmented. "Oneness," "unity" and "agreement" are adjectives used in the Bible to describe God. There is one God, one Lord, one Spirit, one Body, one faith, one hope and one baptism. Furthermore, "There are three that bear witness in heaven: the Father, the Word, and the Holy Spirit; and these three are one. And there are three that bear witness on earth: the Spirit, the water, and the blood; and these three agree as one" (1 John 5:7-8, *NKJV*).

Between Genesis 1:1 and Genesis 1:2, Lucifer and his confederates were cast out of heaven and ended up on earth. Darkness was found on the face of the deep. In Hebrew, the word "darkness" means misery, confusion, wickedness and destruction. It doesn't mean black. It infers wickedness because of the presence of Lucifer. In verse 3, God sent the Holy Spirit to hover over the deep; here God was beginning to restore the earth!

Prior to being evicted from heaven, Lucifer was an anointed cherub who had authority over the angelic community. The book of Isaiah reveals a cunning and prideful Lucifer: "But you said in your heart, 'I will ascend to heaven; I will raise my throne above the stars of God.... I will make myself like the Most High'"(Isa. 14:7-8, *NASB*). Wrong! These are the most deadly "I wills" in the Bible. God could not tolerate such arrogance.

Just as pride is the resemblance of the devil and what brought him to ruin, so humility is the resemblance of Christ, which exalted Him to honor.[1]

In God's estimation, pride is the most dangerous and deceitful sin of all. When Lucifer rebelled against heaven, from where did his rebellion begin? Earth. He came down as Satan—the beguiler, deceiver, accuser of the brethren, serpent and dragon.

The earth and the fullness thereof belong solely to God. While heaven is God's throne, the earth is His footstool. Jesus declared to His Father, "May Your will be done here on earth, just as it is in heaven" (Matt. 6:10, *NLT*). Earth is tangible, and heaven is spiritual; the former reflects the glory of the latter. Satan is the ruler of earth's *system*, not the ruler of earth; he gets confused about that. God's first human creation on earth would become the warden of earth, a kind of prison house, and Satan would be in subjection to his authority before the Fall.

When God created earth, He programmed it to respond to sin (introducing a kind of spiritual DNA to it). "We know that the whole creation has been groaning as in the pains of childbirth right up to the present time" (Rom. 8:22, *NIV*). Although I'm not overly apocalyptic, I'm not so dense that I don't also keep my ear to the ground to listen for certain events or look for signs that may reveal what God is up to.

Some embrace the theology that earth is irrelevant; it's only temporary, and eventually we will all depart for heaven in what is called the Rapture. But the Bible says that God blesses those who are gentle and lowly, for the whole earth will belong to them (see Matt. 5:5). Planet Earth is going to be our base camp. Therefore, Christians should be true environmentalists who take care of the earth, because one day we will rule and reign with Christ right here.

CREATION OF MAN

Adam was created in the image and likeness of God, and he was created to have dominion over the earth (see Gen. 1:26). If you can believe it, when God created Adam, there was someone on the earth that actually resembled God. The creation story reveals that the material God used to make man was taken from the earth; thus man's image and likeness of God was not in a physical form. It was man's inner nature that reflected something vital of the essence of God. It was that image and likeness that set man apart from the animal kingdom.

God's intention in giving man dominion over the animal kingdom was to care for and guard what He had made. God also put Adam in the garden to tend and keep it; thus Adam became the first farmer. God commanded Adam, "You can eat from any tree in the garden, except from the Tree-of-Knowledge-of-Good-and-Evil. Don't eat from it. The moment you eat from that tree, you're dead" (Gen. 2:16-17, THE MESSAGE). This was one of the conditions of the covenant between God and Adam. God's covenant promised him everlasting life based on his absolute obedience to this command. Obedience was apparently possible because Adam did not have a sin nature. On the other hand, the penalty for disobedience was death.

Who named Adam? God did. Pronounced *Ah-dam* in Hebrew, it means "face that is red like blood, flushed, ruddy." Eons later, the *last Adam's* face turned red like blood at Gethsemane, as blood ran down His face from the crown of thorns pressed upon His head.

In Greek, *Adam* means "firstborn." The first covenant began the same way the last covenant did: with the shedding of blood. Jesus was the firstborn of many brethren, and the last Adam.

CREATION OF WOMAN

As important as Adam was to God, He knew that Adam needed a companion. "It's not good for the Man to be alone; I'll make him a helper, a companion" (Gen. 2:18, *THE MESSAGE*). To create woman,

Adam was placed in a deep sleep by the divine anesthesiologist to perform the very first surgery on man. This was also the first place that blood was shed on earth. The significance of Eve's creation lies in the fact that God used a rib taken from Adam as Eve's source. (As the last Adam, Jesus had a scar from a Roman spear on the same side the rib came from to make Eve.) I believe that a deep sleep was necessary; otherwise Adam would have tried to dictate to God some of the terms of the first marriage.

When Adam laid eyes on Eve after surgery, Adam called her *woman* and she became his "helper" or "companion," which means "worthy of comparison, equal to: not under, but equal." By God's design, Eve was created to complete Adam. "A man's greatest treasure is his wife—she is a gift from the LORD" (Prov. 18:22, *CEV*). Woman didn't become Eve until after the Fall.

So here, then, is the sum of the matter: God, not man, created marriage. Marriage is the first human covenant.

THE MARRIAGE COVENANT

As the first human covenant, marriage was created before the Church. God wanted to establish the family before He built the first church. Strong families and societies are built on strong marriages. Not surprisingly, very few people are called to live a celibate life.

God named Adam, but afterwards it was Adam's task to name everything else, including the entire animal kingdom. Whatever Adam called a thing, that is what it became. Adam renamed his wife Eve, a beautiful, blessed prophetic name that means "mother of all living, life giver." Why did Adam bless Eve with that wonderful name—mother of all living? This was covenant lingo in action on Adam's behalf; an expression of *faith* always gets God's attention, and when God is pleased, He responds. Here, her name, Eve, represents restoration and forgiveness. Adam's strong *faith* anticipated with full assurance that God would implement this declaration.

Adam and Eve became "one flesh" physically and emotionally but were not considered of one spirit because each was unique, differing in personality. They were also created with different "plumbing parts" for the purpose of procreation. My wife, Carla, and I are very different spiritually and emotionally, like night and day, really. But when we came together, we became one flesh; and as a result, we produced two children, Sarah and Jesse.

Pure in the sight of God, Adam and Eve were not ashamed of their nakedness. Furthermore, they enjoyed an intimate relationship with God, without the rituals, ceremonies or religious works that usually accompany our modern spiritual quest. They had everything they could possibly need, even the manifest presence of God Himself: "And they heard the sound of the Lord God walking in the garden in the cool of the day" (Gen. 3:8, *AMP*).

THE FALL OF MAN

Satan, in the guise of a serpent, decided to go after the weaker Eve to disintegrate Adam and Eve's relationship with God. While in the garden, Satan cunningly whispered to Eve, "Did God really say you must not eat any of the fruit in the garden?" Casting doubt in her heart, the serpent hissed, "You won't die! God knows that your eyes will be opened when you eat it. You will become just like God, knowing everything, both good and evil" (Gen. 3:1,4-5, *NLT*).

The word "knowing" here means "cunning knowledge." Satan is subtle and cunning and wants us to be like him with cunning and skeptical knowledge. The word "knowing" can also mean intimate and sexual knowledge, as in Adam "knowing" Eve through intercourse. It's not that God didn't want us to have knowledge of sex, because sex predates the temptation and was perfectly fine with God within the covenant of marriage. He knew that along with the awakening of evil consciousness came the consciousness of guilt.

By questioning Eve about God's instruction, Satan impugned God's character. Today we hear the same voices clamoring, "The Bible was written by man; the Bible is an old book—you can't believe it. There are so many translations." This is where Satan uses people to question the validity of the authority of the Bible. Then man descends into situational ethics: "I can't believe the Bible is true, so I'll make up my own set of rules." Soon, man blocks out

God's influence in his life and, unfortunately, becomes a god unto himself.

"When the woman saw that the fruit of the tree was good for food and pleasing to the eye, and also desirable for gaining wisdom, she took some and ate it" (Gen. 3:6, *NIV*). Eating the fruit was pleasurable! Later in the New Testament, the first temptation of Jesus in the wilderness was with food: "If You are God's Son, tell these stones to turn into bread," the tempter imposed. Jesus didn't bite into the snare though. He answered, "The Scriptures say: 'No one can live only on food. People need every word that God has spoken'" (Matt. 4:3-4, *CEV*).

This encounter in Genesis is the first time Satan attempts to get someone addicted to pleasure, and he succeeds. This, too, was where the first lust for knowledge occurred. These seeds of knowledge replaced God in the forms of science, education and secularism. Not surprisingly, Eve wanted to be wise in her own eyes. While Adam had previously been instructed not to eat the fruit from this same tree, he, too, consciously chose to eat the forbidden fruit offered by Eve and thereby violated God's command.

There were other trees in the garden that they were allowed to eat from; but they both chose to yield to the temptation to eat from the one tree that was off limits to them. The *Tree of Life* was the centerpiece and crowning glory of the garden of Eden. Because God's nature isn't that of a tyrant, God gave Adam and Eve a choice; He gave them free will to choose whether or not they would come to the *Tree of Life* to partake of its goodness.

Naturally, Adam's soul was exposed and vulnerable to the woman he loved. He wanted her to be happy, which ultimately led to the choice that compromised the relationship he had already established with God. Perhaps Adam's reasoning hindered his ability to realize the extent of his actions before they were committed. Nevertheless, Eve's influence over Adam changed the course of history. But it's important to note here that even though Eve's actions were attributed to the Fall, the initial instructions to steer clear of the tree in question were directed to Adam, not Eve. "When Adam sinned, his glory was diminished, as was the perfection of all things on earth. The Fall, not God, introduced death and decay into our world."[2]

More than 5,000 years later, the apostle Paul revealed the harsh reality of man's relentless pursuit of knowledge as a result of the Fall. Unregenerate man is driven by an insatiable appetite for knowledge, "always learning and never able to come to the knowledge of the truth" (2 Tim. 3:7, *NKJV*). John Calvin, a leading Protestant theologian in the 1500s, said, "So it has happened that the mind of nearly the whole of Christendom has dwelt for generations within the structure of thought that took its architecture from this one conception of the sin of Adam."

Remarkably, man has not been stripped of the image and likeness of God; but the glory (or presence of God that Adam and Eve once knew) has been distorted through the Fall, and every human being now has a sin nature that hinders his relationship with God, unless or until he finds the saving knowledge of God in Christ.

"Death came because of a man, Adam. Being raised from the dead also came because of a Man, Christ. All men will die as Adam died. But all those who belong to Christ will be raised to new life" (1 Cor. 15:21-22, *NLV*). Some 6,000 years later, Christ—the last Adam—recaptured the ability for us to be able to have fellowship and enjoy the presence of Almighty God as the first couple once did.

The *Tree of Life* is available to us today.

Adam, the first man; Samson, the strongest man; Solomon, the wisest man; David, the "man after God's own heart"—all were brought down by the women they loved. When a man loves a woman and wants to please her beyond what is appropriate in the marriage, he will often acquiesce in spiritual matters. Be wise. Learn from others' mistakes.

In temptation, we are made aware of the ground of our own soul. When temptation exposes the stain and the roots of sin, then these are torn out, humility is born by the fear of God and we are urged to flee to God, to seek His help and to hand our battle against sin over to him.[3]

After Adam's and Eve's eyes were opened, and they knew they were naked, they sewed fig leaves together and made themselves coverings. Formerly, the nakedness with which they were "not ashamed" became intolerable indecency, and it demanded to be covered now that the consciousness of sin had sprung up within them. The word "covering" means "atonement." What were they trying to do? Their actions of covering their shame and nakedness with fig leaves revealed the first seeds of religion and good works. Adam and Eve covered themselves to appease their guilt. In any event, they still hid from God!

Fig leaves can cover up sin but they cannot save, because there is no blood in them. There are many religions that identify themselves as "Christian," but they circumvent the blood of Christ. Failing to reckon with this critical aspect of Christianity, these practitioners only want the teachings of Christ; they want to feel good about themselves but do not want to admit that they are sinners and need salvation. True repentance and belief cause one to conclude: "I'm a sinner and I need a savior."

At the same time sin entered the world, so did death—the spiritual state of those who are separated from God by their sin. The answer to man's dilemma was found in the shedding of innocent blood for the forgiveness of sin (see Heb. 9:22). This was God's way of saving man.

Which part of their bodies did Adam and Eve cover after the Fall? They covered their private parts; hence Satan succeeded in making sex "dirty" so that God's plan for procreation would be inhibited. Today, religion, and the Church in particular, still has a problem with sex. The world declares that sex is beautiful; but the Church doesn't know what to do with it. Ignorantly, the Church has taught Christians that sex is dirty, and many have suppressed the God-given gift of sexual intimacy within their marriage. On the other hand, some have taught that sex in a marriage is only for procreation, not pleasure. As a result, many fall into temptation and commit adultery.

Sex is beautiful between a husband and wife, and the marriage bed should remain undefiled; that's the way God intended it. At the other end of the spectrum, the world rebels against Victorian and puritanical ideas of sex and wants to have unrestrained sex.

Both extremes were birthed out of the Fall. But when legalism and orthodoxy cause people to go to one extreme, the world reacts adversely and mass-produces every type of perversion. This is seen especially through pornography on television and the World Wide Web.

Another result of the Fall is the lack of commitment in marriage. The idea of implementing prenuptial contracts prior to marriage lessens the value of what marriage was intended to be and indicates that many couples approach marriage from a business standpoint to protect their assets rather than as the entrance to a lifelong covenant.

When you enter into marriage as a covenant, divorce isn't an option. The commitment is "until death do us part." Now, that's covenant lingo, and it represents Christ and His undying commitment to us!

HISTORY'S FIRST SACRIFICES

Had Adam maintained his covenant with God, he would have abided in the full blessings of the covenant of life. But because of the Fall, man's rulership and dominion needed to be restored! God was still bound by His covenant with man.

It was time for Adam and Eve to be introduced to the plan of redemption. "Redemption" means to rescue, buy back, to purchase or to pay off a debt. The book of Genesis is the first place that redemption is found in the Bible. God instructed Adam and Eve regarding the cost of their redemption: They were to remove their fig leaves, because their self-made covering could not save them. Only innocent blood would cover their guilt. (This is why an ordinary man could not die for our sins.)

God moved on Adam and Eve's behalf and covered their sin by first taking two sheep and slaughtering them to make coverings of skin to clothe Adam and Eve. The two innocent sheep were history's first sacrifice. Adam and Eve must have watched this in horror. God then wrapped Adam and Eve in hot bloody lambskins and reassured them that their sins were forgiven, but they could no longer go back to Eden because of the judgment of their sin. Life was going to be tough, but God was still with them.

God introduced the principle that this same type of sacrifice would be fixed and permanent, starting in Genesis and going all the way to the Gospels, when the Lamb of God—*Jesus*—became the final blood sacrifice. After the Fall, man's sin would only be forgiven by blood sacrifice. Something innocent had to die to cover guilty man.

Now, in regards to Eve, "though your desire will be for your husband, he will be your master" (Gen. 3:16, *NLT*). God didn't curse Eve, but her role was diminished. Even though at creation both man and woman were formed with equal rights, she was now in subjection to her husband as a consequence of sin.

Adam and Eve were removed from the pristine garden to face the harsh elements in an alien environment called fallen Planet Earth, where the prince of the power of the air (Satan) resided. Tragically, the first divorce had just occurred: Adam and Eve were now without the intimate relationship they once knew with God. No longer were they in Paradise, enjoying the good life. After Adam and Eve transgressed, God cursed the ground. From that time on, by the sweat of his brow, Adam was going to have to work to eke out a living.

Some 6,000 to 10,000 years later, man continues to toil. We who live in the First World may live comfortably, but a third of the world goes to bed hungry. Third World country dwellers work 12-hour days for a bowl of rice. Why? The earth is cursed because of man's transgression.

The genesis of human life outside of the garden included elements regarding human potential for the best and the worst: from creating life to destroying life; from intimacy to jealousy and resentment; from appealing to the name of the Lord to lying to God; from living in the presence of God to alienation from God. Even with all the ramifications of the Fall, man had not yet learned what it meant to be in covenant with God.

Life Lines

- The cause of Lucifer's downfall was pride, and pride continues to be man's stumbling block today. Search your heart on a continual basis. If you find that you fall short, ask the Lord to forgive you and teach you how to be more Christlike with others. Attitude adjustments are important to spiritual maturity.

- The sinless nature of man created in God's image resided in Adam before the Fall but became flawed by sin in the Fall. From the Fall onward, we begin to recognize our own sin nature and that, as the saying goes, the apple doesn't fall far from the tree.

- After the Fall, Adam's attempt to cover up his sin drove him to flee from God's presence. Have you found yourself guilt-ridden in sin, fleeing from God instead of running to Him for comfort and forgiveness? The fear of approaching God will always keep you at a distance from Him. He is a loving Father who wants to restore you in those areas of weakness. Seek forgiveness and let the promise of God's covenant restore you.

- The covenant of redemption is God's idea. Fig leaves were Adam's way of covering himself in good (religious) works. Are you caught up in a performance trap that has kept you bound in religious works? If you are willing to surrender this area of your life, you will be reciprocated with a genuine relationship with a God who understands.

- When Adam succumbed to Eve's innocent suggestion to disobey God, their actions cost them the supernatural life they enjoyed in the garden. Do not fall into that trap;

seek the counsel and accountability of others. "Where no wise guidance is, the people fall, but in the multitude of counselors there is safety" (Prov. 11:14, *AMP*).

- In covenant, God always takes the initiative—the greater seeks out the lesser.

CHAPTER THREE

Covenant with Noah

Behold I, even I am bringing the flood of water upon the earth, to destroy all flesh in which is the breath of life, from under heaven; everything that is on the earth shall perish. But I will establish My covenant with you; and you shall enter the ark—you and your sons and your wife, and your sons' wives with you.

GENESIS 6:17-18, *NASB*

Not long after the Fall, the prince of the power of the air was busy contaminating the minds and hearts of the human race. One such example of his handiwork was his influence in the first murder. The venom of the "serpent" was poisonous and deadly, seducing Adam's son Cain to kill his brother, Abel, over an offering they both made to God. After murdering his brother, God inquired of Cain Abel's whereabouts. Cain's callous disregard for his brother revealed that the poison lodged in his heart continued to work with serious side effects. "'How should I know?' he answered. 'Am I supposed to look after my brother?'" (Gen. 4:9, *CEV*).

Another example of Satan's work was evident in the world in the time of Noah. Noah, the first patriarch to be born after the death of Adam, was unusually old by the time he began his family. Noah lived on earth 10 generations after Adam and Eve and 10 generations before Abraham and Sarah; so you can well imagine how much evil Satan continued to incite on earth, taking advantage of God's prized creation—man: "The LORD saw how great man's wickedness on the earth had become, and that every inclination of the thoughts of his heart was only evil all the time" (Gen. 6:5, *NIV*).

If you've ever wondered whether God has any sentiment as you and I do, the Bible says that it grieved the heart of God that

He made man on the earth (see Gen. 6:6). God's fatherly heart expressed sorrow for what the people had done to themselves in choosing an immoral and destructive lifestyle.

Carefully calculating His overall plan and considering the condition of the people of Noah's day, there was no hope that God would relent in destroying the earth; not even righteous Noah would be a shield against God's coming judgment. God had to judge sin in order to preserve the covenant He had planned for man. Recall that Satan started out right, but through his rebellion, he was thrown out of heaven. For justice to prevail, divine judgment had to be meted out. But one day, God knew, man would be completely restored in fellowship and union with Him as Adam was before the Fall.

We don't always understand the ways of God, especially in His decision to annihilate an entire population, but I know that the character and nature of God is love, and all of His actions ultimately stem from love. Although God destroyed the earth in a flood, He did spare Noah and his entire family. It is helpful to know that during this "dispensation," or divine management of affairs and events of the world, God dealt with man differently from the way He does today. Today man lives under the grace and mercy of God. In other words, when God deals with man in his sin today, His judgment is based on mercy and grace. This doesn't give us license to sin; rather, it reveals another side of God.

Before judgment was meted out upon the people of Noah's day, God's gaze turned toward Noah with favor precisely because his life was pleasing to Him. "Favor" means to treat someone or something with particular approval or kindness; to distinguish somebody by giving him or her something valuable.[1] Favor is the distinguishing feature of a believer whose life is blessed by God.

God's purpose for favor is not only for individual enjoyment, but also for accomplishing His will upon earth. Every individual receiving salvation has the potential within to be highly favored by God.

There are many ways to gain the favor of God, but one of the most important ways is when we, like Noah, learn to live the

Christian life in the midst of the wickedness and perversity surrounding us. But Scripture also gives a caution about living in this world. Jesus knew how critical the disciples' witness would be when He instructed them, saying, "You are the salt of the earth; but if the salt has become tasteless, how can it be made salty again? It is no longer good for anything, except to be thrown out and trampled underfoot by men" (Matt. 5:13, *NASB*).

Despite the passage of many centuries, human nature remains corrupt. Jesus warned that when He returns, man will be just as indifferent to God and just as wicked as in Noah's day (see Matt. 24:37). I've seen the descent of our society in my own lifetime: from *Happy Days* to evil days in 30 years; from *Ozzie & Harriet* to Ozzy Osbourne!

God gave us a permanent example of covenant in the story of Noah. His story is the first place where the word "covenant" appears in the Bible. God made Noah His covenant partner to preserve the human race.

THE ARK

God took great care to instruct Noah in every detail of the construction of the ark to preserve a remnant of living things from the great flood that was about to engulf the earth. Imagine! They were situated in the middle of dry ground, and there had never been rain on the earth. Mankind had no idea what rain was! God's mysterious irrigation system at this time included a mist that went up from the earth and watered the whole ground (see Gen. 2:6).

For Noah to take on the task of building the ark was a step of faith. The public ridicule and scorn that surrounded Noah and his family must have been incredibly strong and, at times, discouraging. "Noah, why are you wasting your time building this humongous boat—have you lost your mind?!" I am sure that others just ignored Noah, writing him off as a lunatic. Nevertheless, Noah continued to declare God's message of righteousness and impending judgment, and remained faithful to the task at hand.

The ark took Noah 120 years to finish. Imagine the patience God extended to these sinful people to change their ways. Uncertain of his future, Noah had to trust that God's plan for the ark was part of a bigger picture that he was unable to see at the time.

When the ark was finished, Noah loaded up his family, and the animals soon followed in formation, two by two. Many scholars estimate that almost 45,000 animals could have fit into the ark. Once they were all safely inside the ark, God sealed them in.

Then it began to rain, and the rain lasted 40 days and 40 nights. The earth responded by opening the fountains of the deep. Picture for a moment the waters slowly covering the earth as the days passed, and masses of people running in every possible direction to find refuge. The panic-stricken soon headed for the ark they had once criticized, and tried to claw their way to safety only to be swept up by the torrential rains that drowned out their voices. There was simply no way of escape. Every living thing that moved on the earth perished.

Apparently, no one outside of Noah's family believed Noah's message; otherwise, perhaps others would have been added to the ark. A vivid scene in the Hollywood movie *Titanic* shows a peculiar, yet similar, scenario. Unable to avoid an iceberg in its path, this massive ship's cargo hold suffered a devastating blow that sent the entire crew and its passengers scrambling in panic for their lives. As the waters slowly submerged this supposedly unsinkable luxury liner, it became the greatest maritime disaster in history. Lives were spared from that tragedy due to the use of life rafts that kept them afloat until they were rescued; in Noah's day it wasn't so.

It was not the ark that protected Noah and his family; it was the covenant he had with God. The covenant supplied everything that Noah and his family needed to survive the world's greatest catastrophe.

Noah and his family had been in their floating "zoo" for more than a year when the rains stopped and the waters receded. It was time for Noah and his family to disembark from the ark, along with the animals. They were now in a new environment, a fresh new world, to begin again the process of populating the earth. Noah was 600 years old.

AN ALTAR OF WORSHIP ON DRY GROUND

The first order of business for Noah and his family was to build an altar and offer a burnt offering unto the Lord. What was Noah going to do for food? All vegetation had been destroyed. Noah could take inventory of his animals for food, yet the first thing Noah did was take the choice animals and offer them to God! Now that was a sacrifice! Noah and his family were grateful to God and wanted to give their best to Him in worship and thanksgiving.

The first rite performed in the new world was worship. God smelled a sweet aroma and received Noah's sacrificial offering! Today we don't need to offer animal sacrifices in our worship to God. However, we are called to worship Him with our whole heart. "But let all who take refuge in you be glad; let them ever sing for joy. Spread your protection over them, that those who love your name may rejoice in you. For surely, O LORD, you bless the righteous; you surround them with your favor as with a shield" (Ps. 5:11-12, *NIV*).

Indeed, God was happy, and declared to Noah, "As long as the earth remains, there will be springtime and harvest, cold and heat, winter and summer, day and night" (Gen. 8:22, *NLT*). What God was essentially saying was that His providence would carefully preserve the regular succession of times and seasons and cause each to know its place.

God further promised that He would never again destroy the earth by water, even though man's heart remains evil. God's promise to Noah was confirmed with a sign: "I am putting a rainbow in the cloud—it will be there as a sign of the covenant between myself and the earth" (Gen. 9:13, *CJB*). God will never again judge the earth and its people with an all-encompassing flood. This promise included the animals that were considered a part of "all flesh." God cares for all life forms.

The matter of repopulating the earth was on God's mind and thus He instructed Noah and his family to be fruitful and multiply and replenish the earth. After the flood, however, the days of man on earth were shortened to 120 years.

THE PLOT THICKENS

Shortly after Noah's remarkable feat, the Bible records an indiscretion that occurred in the life of this righteous man who found favor with God. Noah was just as human as the rest of us and was affected by the aftermath of the Fall in the garden, even though his environment had dramatically been altered by the Flood. I draw the following point for those who aren't able to relate to Noah and feel they can't achieve the obedience, long-suffering, endurance and faith this man had.

Settling into his new life after the Flood, Noah and his family began farming, and they planted a vineyard. This vineyard produced some of the finest wines that even Noah indulged in—a bit too much, I'm afraid. One evening, while he was enjoying the fruit of his labor, he ended up in a drunken stupor and became "uncovered" in his tent (see Gen. 9:21). While he was passed out that night, in walked his son Ham and apparently Ham's son Canaan, and the two discovered Noah in his nakedness. Noah, who had kept sober in drunken company was now drunk in sober company.

Acting without discretion, they couldn't wait to blab to brothers Shem and Japheth. The matter entails not simply a breach of a son's fidelity, but the public disgrace of a father. Upon hearing about their daddy's shameful deed, Shem and Japheth immediately scurried to the tent, entered in backward with a blanket and covered their father's nakedness. A sober and shameful Noah appeared from his tent the next morning looking for his son Ham to address his careless behavior the night before. His fatherly correction to Ham and Ham's son Canaan resulted in a curse being pronounced upon Canaan's life. In antiquity, parent-child relationships were considered to be of the highest importance in Israel, which prescribed capital punishment for sons who rebelled.

This story illustrates a profound lesson on how we handle people's mistakes.

Most of us wrestle with the temptation to repeat things we hear about our enemies, or even, perhaps, our parents. Though you might be an eyewitness to another's weakness or sin and have cold, hard, documented facts, the trumpeting of another's sin is blatantly inviting a curse upon yourself. Your parents may have weaknesses that anger you, but to expose them is wrong.

Ham told his two brothers what he saw, which was an obvious violation of a natural law, let alone a spiritual one. What Ham and Canaan saw was true. What they said was true. One can repeat truth and still be cursed! How we handle truth is continually under heavenly surveillance. If you find yourself relating to this story because you have gone after another to expose his or her sin, beware! You could reap a curse upon your life.

No one's petty actions are ever justified when it comes to living above reproach. Christlike conduct and character in any given situation is important. Consider Shem and Japheth's godly actions in quickly covering their father's nakedness, honoring him even in his shame.

It was unfortunate that the curse came upon Canaan, even though his father was the one who did the evil deed. Why Ham wasn't cursed is much debated. I am a father, and I know that if my sons were cursed because of my careless actions, I would be in a world of hurt. Let's not forget that love covers a multitude of sins. There is a blessing in covering sin and a curse in exposing it.

Noah died 350 years after the Flood, at the ripe old age of 950. He was the last of the immensely long-lived patriarchs.

FAITH IN ACTION

Even though Noah had weaknesses, he knew instinctively that God was with him and that His Word would eventually come to pass. Noah's life was marked by obedience and trust; these character traits were vital links to fulfilling the divine call on his life.

How can we apply Noah's experiences of obedience and faith to our life? We all have to start somewhere. Trusting God as a young Christian can be difficult because you haven't yet built a relationship from experiences you can draw from. Even though the Bible is full of experiences that can become life lessons for us, ultimately the greatest impact God will have on us is when we have our own experiences with Him and build our own track record with Him. Then we will learn to appreciate and embrace the Bible in a more meaningful way.

You can be sure that God is faithful; but if you have no personal experience of His faithfulness to draw upon, you will be more likely to mentally agree with God's Word but lack the ability to move forward in action. Faith requires action and is risky. To borrow the words of experienced veteran missionary J. Hudson Taylor, "In your pursuit of God, if there is no element of risk then there is no need for faith." "Risk" means to incur the chance of harm or loss by taking an action. Rest assured that God will require your action as you learn to trust Him. There are no loopholes on the journey of faith. You will face hard times in your obedience to God, just as Noah did. But let me assure you, God cares, and He will bless you on His timetable.

The covenant that God made with Noah was designed to renew the original dominion of man over the earth. It was a covenant that dealt with the preservation, propagation and protection of man and culminated with the promise that God would never again curse the earth with a universal flood. Notice that God initiated the covenant and kept the conditions of it. It was totally unconditional, being promised not only to Noah, but also to all flesh. Though it did not deal directly with the redemption of man, it provided the necessary backdrop for further development of God's covenant of grace.

The book of Genesis makes clear that despite the purging of earth's population in the Flood, our world was hardly purified from sin. Noah and his family still carried within them the sin nature that was a consequence of Adam's Fall in the garden. If you couple that with Satan's invasive nature to kill and destroy mankind, then we witness God raising up another man who would be instrumental in his generation to establish God's covenant: Abraham, the father of our faith.

Life Lines

- Even in the midst of widespread wickedness, God recognized and rewarded Noah's righteous life. Are you surrounded by evil while trying to live a decent life? When you make a stand for God and live righteously, you may be ridiculed and persecuted, but God's covenant will preserve you. Meditate on Psalm 1.

- With the ridicule and scorn of Noah's contemporaries, they condemned themselves. It is no different today.

- Many are judged and condemned already when they don't embrace the opportunity of God's salvation.

- Has God called you to do something that appears ridiculous to others? Your faith will be tested at times; will you persevere and commit to put your hand to the plow until the job is complete? Many start, but few finish. It is more difficult to complete a task when it requires years before one sees the end result. Be patient! Realistically, God is more than likely working on other areas of your life in the process.

- It took Noah 120 years to build the ark. In that time, he pleaded with the people to turn from their wicked ways. God's patience with them demonstrated His mercy. Are you straddling the fence in your commitment to Christ? Have you been running from God? There is a window of opportunity for all of us to turn wholeheartedly to God; we have no guarantee of tomorrow.

- When Noah's son Ham exposed his father's sin, his son Canaan reaped a curse as a result. Consider your actions before you expose another's sins.

- Noah's experience should remind us that in our day, we, too, must deal with issues of faith, judgment and personal sin before the day of the return of our Lord.

- The creation promise to Noah provides groundwork for the covenant with Abraham. We will discover that the sign of Abraham's covenant—circumcision—becomes a sign for Abraham to keep; whereas the sign of the rainbow serves to remind God of His promise.

CHAPTER FOUR

Covenant with Abraham

I will keep my promise to you and to your descendants in future generations as an everlasting covenant. I will be your God and the God of your descendents.
Genesis 17:7, *GNB*

There is no greater example of covenant in all of biblical history than the covenant that God made with Abraham, the father of our faith. Abraham was the first patriarch of the people of Israel. As the father of both Isaac and Ishmael, Abraham is the common ancestor of both the Jewish and Arab peoples.

Abraham is not considered the greatest patriarch because of his personal attributes, but rather because he became the turning point in salvation history. In Abraham, we identify the role of faith in reestablishing relationship with God, and we are given our first glimpse of God's plan to restore the damage done by Adam's sin. There are many life lessons from this patriarch that can instruct us, some of which we will uncover in this chapter.

For years, I struggled with "father" Abraham because of my absentee father. My father drank and partied too much; he was also a womanizer, but he was a fun father when he was around. He had a hard time staying married and a hard time with relationships. My friends used to love to hang out with Dad.

I was raised by my grandparents, but my dad would visit every three months or so and promise that he would take me fishing on his weekend visits. To a five-year-old, that promise was the gospel. I recall a few times when I stood outside in front of our house waiting for Dad for eight hours with my fishing pole and lunch bucket, watching every car pass by, only to be terribly disappointed by the end of the day.

My dad would call me on the phone and say, "Dickie, we're going to the ball game next weekend." The excitement of spending quality time with Dad soon wore off when I began to realize that his promises were empty words. I was never affirmed or shown love by my father, and as a result, the image I had of a father was that he was there at times, but I couldn't trust him. Unfortunately, my father died an untimely death in 1970, at the prime of his life—age 52! The cause of his death was primarily due to alcohol and cigarettes—he smoked three packs of Camels a day.

After I became a Christian, I could relate to Jesus: He had long hair, was a construction worker like I had been and liked to fish, a sport I have enjoyed to this day. Oh, and He could turn water into wine!

When I heard about the idea as a young Christian that God keeps His promises, I thought, "Well, we'll see." I had heard preachers say, "God is not a man that He should lie." Every time I heard those words my mind immediately retorted to programmed thoughts of doubt and unbelief. It took years for me to believe that God would keep His word when it came to my personal life and needs.

I continued to struggle in this area even after becoming a pastor. I don't think I preached a sermon series on our Father God until 15 years into my pastoral ministry. Fortunately, a revelation of the Father's love for me helped break the cycle of pain in my life.

I have now come to admire "father" Abraham, because although he was a man with many problems and great weaknesses, he was a man who walked with God by faith.

When my four-year-old grandson, Michael, was about a year old, he was afraid of me. I would walk into the room and he would cling to his mom or dad. Later, when he was about two years old, he changed. It is perhaps not surprising that now I can't shake him off of me! I'm his best friend. Why? He lives across the street from me and is used to seeing me; he calls me up on the phone now! He wants me to come over and play with him and watch the children's cartoon program *Sponge Bob Square Pants* on television. That's the way it should be with our heavenly Father. We should be that close to God.

If my daughter and son-in-law lived in New York, and I was only able to see them twice a year, do you think Michael would be that close to Grandpa? No, because there would be less fellowship between us. That's the way many Christians are. They only attend church now and then, and when it's time to go to God about something that needs His attention, they are apprehensive and insecure because they are not quite sure if God is going to even listen to them.

THE FATHERLESS GENERATION

One day, I was talking with a couple of friends over dinner. I was curious about their upbringing, especially their relationship with their fathers. Mike Hayes told me that his hyper-religious father raised him, and Steve Hage said that he was raised on the streets and that his dad was a druggie. As we continued sharing stories about our childhood, I thought it would be a good idea to plan a conference dealing with childhood issues, especially about fathers.

When the conference became a reality, Mike and Steve came to Jubilee Christian Center and shared their experiences so that others could receive healing and restoration much like these men had. My son Adam, and sister, Juanita, also shared their experiences. It was a special time, and we witnessed broken families set free from generational bondages; many also experienced emotional healing from childhood traumas and abuse. This type of ministry is often necessary, especially at the time you begin your new life in Christ.

While the desire to procreate may be innate, responsible fathering practices are learned. "Most men long to feel secure in their manhood. But they are locked in, paralyzed by sin, overwhelmed by loneliness of their father wound and the emptiness of having been abandoned by their dads," writes author Gordon Dalbey in his book *Father and Son: The Wound, the Healing, the Call to Manhood*.[1]

When fathers are absent, children suffer. Today's young generation has become known as a fatherless generation. Without a father to bond with or provide the balance of a strong family structure, many teens are turning to other alternatives or vices to mask the pain and fill the void in their hearts. I have no doubt that fatherlessness is linked to poverty, high school dropout rates, crime, adolescent drug use and teenage pregnancy. These problems have become systemic as one generation passes on the legacy of dysfunction to another.

It is sad but true that 50 percent of the children in America wake up each morning with someone other than their natural birth father in the home. All too often this unrelated "father" figure does not have a strong interest in meeting the emotional and spiritual needs of the child in his care. A generation is crying out for responsible fathers and father figures to lead children to their God-given destinies.

Embracing today's youth is a priority at Jubilee Christian Center; we have built a state-of-the-art youth facility that provides a wholesome environment to build important relationships through social interaction, discipleship and meeting corporately for church. Making God relevant to their everyday life will provide the impetus this generation needs to change.

The idea of restoring the image of a father might seem foreign and unnecessary when you are approaching the subject of covenant. Many sincerely believe that what happened in the past should stay there—let bygones be bygones. Quite the contrary!

I'm living proof. I was married when I was 18. It was a "shotgun" wedding, if you know what I mean. It was the mistake of two young foolish kids. The fact is, however, that a beautiful son named Adam was born. I wasn't ready for marriage, and I wasn't a Christian. I was young, I was wild and I still wanted to hang out with my buddies. I wasn't interested in staying home and changing diapers.

Eventually, I was handed divorce papers. I knew I deserved it, so I didn't fight it. I shrugged it off until one day when I was out partying and afterwards a couple of buddies and I went to a local restaurant for a bite to eat. My ex-wife and a man walked into the restaurant with my son, Adam. It was as if someone had stuck a knife in my heart.

I should be that man, I thought. *What's he doing with my son? Oh, that's right. I gave up on my marriage.*

She deserved somebody good. It was a horrible feeling. So it is perhaps not surprising that what I hated in my father I had become.

As fate (or providence) would have it, years later I met Carla. And this Baptist girl introduced me to Jesus. It wasn't long after we married and had kids that we were off to Bible school in Oklahoma. When we returned to the Bay Area, we started Jubilee Christian Center. My life was now a whole new experience. But in the recesses of my mind, I still had regret for not raising my firstborn son. I guess I believed that that was simply a part of my life that would never really be closed; it was part of the fruit of sin, and my penalty for not being good in the first place—that is how I saw it.

I underestimated the goodness of God.

Thankfully, my son Adam has found it in his heart to forgive my shortcomings as his father. His story doesn't have a hopeless future chained to the bondages of past generations. Adam surrendered his life to Christ at the age of 25, enrolled in Bible college, and began working and traveling with me in the ministry. Our times together are now enjoyable, memorable and instructive, like a father and son's time together should be.

Though the moral fabric of our society is being torn to shreds, none of us are doomed to failure if we surrender our life to the Father of all fathers. You don't have to remain wounded, carrying the painful memories of your father issues in your heart. Forgive your father for his shortcomings and release the wounds caused by him to the One who can heal you. The power that raised Jesus from the dead is the same power that will break the spiritual shackles off of your life, removing your limitations so that you, too, can become the father your children need you to be.

Gordon Dalbey points out that Jesus came to reconcile humanity to the Father and that "nowhere else is the impetus for that reconciliation more keenly felt than in the relationship with our earthly fathers. That is why the enemy is hell-bent to make us deny not only the father wound itself but also the fatherhood of God."[2] Freedom in Christ comes when this truth is made known.

CHOOSING A COVENANT PARTNER

Back to patriarch Abraham. In pursuit of fulfilling His purpose to be reconciled to man, God chose a pagan named Abram. The meaning of Abram's name, "exalted father," is key, as names given to children were important to the Hebrew culture and family line ancestry. Names expressed character traits hoped for the child. "Ab" means "father" (*abba* in Greek). His name would later be changed to Abraham, or "father of a multitude." It is worth noting that throughout the Bible, God renamed key individuals to convey a divine personal message to them, to their generation or to future generations.

When God chose this wealthy pagan, He was aware that Abram knew nothing about covenant. Abram had no Scriptures to refer to, no believing parents to serve as an example. When God called Abram and his family, they were moon worshipers, minding their own business, living well in the land of Ur, in what is now Iraq. To make his life more complete, Abram had the companionship of a beautiful wife, Sarai, and was looking forward to having a son. But in all his wealth and pagan ritualistic lifestyle, he and his wife were unable to produce children, because Sarai was barren. All that this 75-year-old man wanted was a son.

Let's review this very ordinary pagan's first recorded unusual encounter with Jehovah God. When God approached Abram, He gave him several divine instructions. He was to leave his country, his father's house and his relatives to travel to an undisclosed location that would later be revealed to him. Imagine how Abram must have felt—he was challenged to obey not just any ordinary request, but a request that would affect everyone around him and test his obedience to a God neither he nor his family knew. Naturally, Abram would attempt to decipher and obey what God required of him and would be challenged to consider his family. No doubt his relatives had their own opinions and conclusions about what God had communicated to Abram.

Even when Abram left his comfort zone and his kinfolk and set out for Canaan, he took his nephew Lot with him. (Sometimes the greatest hindrance to your spiritual progress is family or those closest to you. They don't want you to experience any pain or separation in your life.) Abram left Ur but, unfortunately, brought his extended family along. Rather than go directly to the land God would show him, he settled in Haran until his father, Terah, died. Abram's initial steps of faith were painfully faltering and only partially complete.

I have to applaud Abram's efforts though! God still honored his faith. "Abram believed the LORD, and he credited it to him as righteousness" (Gen. 15:6, *NIV*). God accepted the sinner Abram and his natural faith in place of a righteousness or "right standing with God" that he did not have, and his faith was attributed to him as if it were righteous.

God also revealed to Abram His future plans for Abram's life, his people and the nations of the earth. "And I will make you a great nation, and I will bless you and make your name great, so that you will be a blessing. I will bless those who bless you, and him who dishonors you I will curse, and in you all the families of the earth shall be blessed" (Gen. 12:2-3, *ESV*). Here, covenant lingo speaks of the future. God was prophesying Abram's future should he trust God to fulfill the promises spoken to him. Abram must have trembled in his sandals when Yahweh spoke. These were unbelievable promises! It was hard for Abram to believe that God actually wanted to do these things for him. Recall that this man knew nothing about God, yet he was willing to step out and trust what he was hearing. God was building relationship with him.

Yahweh made yet another promise to Abram: "'Look now toward heaven, and count the stars if you are able to number them.' And He said to him, 'So shall your descendants be'" (Gen. 15:5, *NKJV*).

Abram asked, "How shall I know that I will inherit this land?"

In order to convince Abram that He meant what He said, Yahweh instructed, "Take me an heifer of three years old, and a she goat of three years old, and a ram of three years old, and a turtle dove, and a young pigeon. And he took unto him all these, and divided them in the midst, and laid each piece one against another: but the birds divided he not" (Gen. 15:9-10, *KJV*).

A blood covenant was in order. By cutting a covenant with Abram, Yahweh communicated His unfailing love and fidelity on a level Abram could understand. This was serious business! God wanted Abram to know, without a doubt, that He loved him and that He would care for him. By making a blood covenant with Abram, Yahweh further proved that He wanted to exchange His strength, His weapons and His authority with Abram.

The apostle Paul recounted Abram's faith in God, noting that Abram became fully persuaded that God was able to perform that which He had promised (see Rom. 4:21).

THE REAL JOURNEY BEGINS

The journey Abram took finally landed him in Canaan, where some 10 years later, God repeated the same promises He had declared earlier to include the promise of many descendants. Although Abram was old and his wife, Sarai, was barren, the Bible says that Abram believed in the Lord. Abram had been walking with God for about 40 years and still he had no son.

Abram's faith was getting a little shaky, and reasoning began to kick in. Sarai was more than likely feeling the pressure of her inability to bear children in a culture where childbearing was the primary source of a woman's fulfillment and self-esteem. Barrenness was an extreme source of shame and disgrace in ancient Israel. A woman who was barren was considered cursed. Was Sarai too old to bear children? They both were beginning to wonder.

Because they both believed that God would grant them a son, they thought it might be through the avenue of one of her servants. In those days, it was common for marriage contracts to include a provision of surrogacy should a wife be unable to produce an heir within as little as two years. Sarai and Abram waited at least 10 years before taking this action. Sarai chose her Egyptian servant, Hagar. Her servant had no choice or rights in the matter;

she was simply given to Abram. Although Sarai treated Hagar harshly, Abram tacitly participated as well. Consequently, Ishmael was born to Hagar, their servant girl. Nevertheless, the promised son would still come the way God had promised. Abram was 86 years old when Ishmael was born, and he had 14 years to bond with his son before Isaac's birth.

This father-son relationship had a bittersweet ending when it came time for Ishmael and his mother to be sent away. The rivalry that ensued between Sarai and Hagar was much too great for the two to remain in the same dwelling. Sarai repeatedly made reference to Hagar as the "slave woman" and had concern about inheritance rights.

Even though Sarai's actions were unnecessarily harsh, God revealed to Abram that Sarai's decision was right. Sarai's predicament would cause any woman to experience the same disappointment and justifiable impatience.

Later, Ishmael married an Egyptian woman, by whom he had 12 sons. God still blessed Ishmael, who was circumcised by his father in childhood. The descendants of Ishmael have grown into a mighty nation as part of today's Arab nations. "I will make the son of the maidservant into a nation also, because he is your offspring" (Gen. 21:13, *NIV*).

THE BARREN WOMB

Women played an important role in biblical history; many remained nameless in their exploits for God, while others became prominent figures influencing the way we see women today. From the widow and her small coin offering to the prophetess Deborah who judged Israel in her day, their undying love and devotion to God were evident.

Children, especially male children, played a more prominent role and were coveted because they continued the patriarchal family line.

There were many other notable women in the Bible who were barren and who desperately wanted children. They all eventually conceived: Rachel, Jacob's wife and the mother of Joseph; Hannah, Samuel's mother; and Elizabeth, John the Baptist's mother, to name a few. Hannah was ridiculed by her husband's other wife for her inability to conceive children. In her desperate plea to God for a miracle, Hannah's prayers were answered and Samuel, destined to become a prophet, was born. Hannah dedicated him to the Lord. God used Samuel to raise up a king for Israel. His birth was critical to Israel's future because of the condition the nation was in. "In those days Israel wasn't ruled by a king, and everyone did what they thought was right" (Judg. 21:25, *CEV*).

Jacob's first wife, Leah, was "unloved" but gave him six sons in hopes of gaining her husband's love and affection over her sister, Rachel, who was barren. Like Hannah, Rachel was also subject to ridicule and humiliation as a result of her barrenness.

In our society today, barren women turn to fertility drugs, surrogacy and adoption in an attempt to reverse their impossible situations. Barrenness in our society doesn't have as strong a public scorn as it does in other countries where women are ridiculed and ostracized for their inability to conceive offspring, especially male children.

Today, Israel's barren women arrive in droves to the outskirts of Bethlehem to pray at Rachel's Tomb, a site that has been venerated since at least the fourth century A.D. Amazingly, the Jews consider this tomb the third holiest site in the world. In desperation, these barren women bring their prayer books, handkerchiefs, their heartaches and tears, hoping for a miracle. Some weep quietly while others cry uncontrollably. And miraculously, many later give birth to children.

Several years ago, my daughter-in-law, Michelle, and my son, Adam, took a group from our church on a pilgrimage to Israel. While they were touring the sites, they came to Rachel's Tomb. Immediately, Michelle got off the bus, ran to the site and prayed for a miracle to conceive. Nine months later, she had my granddaughter, Hannah.

If you are believing God for a child, do not lose hope. God can and wants to bless you with children. Do not look at your inability—look at God's ability. Faith anticipates and waits for God, who is the giver of life.

My wife has prayed over many barren women who later bore children. If you have lost a child, give your hurt and pain to the Lord. The loss of that child is a terrible trauma that only the Father can heal. Never determine your future by the outcome of the present or the experiences of the past. I nearly lost my wife after she gave birth to our first child, Sarah; she was rushed to the hospital because she was hemorrhaging profusely. She survived, and that miracle not only birthed our daughter, but it also birthed our ministry. We don't have all the answers to life's most difficult setbacks, but we have confidence that God works all things out in the end.

SHE'S MY SISTER

Abram was as flawed by sin as any human being, but as he continued to persevere on his journey of faith with God, none of Abram's mistakes were fatal, and this is why he is a great role model for all of us who make mistakes.

On two occasions while in Canaan, Abram was terrified that the Egyptians would kill him in order to steal his wife; so he begged Sarai to lie about their relationship and claim that she was his sister (see Gen. 20:11). She happened to be his half-sister, because they had the same father; but she was, nevertheless, his bride. Being the submissive wife that Sarai was, she was willing to obey and protect her husband at the risk of her own life.

God was merciful to protect them both from the possible consequences. Fear can create a strong temptation to do wrong—whatever the motive may be. If you find yourself in a compromising situation, it is never wise to be untruthful, no matter the consequences. You can be certain that with integrity and uprightness God will preserve you.

Though our faith may falter at times when it is tested, as we continue to experience more of God's intervention in those weak areas of our life, our faith muscles will become stronger.

ABRAM GETS A NEW NAME

The 99-year-old Abram was still without a son. Again, God reaffirmed His covenant with Abram: "As for Me, behold, My covenant is with you, And you will be the father of a multitude of nations. No longer shall your name be called Abram, But your name shall be Abraham; For I have made you the father of a multitude of nations" (Gen. 17:4-5, *NASB*). In the 40 years that Abram had walked with God, God never addressed Abram this way.

On previous occasions, God identified Himself as *Jehovah*, He who saves; or as *Elohim*, I am the God who creates nature. God would now reveal Himself as *El Shaddai*, translated "Almighty." *El* means "all." *Shaddai* means "provision."

Although Abram was 99 years old, *El Shaddai* was great enough to do anything, including give Abram and Sarai children in their old age. God had already declared Abraham the father of many nations. This is the dynamic nature of covenant lingo.

The difference between the names Abram and Abraham is the "ah" in the middle, and it means "connected to God in covenant." "Ah" is the sound of God: YAHweh, JehovAH, YeshuAH. Other religions understand this sound of divinity: AllAH, KrishnA, BuddhA. Not only is this sound the sound of God, but in Hebrew it is also a connection to God.

My full name is Richard William Bernal. Richard means "strong leader." For the first 30 years of my life, I was not living up to my name, that is, until I encountered God. Then He managed to become a part of my everyday life, impacting who I was and who I became—Pastor Dick. And that is how I learned to be a leader, a father, a husband and a friend—so I can certainly relate to Abram's name transformation.

Abram's amazing journey of faith was beginning to take a new direction.

CIRCUMCISION

"This is My covenant, which you are to keep, between Me and you and your offspring after you: Every one of your males must be circumcised. You must circumcise the flesh of your foreskin to serve as a sign of the covenant between Me and you" (Gen. 17:10-11, *CSB*).

The time had come for the relationship between Yahweh and Abraham to become a partnership. Abraham was increasingly learning about covenant and drawing closer to God. Both were entering a dimension of covenant that would reveal their partnership in a new way. Abraham would inevitably become the father of a multitude of nations and the founder of a line of kings.

The agreement thus formed was permanent and everlasting; Abraham's posterity was to come within the scope of it.

This covenant of the highest spiritual fellowship between Yahweh and man would be sealed with the physical sign of circumcision. The cutting of flesh and the shedding of blood would validate the covenant. Why the male organ? Because it represents the fountain of life, having to do with procreation. Covenant with Yahweh had to be personal and sacred.

"And I will establish My covenant between Me and you and your descendants after you throughout their generations for an everlasting, solemn pledge, to be a God to you and to your posterity after you" (Gen. 17:7, *AMP*). This was the sovereign connection that Adam had in his original created state and which he lost in the Fall. This is one of the most repeated themes throughout the rest of the Bible. It is the theme of the rest of the covenants, regardless of their particular area of focus.

Circumcision was the most intimate and personal sign of covenant in the Old Testament—a perpetual sign by which God's people would be identified. For the Jews, the only outward covenant cutting was circumcision. Abraham's adult circumcision probably hurt! But his willingness to be circumcised demonstrated a higher level of commitment than, say, a handshake or a loyalty oath. To walk with God meant there would be some pain; man would have to bleed, and there would be a mark in the most private part of a man. Why? When it comes to the vertical relationship between *flesh* and *spirit*, between *earth* and *heaven*, the most precious and private thing we have is our walk with God.

The rite of circumcision was a requirement that included certain religious privileges. "No foreigner, uncircumcised in both heart and flesh, is to enter My sanctuary—no foreigner living among the people of Israel" (Ezek. 44:9, *CJB*). The fact that Yahweh only allowed the "circumcised" to enter His presence might provide more insight into why Abraham was willing to submit to circumcision as an adult. Circumcision was necessary upon arrival into Canaan in view of the possible intermingling of Jew with Gentile; the distinctive marks of the Abrahamic covenant had to be preserved. Israel's enemies, the Philistines, were continually referred to as the "uncircumcised."

Today, circumcision for Christians symbolizes the cutting away of the flesh-life, rather than earning one's way through personal achievement. "When you came to Christ, you were 'circumcised,' but not by a physical procedure. It was a spiritual procedure—the cutting away of your sinful nature" (Col. 2:11, *NLT*). An "uncircumcised heart" refers to a believer who is ruled by his flesh. As circumcision in the Old Testament was an outward sign of an inward commitment to become one with God, so we are called to fulfill this same covenant requirement spiritually in order to reap the benefits of our union with God.

The benefits of covenant commitment far outweigh the physical discomforts of the moment. You may be having a hard time with fleshly sins that seem to hinder your walk with God. Examining Abraham through the eyes of mortal flesh will help you understand that God is more concerned about your obedience to Him.

The Christian life is not for the fainthearted. Perseverance is a precious commodity not to be underestimated when you are attempting to overcome the life of the flesh. Surrender those weaknesses to God on a daily basis and become established in your faith. That may be a tall order for some, but at least you know that this supernatural life in Christ isn't going to come without some tenacity and willpower.

Abraham may have waited, but God answered—maybe not according to Abraham's timing, but He did answer.

God is not slack concerning His promises; He is faithful.

SARAI GETS A NEW NAME

"Abraham, your wife's name will now be Sarah instead of Sarai. I will bless her, and you will have a son by her. She will become the mother of nations, and some of her descendants will even be kings" (Gen. 17:15-16, *CEV*).

Sar means princess. The last part—*ai*—has a multitude of meanings, namely: injured, contentious, obstinate. Every time Abram called his wife by her name, "obstinate, injured princess," she was living up to that image. She was beautiful to look at, but she also was fruitless. *Ai* was replaced with *ah* in Sarah's new name, which now meant princess with promise. It also meant mother of many nations.

COVENANT CHILD—ISAAC

Abraham was 100 years old and Sarah 90 years old when God delivered the son of promise and God revealed Himself as El Shaddai. Abraham's understandable mixture of respect and shaky optimism exuded in laughter. At God's instruction, he called his son "Isaac," which means "laughter" in Hebrew.

Sarah proved that she too was just as elated as good ol' Abraham. "God has blessed me with laughter and all who get the news will laugh with me! She also said, Whoever would have suggested to Abraham that Sarah would one day nurse a baby! Yet here I am! I've given the old man a son!" (Gen. 21:6-7, *THE MESSAGE*).

Like any good father, Abraham was enjoying life, bonding with his covenant son, teaching and instructing him concerning Yahweh and the many lessons of faith he had learned over the years. His greatest joy was that one day he would see his son grow to manhood and become heir to his inheritance. Living under the magnitude of a calling that far surpassed his personal family life, Abraham had to wonder about some of the words God had spoken over him and how they would be fulfilled. Another visit by the Initiator of the covenant was about to occur. This particular visit would forever change Abraham's life and be the ultimate test of faith for him.

COVENANT SACRIFICE

Abraham's first visit with Yahweh required that he leave his country, leave his family and go to a land that would later be revealed to him. After Abraham had fulfilled these commands, God faithfully kept His end of the deal by giving Abraham the son of promise. Now, God was ready to reveal more pieces of the redemptive puzzle in the form of a test. Abraham was asked to offer his beloved son Isaac as a burnt offering on Mount Moriah (see Gen. 22:1-2).

The Hebrew meaning of a portion of that command actually reads: "I pray that you would do this for me." The story reveals that God's only desire was to test Abraham, that it was never His intent to have Abraham sacrifice his son. In other words, God was more interested in Abraham's willing submission to this test rather than performance of the actual deed. Therefore, God entreated, or pleaded, with Abraham to willingly follow His request. God had just as much at stake in this matter as Abraham did. God needed to know where Abraham's faith lay.

Though Abraham's heart must have agonized over this request, he didn't argue. This event is probably one of the most complex, mystifying and perhaps ethically troublesome in the entire Bible. History suggests that Isaac was probably in his early thirties, a full-grown man, strong enough to prevent the elderly Abraham (who was around 125 years old) from tying him up had he resisted.

Abraham and God were in blood covenant with each other, and therefore close partners, and whatever a covenant partner asked for, the other complied, as evidence of the covenant bond.

Abraham awoke early the next morning, cut the wood that was needed for the burnt sacrifice, bundled it and then set out with Isaac for Mount Moriah, a three-day journey. Ignorant of God's request, Isaac willingly helped his father prepare for one of the most historic occasions in biblical history. Geographically, Jerusalem is located 2,900 feet high in the Moriah mountains. *Moriah* means "seen of God" or "seen of Yah" or "watched by God." From this vantage point, God would observe Abraham while he was being tested.

When they reached their destination, Abraham left his servants at the foot of the mountain, affirming to them that he and his son would return. On the way up the mountain, Isaac noticed they were missing a lamb for the sacrifice. Inquiring of his father, Abraham replied, "My son, God will provide for Himself the lamb for a burnt offering" (Gen. 22:8, *NKJV*).

When stepping out in faith, not knowing what the future holds, it is easy to rationalize yourself out of following God's commands. The voice of reason will often ask, "Where is the proof?" before venturing out in faith. Faith doesn't grow in the realm of reason, where you feel, sense and see before the answer comes. No, in order to pass this test, Abraham had to resist the reasoning of a father and maintain his confidence in God. Abraham knew the promises of the covenant well.

How could the promise that he would be the father of many come to pass if Isaac was sacrificed?

Abraham knew that his covenant partner, God, could not lie. God had assured Abraham earlier that through his son all the families of the earth would be blessed. So Abraham therefore concluded that God would raise Isaac from the dead if He had to, to keep His promise.

Trusting God does not mean responding in an unquestioning manner. The dialogue between Abraham and Isaac doesn't signify passivity before God. Rather, the confession that "God will provide" suggests times of questioning and challenging God, as well as "blind" trust. Abraham does not simply obey—he obeys because he trusts. Trust must be experienced relationally, not legalistically.

Relationships will inevitably be tested and individuals will often experience situations where their loyalty is at stake. What constitutes testing depends on the nature of the relationship and the expectations the parties have. When the relationship between you and God matures and a high level of trust is formed, faithful responses to God's tests will become second nature.

The allegory culminates at the top of Mount Moriah, where Abraham built an altar, tied Isaac to it and stacked the wood around it. A sense of awe and fear must have overwhelmed this troubled father as he raised his knife to kill his son. It was at that moment that Yahweh summoned the Angel of the Lord to intervene, preventing the sacrifice of Isaac. Abraham's attention was immediately turned to a ram caught in a nearby thicket (see Gen. 22:15).

Relief and elation must have flooded Abraham's soul as he marveled at God's providence. Abraham immediately untied Isaac and pulled the ram from the thicket to prepare an offering in Isaac's stead. The thicket that entangled the ram is the same type of bush that Jesus' crown of thorns was made of.

Descending from the mountain, both Abraham and Isaac returned renewed. This indeed was an offering that had eternal significance. I would imagine they both reflected on and testified about this experience for the rest of their lives.

Yahweh had found a man in Abraham who would enter into covenant with Him and who was willing to sacrifice his own son for the benefit of the covenant. Yahweh in turn was bound to send His Son, Jesus Christ, as a sacrifice in order to fulfill His obligation to His earthly covenant partner! The significance of the promises made to Abraham is not merely historical or theological. As the covenant with Abraham developed into a relationship where he was considered a "friend of God," so also does the covenant we have in Christ's blood provide us with the same opportunity for this type of intimate relationship. Author Larry Richards wrote, "When looking back to Abraham and the promises made to him, we discover a firm basis for our own faith in God."[3]

Life Lines

- Are you struggling with the father-image just as I was? Whatever your upbringing, the father-image will be a healthy one or one of disdain. "God understands and cares" seemed like a cliché to me and evoked no understanding in me until the damage of that distorted, meaningless father-image was restored. I am certain that what

God did for me in restoring my father-image, He will also do for you. It takes courage to face your past; but as you do, I know that God is faithful and can surround you with godly role models or fathers in the faith to restore you.

- When God called Abram to covenant with Him, Abram was a pagan, much like us when we were called out of the world and surrendered our lives to Jesus. Ever feel like you aren't qualified to covenant with the Almighty God? Take heart from the lessons learned by this ordinary man turned extraordinary through the power of God.

- God works through complex situations and imperfect human beings to accomplish His purposes.

- The request made by God to Abram to leave the familiar comforts of life was a severe test. Letting go is hard. What are you afraid to let go of that you might learn to rely on God alone? Surrendering to God's will can be painful and uncertain; it is a gradual process that won't happen overnight. God will never ask you to do something that He is not willing to provide the ability for you to accomplish.

- Ishmael, who was not a part of God's plan for His chosen people, is a perfect example of what happens when man is impatient when God appears to be silent. Those years when God was silent on His promise to Abraham and Sarah were a time of discipline, not a sign of God's displeasure. God's silence caused Abraham to rely on his self-sufficiency. There are times when God will wait until it is literally impossible for your dream or promise to come to pass before He moves. Wait for His timing; God is faithful!

- Abraham was as flawed by sin as any of us. Consider your mistakes as learning experiences.

- Circumcision is fulfilled for us today when we lay aside fleshly habits and vices that hinder us from pursuing the ultimate union with our Savior.

- Isaac's miracle birth was a lesson in God's faithfulness. "Anyone who comes to him must believe that he exists and that he rewards those who earnestly seek him" (Heb. 11:6, *NIV*). Believing is essential to receiving. If you are barren, through faith and patience you, too, can give birth to your "Isaac."

- Abraham's life demonstrates that patience is an important part of faith.

- There is a faith that goes beyond believing that God will someday do something important in our life. It is faith that realizes God is calling us to significance now.

- The goal of covenant is to provide a display of divine power through man that ultimately brings glory to God.

CHAPTER FIVE

COVENANT WITH JACOB

*And the Lord appeared to him the same night and said,
I am the God of Abraham, your father. Fear not, for I am with you
and will favor you with blessings and multiply your descendants
for the sake of My servant Abraham.*

GENESIS 26:24, AMP

The next patriarch profiled in our line-up is Isaac's son, Jacob. You recall that Isaac was the miracle child spared on Mount Moriah, being his father, Abraham's, most notable sacrificial offering. Jacob was also a miracle child; but of all the patriarchs, Jacob was one of the most dysfunctional. He possessed a shady character that got him into trouble on more than one occasion.

The highly dramatic story of Jacob's life was marked by conflict and struggle. There were tense moments of sibling rivalry, conspiracy, favoritism and disdain for God's covenant that was passed on to a man known for his cunning and impetuous nature. Jacob's story reveals the depravity of human nature when it is not harnessed by the Lord.

One might wonder what was Jacob's "claim to fame." Believe it or not, Jacob had a prominent role in Jewish history, having fathered 12 sons who became the 12 tribes of Israel. How Jacob became the father of the 12 tribes was not by his own design or by chance. God knew that Jacob would be suited for the job, but He wasn't relying on Jacob's fleshly schemes to do it. By the time God was through with him, Jacob became one of the greatest examples of character restoration in Scripture, proving that we don't have to remain enslaved to the vices that control us. There is much to be said about Jacob's twin brother, Esau, who is covered in this chapter as well. The character analysis of these twins is sure to relate to all of us in one area or another.

THE BIRTH OF TWO NATIONS

Twenty years into marriage, Isaac's wife, Rebekah, was still barren; so Isaac pleaded with God for a child. God answered his plea and, to their surprise, Rebekah was pregnant with twins. Throughout her pregnancy, Rebekah was troubled because she could feel the twins in a constant struggle within her womb, so much so that she began to inquire of the Lord as to why this was so. She was amazed by God's reply: "Two nations are in your womb, two peoples shall be separated from your body; And one people shall be stronger than the other; And the older shall serve the younger" (Gen. 25:23, *NASB*). (This struggle between Jacob and Esau in the womb symbolizes the struggle between the kingdom of God and the kingdom of Satan.)

When Rebekah was ready to give birth, the first baby to come forth was the stronger, Esau; but on the heels of his birth, Jacob followed—literally. This was indeed a message that symbolized younger Jacob's pursuit of the older brother's birthright and blessing. Though they were twins, their traits were as different as night and day. Esau was a man of the world, a true outdoorsman, while Jacob was like his father, with a quiet and gentle disposition, who became a tent dweller and a shepherd. The brothers had nothing in common and didn't appear to get along growing up. The Bible clearly states that Rebekah loved Jacob more than Esau, and that the firstborn, Esau, was favored by his father.

ESAU GETS STEWED

One day, when Esau returned from hunting, he was famished and felt faint. Smelling the aroma of food being prepared in their makeshift kitchen, he saw Jacob cooking stew. "Hey, Jacob, can I have a bowl of that savory stew you're making?" Esau asked. "I'm famished. I haven't had a thing to eat all day." Instead of obliging Esau's simple request, Jacob manipulated the situation by proposing a trade: the stew for Esau's birthright. Being largely a creature of impulse, Esau was ready to satisfy his desire of the moment without regard for the consequences. Esau's willingness to easily abandon his birthright also showed how indifferent he was to spiritual matters as well.

By reducing the birthright exchange to a meal of stew, they both lowered themselves, much like Judas did when he accepted a bribe of 30 pieces of silver in exchange for identifying Jesus to His captors (see Matt. 26:14-16).

It would be wrong to suppose at this point that Jacob had a personal relationship with God. But what Jacob did have was enough faith to see the value of the spiritual.

A BLESSING IN DISGUISE

The aging Isaac, who had lost his eyesight by this time, believed that his death was near, so cultural tradition compelled him to bless his eldest son, Esau. He sent for Esau, giving him specific instructions to go out and capture some game and prepare his favorite meal so that afterward Isaac could pronounce the covenant blessing on him. The meal was an integral part of the blessing ritual, without which it would not have been valid.

Rebekah was within earshot of that intimate conversation when she began to conspire with Jacob to quash Isaac's intentions. Rebekah's determined and deceptive coaxing of her son Jacob into pretending to be his brother played right into her scheme. Now that Esau was gone hunting, Rebekah immediately prepared the meal for Jacob to present to her husband before Esau returned.

Blind Isaac blessed Jacob (thinking he was Esau) with a double portion of the paternal inheritance, the priestly office of the family, and the promise of the Seed in which all nations of the earth were to be blessed.[1] Jacob willingly deceived his father by taking the blessing that Isaac had meant for Esau. When Isaac realized that he had been hoodwinked by his wife and by his clever son Jacob, he bowed to God's will and confirmed the covenant to Jacob.

Meanwhile, Esau returned to his father's tent and prepared a savory stew with the game he captured. Anxiously waiting on his father to eat, Esau reminded Isaac of the blessing but was told that Jacob had cunningly deceived him and hurriedly took it before he returned. After begging his father for the blessing, Esau wept bitterly because even though his father blessed him with the promise that his dwelling would be of the wealth of the earth, he also declared that Jacob would be his master.

Despite the fact that Esau was only seconds older than Jacob, and thus the eldest, God intended the younger Jacob to inherit the covenant promise He had given to Abraham. This covenant, you will recall, was made known to Rebekah before the brothers were born. But rather than patiently waiting for God to work this out, Jacob and his mother took matters into their own hands. Rebekah and Jacob's deceit gained them their objective, but at a terrible price. While their actions can be explained, can they be justified? God chooses to work in and through what man makes available to Him. This reveals a risk on God's part; it links Him with people whose reputations are not stellar and opens God's ways to the world of public scrutiny and sharp criticism.

Because Esau was rejected, he held resentment and anger toward his parents and his brother. Esau's hatred resulted in a death threat against Jacob that he intended to carry out after their father died. As a result, and at the suggestion of Rebekah, Isaac sent Jacob away, apparently to obtain a bride from her own family back in Haran. "Little did Rebekah realize when she plotted with Jacob that once her best loved son left home, she would never see him again. Jacob was gone from Canaan for twenty years, during which time his mother died."[2]

Even though Jacob departed with his father's blessing, he would bear the burden of the devious acts he had committed against his brother, Esau, and it would later revisit him in a haunting way.

A DIVINE COURSE OF INSTRUCTION

Determined to start a new chapter in his life and gain a fresh start, Jacob headed for Uncle Laban's to find a suitable cousin to take for a wife. While making the journey to Haran, some 400 miles away, he made a pit stop and pitched his tent under a shaded tree to retire for the evening. As he lay there sleeping, he had a significant dream. In the dream he observed angels coming and going between heaven and earth by the use of a ladder, with God directing the divine flow of traffic. In the dream, God promised Jacob the same blessings He had earlier promised to Abraham and Isaac.

When Jacob awoke from the dream, he was inspired and encouraged, feeling new confidence that the Lord was with him despite the guilt he felt leaving his furious brother behind. He then made a vow: "If God will be with me and will keep me in this way that I go and will give me food to eat and clothing to wear, So that I may come again to my father's house in peace, then the Lord shall be my God" (Gen. 28:20-21, *AMP*).

This experience partially convinced Jacob to trust the Lord with his brother and his future. Although this vow sounds self-serving and lacking in maturity, God was merciful and willing to teach Jacob the true nature of a relationship that still needed development. It was then that God began to bring Jacob under a divine course of training and instruction. Previously, he had referred to the Lord as "your" God, but Jacob was beginning to realize just who he was contending with.

This was the first significant step in welcoming God into his life for the arduous journey ahead. Like our own first steps in learning how to walk with God, this one seems to have been taken for selfish reasons—a conditional surrender, you might say.

BELABORING FOR LABAN

Jacob finally arrived at the hometown of Rebekah's brother, Laban. He stopped by the local well to fetch a drink of water from a commoner who happened to be there for the same reason. As he stood by the well, his cousin Rachel approached the well from afar to give her father's thirsty sheep a drink. The Bible says that when Jacob saw Rachel, he was captivated by her beauty and kissed her.

As the story goes, Laban took his nephew in and soon Jacob fell deeply in love with Rachel. Lacking a dowry, Laban agreed to marry off his younger daughter, Rachel, to Jacob in exchange for seven years of work. Jacob agreed and the time seemed to fly by because they were both in love. However, Jacob was about to reap some consequences for the bad seeds he had sown in his father's house with Esau. God used Uncle Laban to do some much-needed character building in Jacob's life.

At the end of seven years, it was time for a wedding celebration. However, a greedy and crafty Laban had a plan up his sleeve: "I will substitute my oldest daughter, Leah, for Rachel, and he won't know the difference until after it's over. By then, I will demand of him another seven years to marry Rachel." When the festivities were over, Jacob was ready to consummate his marriage with the love of his life, Rachel. When he entered the nuptial tent, Leah was dressed for the occasion. She had a veil covering her face and a candle dimly lighting the room while she lay under the canopy of their bed anxiously waiting for her new husband. The ambiance was perfectly staged for a ravished lover to satisfy his longing for the wife of his youth.

When dawn came, Jacob discovered that he had been deceived by Laban's plot and stormed out of the tent to confront his uncle, leaving a distressed and rejected Leah behind. Jacob went from wedding bliss to wedding blues. Laban made the excuse that it was their custom to marry off the eldest child first. Laban's plan went off without a hitch. By withholding Rachel, he extracted seven more years of labor from Jacob.

The younger son who schemed to pass himself off as the elder brother had been fooled into taking the older daughter in place of the younger. The son who took advantage of his father's blindness had himself been blinded.

Shortly after Jacob married Leah, Laban gave him Rachel's hand in marriage. Leah knew that her husband did not love her, and it was an unbearable rejection for her. Leah's jealousy blindsided and deceived her into thinking that if she bore sons for Jacob he would reciprocate by giving her the love she was starving for. Providence intervened, and she bore him six sons and his only daughter, Dinah. The names she gave to several of her sons reflected her dwindling hope to win her husband's affections. Laban, a scheming, greedy and deceitful man apparently valued sheep and goats more than his daughters, pitting the two sisters against each other, making them rivals for the affection of one man.

For 13 years they competed with each other until Rachel's death while giving birth to Benjamin. A noteworthy point: Leah did earn the place of being buried next to her beloved husband when he died, unlike Rachel, who was buried alone in exile.

REJECTION AND FAVORITISM

Much of what we have learned thus far about Jacob's life has revealed the rejection and favoritism of family members and their consequences. Rejection and favoritism are barriers that will keep a believer from walking in the fullness of the covenant.

Being cast aside or rejected by a parent or other significant person can motivate destructive behavior in some to gain the attention of the one who rejected them. Strongholds of jealousy, anger and retaliation can mount, creating a distorted view of relationships. For example, when Esau realized how much his parents disapproved of his Canaanite wives, he spitefully went out and married yet another wife they would disapprove of, a daughter to his Uncle Ishmael.

For many years, Jacob's love, Rachel, was barren. When she finally had a son, Joseph, he became his father's favorite. Just as the destructive nature of favoritism had ruined the harmony of Jacob's childhood family, the favor he showed toward his son Joseph, when he had many other sons as well, destroyed any healthy relationship Joseph hoped to have with his brothers until much later in life. The brothers hated Joseph and plotted his demise, selling him to traders bound for Egypt. You will hear more about Joseph's life in the next chapter.

Unfavored siblings in childhood can become embittered adults. Favoritism doesn't just occur in childhood; this flawed disposition can emerge in any dysfunctional relationship. If favoritism has affected your life, the Lord can restore you to wholeness.

Often the scars of favoritism cover anger and resentment; and when those toxic emotions are brewing underneath, they will hinder your believing the truth of the Word of God in every area of your life. Rejection is a terrible pain to overcome, because over time you become hardened to it and it becomes a mindset that produces wrong thinking that is contrary to the principles of covenant.

Jesus said to His disciples, "And you will know the truth, and the truth will set you free" (John 8:32, *NLT*). Are we not His disciples today? This promise is for us.

Another aspect of restoration is forgiveness. You may have to go to a parent, or to someone else who has hurt you, and release forgiveness. I must say that in many instances, denial is the first line of defense; but if your heart is right in your pursuit of reconciliation, it isn't necessary to gain approval or acceptance of others to be free. However, if your faith remains hindered, consider the other examples in this chapter.

During the years that Jacob worked for Uncle Laban, God blessed his efforts. And because of God's covenant with his fathers, Jacob gained large flocks and herds. When Laban realized that God had blessed him because of his nephew Jacob, they worked out other agreements to keep Jacob in his employ for another six years. To Jacob's frustration, Laban kept changing the terms of their agreements. Jacob learned by experience the frustration his brother Esau must have felt when Jacob tricked him! Finally, after 20 years, God directed Jacob to return to the promised land.

CONTRASTING CHARACTERS— ESAU VS. JACOB

Both Esau and Jacob had some serious character flaws. Character is derived from human nature, and when these flaws become a part of the way you live, they are more difficult to recognize as being damaging or destructive.

Many believers today struggle with the same weaknesses, not realizing that in order to maintain a healthy relationship with our

Divine Covenant Partner, these obstacles need to be dealt with. God has given us access to His presence to be cleansed, purified and ultimately made ready for His covenant purposes. So let's examine these character flaws to gain God's perspective on them. Solomon wisely stated that it is "the little foxes that spoil the vines" (Song of Sol. 2:15, *NKJV*).

ESAU

Fleshly Appetite: Esau was desperate for a meal, and he wanted it to the point of exaggerating his condition in order to fill that temporary need. "Look, I am about to die . . ." was his plea. Because of His impulsive nature, Esau had no self-control to restrain from the demand of present gratification. He could not withstand present need. He had an ungovernable fleshly appetite.

Giving in to temptation and ignoring the consequences because of the temporary satisfaction you gain is deceiving. Consequences keep us in check and establish the fear of the Lord in our life. This is the beginning of wisdom. Lack of self-control and self-discipline can rob anyone of happiness, respect and peace. True self-control requires a willingness to forsake the small for the sake of the great, the present for the sake of the future, the material for the sake of the spiritual; and that is what faith makes possible. A morsel doesn't last, but the spiritual discipline of self-control provides the anchor you need to gain God's perspective when you are tempted to discard the spiritual.

Spiritual Indifference: Spiritual values had no priority in Esau's life. Esau is always referred to in the Bible with a certain contempt. The author of Hebrews calls Esau "a profane person . . . who for one morsel of food sold his birthright" (Heb. 12:16). "Profane" means secular, a person who judges things by earthly standards without spiritual insight. Esau's response provides obvious proof of his indifference: "What profit shall this birthright do to me?" Of course, Esau didn't think he was losing the great by grasping at the small. He had no patience to wait, no faith to believe in the real value of anything spiritual. After all, he concluded, "Who wants an ethereal insubstantial thing like a birthright?"

For the new believer, there is much grace to develop an appreciation for spiritual matters. It is important to realize that at some point on your spiritual journey, if you gain no value for the spiritual, indifference will set in and keep you, as it did Esau, from your covenant blessings. Without faith it is impossible to walk in your covenant with God.

> Dear brothers and sisters, when I was with you I couldn't talk to you as I would to mature Christians. I had to talk as though you belonged to this world or as though you were infants in the Christian life. I had to feed you with milk and not with solid food, because you couldn't handle anything stronger. And you still aren't ready, for you are still controlled by your own selfish desires. . . . You are acting like people who don't belong to the Lord (1 Cor. 3:1-3, *NLT*).

JACOB

Manipulative Manners: Jacob was his mother's favorite, and it is likely that growing up she filled his mind with ideas of promise as the one who stood to inherit his father's blessing. Since Satan's operation is to kill, steal and destroy, it is likely that his cunning suggestion to Jacob to deceive his brother was a part of Satan's plan to destroy both of their futures. Recall that Jacob wasn't all that spiritual when this occurred; so with a manipulative and controlling nature, he was more prone to the power of suggestion. Jacob had a spiritual heritage to admire, but he was not concerned with knowing the God of his fathers, because he was too distracted with his natural pursuit of attaining what God had promised. In truth, Jacob was no better than Esau.

The Bible says that the sins of the fathers rest on the bosom of the children. Even though Jacob bore his father's tranquil nature, he also bore his mother's shrewd ways (see Deut. 5:9; Jer. 14:20; 32:18; Lam. 5:7). Sins that are passed down through the generations can have a strong influence on who we become, as we are learning from Jacob and Esau's story. Manipulation can definitely be an inherited temperament that carries with it other destructive quirks that vie for your attention when you are consumed with getting your way.

In his book *The Three Battlegrounds,* Francis Frangipane helps us discover what strongholds may be affecting us:

> If you want to identify the hidden strongholds in your life, you need only survey the attitudes in your heart. Every area in your thinking that glistens with hope in God is an area which is being liberated by Christ. But any system of thinking that does not have hope, which feels hopeless is a stronghold that must be pulled down.[3]

Without a relationship with God, Jacob was left to pursue God in a fleshly manner while chained to his strongholds. Given his deceptive nature, compromise for spiritual gain took no thought at all—it was second nature. This behavior has no regard for others, not even for God; it is only after selfish gain. Whether or not generational sin is passed on through our DNA, generational sin is a fact of life. It was passed down to us and we will pass it on to our children unless we understand God's remedy for the matter.

Therefore, a major key to walking in covenant with God is an understanding of the generational sins and iniquities that we have inherited. We can never be released until we recognize our afflictions.

Lust for Spiritual Gain: Isaac favored Esau, not Jacob. This alone reveals much about the relationship Jacob had with his father, or lack thereof. Jacob and Rebecca conspired to deceive Isaac through a series of deliberate acts. When the heart is hardened, it commits one lie after another in order to maintain cover.

Perhaps his willingness to conspire with his mother was part of the resentment Jacob had toward his father for rejecting him. As mentioned before, those who have been rejected by someone near and dear to them go to great lengths to get even or take advantage of a situation. The temptation to take matters into our own hands, even when God promises to intervene in His timing, strikes at a weak spot in most, if not all, of us. We have our birthright as children of God; and how it is realized in our lives is key.

A DIVINE CURE

Cutting himself loose from Uncle Laban must have given Jacob a sense of relief. As he journeyed home with his family, the farther Jacob traveled from Laban, the closer he got to his brother, Esau, who had murder on his mind the last time Jacob had seen him. Terrified of his brother's impending wrath after a long absence, Jacob tried to pacify Esau by sending elaborate gifts to him before they met.

When he reached the borders of Canaan, Jacob saw a band of angels in a vision, waiting to accompany him home. In spite of this encouraging vision, Jacob was still not convinced of his safe return. Instead Jacob pleaded for mercy, reminding God of His covenant (see Gen. 32:10-12). Sounds like Jacob was getting desperate. He took all the precautions humanly possible to secure his family in case Esau attacked him. The night before entering Canaan, Jacob sent his herds and family across the river while he remained behind.

The fear and stress Jacob had been living under for years finally caused him to go after God, alone. There he wrestled with a "Man" whom Jacob identified as an angel. This was not only a physical wrestling match, but also a spiritual one. Jacob refused to release his hold on the angel of the Lord until the angel blessed him; and in that encounter, the angel put a perpetual mark of honor upon him by changing his name to Israel, "prince of God." The angel then touched the socket of Jacob's hip, putting it out of joint so that when Jacob walked away from that encounter, he walked with a limp in his gait.

The fact that the struggle involved a figure in human form revealed that this experience was more than just a "dark night of the soul." This was no nightmare; Jacob remained fully awake. He struggled with more than just his conscience or fears. His entire person was engaged. When the struggle was over, Jacob named the place Peniel, which means, "I saw God face to face and my life was preserved." Jacob's Peniel experience cured his deceptive nature and ushered him into his promise.

NATURAL PROGRESSION OF JACOB'S SPIRITUAL LIFE

The fact that Jacob's total surrender didn't take place overnight should not be overlooked. His infamous nocturnal wrestling with the angel of the Lord should be brought into proper perspective. Notice how God mercifully drew Jacob to the end of himself in order for complete restoration to be initiated. This correlates in many ways with the believer's life today.

1. GOD USED LABAN

Jacob was under divine correction during the 20 years he served Laban, even though Laban was just as deceitful as Jacob. God has a redemptive purpose for bringing difficult people into our life. However, we often have a hard time getting God's message because we can't get past the messenger. Yet, the very people we shun are often sent by God to alert us to our shortcomings and weaknesses.

If God has sent a Laban into your life, his intent is to correct your character flaws. He often does this by setting you up to become victim of the same kind of hurt or abuse you inflict on others. Perhaps you have found yourself going through the ringer with someone. Is it possible that your circumstances have been designed by God to help you on your journey to encountering Him?

As strange as it might seem, Jacob's Uncle Laban was instrumental in leading Jacob back to God.

2. GOD USED ESAU

When Jacob walked away from his brother, Esau, that wound remained like a goad in Jacob's conscience, prodding him for 20 years, until he and Esau were restored. Conviction is important to the believer whenever offense is meted against another. You can't live in total peace until the broken relationships that are dear to you are restored or given proper perspective by God.

3. GOD USED A DREAM

Jacob was on the run but was stopped dead in his tracks for his first encounter with God through a dream. After the dream, Jacob responded with a vow and a half-hearted, conditional surrender. This is when God began to soften Jacob's heart to the idea of establishing a relationship with his brother. Even though God's initial wooing was purely merciful, God's intent was to have their relationship restored so that the covenant could be transferred to the next generation with greater appreciation and understanding. God may not give you a dream, but He uses ways to draw you into an initial step of commitment. God may use an angel in disguise. Stranger things have happened to me—don't think they can't happen to you too.

4. GOD USED ANGELIC HOSTS

Jacob was done with Laban's shenanigans and was ready to return home. With fear tormenting him and the agitation from his father-in-law's abuse, God's messengers showed up to greet Jacob at the border of his hometown. Still afraid, Jacob made a lengthy plea with God for mercy. Notice, he wasn't relieved from the fear and torment yet, even though he had convincing angelic evidence.

In the same manner, God has convincing evidence for you when you are overwhelmed by the influx of emotions that accompany a difficult reconciliation. Look around you; God is confirming His reassurance so that you may pursue the path He has for you. Take heed, the human heart has a tendency to focus more on the problem than on the One who can solve it. Fear has a voice and can override any heavenly assistance if it isn't dealt with. Jacob needed to draw closer to God to deal with his fear and other issues in his heart. Don't draw back; draw near!

5. JACOB WAS ALONE WITH GOD

In desperation, Jacob isolated himself from family to get alone with God. It was then that Jacob wrestled with the angel of the Lord and was delivered from his sinful nature. God allowed Jacob to sense that he was about to lose it all. By this time, Jacob could no longer rely on his ability to connive his way out of trouble and into blessing through his own strength and manipulation. God wasn't angry with him but rather wanted to move Jacob toward his destiny, which was to birth the nation of Israel. His unrefined nature stood in the way, and God needed to change that. A conditional surrender would not do. When it became an absolute surrender, Jacob was liberated.

God will challenge us when it comes to the struggles of daily life. Yet, when we come to the end of ourselves, God is there to contend with us as He did with Jacob. This encounter occurred before an audience of One. There are seasons in life when we must pursue God alone. Fear not when that day comes! "But now thus says the Lord, he who created you, O Jacob, he who formed you, O Israel: Do not fear for I have redeemed you; I have called you by name, you are mine" (Isa. 43:1, *NRSV*).

Notice that God "created" Jacob but afterwards Israel was "formed" through the crucible of life. There is a huge difference between "create" and "form." As a result of the Fall, Jacob was found to be impetuous, a deceiver and a manipulator. But Jacob became Israel because he was transformed through his encounters with God. Fear was Jacob's Achilles' heel, hindering him from believing God was with him. Notice how God encouraged him: "Do not fear!"

Jacob's name was changed to Israel. The change in his name meant a change in character. What are you known for? What do others call you? Perhaps you need a Peniel experience with God like Jacob did to find out who you really are.

RETURNING HOME

After this anxious night of wrestling, Jacob went on his way with a limp, physically weakened by the conflict but spiritually strong in the assurance of God's favor. Esau and his 400 men came into Jacob's line of sight, and when they were finally close enough, Jacob bowed seven times before Esau, demonstrating his complete submission.

To Jacob's amazement, after 20 years, Esau was ready to make peace with him. During the years they were apart, Esau had become as rich as his father, Isaac, had earlier spoken over his life when Jacob stole the paternal inheritance. In his wealth, Esau's contentment pacified his anger toward his brother. Following that miraculous convergence, they maintained friendly relations throughout the rest of their lives.

God told Jacob to return to Bethel, the place where he began his journey with God. At Bethel, God once again appeared to Jacob and renewed the Abrahamic covenant with him. God's promises may have been an enigma to Jacob years before, but after his wrestling match, Jacob gained a new appreciation for them. Jacob returned to the old family home to wait at the deathbed of his father, Isaac. The complete reconciliation between Esau and Jacob was evident when they united with their families at the burial of their father.

THE CONCLUSION OF THE MATTER

Apparently, God shows up to demonstrate His power when man is at his weakest point. Man is pretty self-sufficient and can easily turn away from God. When everything is running smoothly, he may be fairly self-controlled. But if he is offended and loses his temper, he's not as self-controlled or self-sufficient as he thinks. God is patient and waits until the circumstances are right to intervene in the affairs of man.

It is necessary for God to guide His children into that all-important place where He can mold and shape them into His image and likeness. Fiery trials have a way of burning up the dross in our life—the superficial commitments, the time-wasting activities and wrong attitudes. Relying on our own understanding and self-confidence can be the greatest detriment to our spiritual development. Fully surrendering to God only comes in an atmosphere where repeated tests and trials have allowed us the opportunity to learn to trust Him in the midst of them. The Bible says that the testing of our faith produces patience.

Building character requires intense work deep in our inward parts; it is work that requires patience before fruit comes. The apostle Peter's pride and impulsivity tripped him up at every step. He was anything but a solid rock, yet our Lord knew that Peter would grow from the trials he suffered. Peter's name was changed to his new identity—Cephas, a stone—to point to the greater Rock,

Jesus Christ (that Peter had just confessed), as the rock upon which God would build the Church. That is covenant lingo, declaring what Peter would become in terms of God's purposes for His kingdom. Indeed, Peter had a character change that eventually coincided with his new name. Here is what Peter learned about character after years of walking with the Lord:

> Add to your faith goodness;
> and to goodness, knowledge;
> and to knowledge, self-control;
> and to self-control, perseverance;
> and to perseverance, godliness;
> and to godliness, brotherly kindness;
> and to brotherly kindness, love (2 Pet. 1:5-7).

By nature, Jacob was a deceiver who came from a very dysfunctional family. He had problems with his dad, his father-in-law and brother. The closest people to him were women. In the end, Jacob earned the respect of his father and his brother because he honored his covenant with God.

Ultimately, to get release from our fleshly character weaknesses, we must come to the end of ourselves and be willing to endure the refiner's fire of God's presence. We are helpless to fix ourselves. Believers with mature character are those who most rely on God. God is looking for people of character.

Life Lines

- Each of us has a multitude of character deficiencies that need to be perfected. God uses those in authority over us to do this.

- In his book *Winning with People,* John Maxwell makes an important statement on the subject of character: "The question I must ask myself: Have I examined myself and taken responsibility for who I am?"[4]

- Jacob and Rebekah, the formidable duo, conspired to obtain father Isaac's spiritual blessing, and for this, Jacob suffered harsh consequences. Unfamiliarity with God's ways can lead to impatiently handling matters without His leading. Left to their own devices, many people try to exalt themselves by degrading others. There is no peace or happiness apart from God's way of doing things.

- Making restitution can be difficult, as illustrated by the family conflicts of Jacob and Esau. Nonetheless, God intervened to make it possible. Dealing with Jacob's character flaws was necessary for him to overcome and realize that restoration was possible.

- Is there someone in your life that you have had long-standing resentment toward because of some mistreatment? What is keeping you from taking the first step toward reconciliation? Allow God to set up your divine appointment to restore the matter. Holding a grudge will hinder your covenant blessings.

- The apostle Paul testifies to the importance of a clear conscience: "I myself always strive to have a conscience without offense toward God and men" (Acts 24:16, *NKJV*).

- Discerning God's direction is not a formula-driven science but an inner conviction from God that will help sort out feelings of anxiety, deceit and covetousness.

- In what ways are you trying to live life in your own strength? Encountering God will change your perspective on life's most difficult seasons.

- God measures us by the character of our inner being, not by what we accomplish or what we do for Him.[5]

CHAPTER SIX

COVENANT WITH JOSEPH

The blessings of your father have excelled the blessings of my ancestors . . . They shall be on the head of Joseph, And on the crown of the head of him who was separate from his brothers.
GENESIS 49:26, NKJV

Our story begins with the birth of Joseph to his aging parents, Jacob and Rachel. God sure takes a liking to barren couples who desperately want children and are beyond their childbearing years. Already we've noted that Isaac was Sarah and Abraham's miracle child; Jacob was Isaac and Rebekah's miracle child; and Joseph was a miracle birth too.

Joseph's miracle birth tells us that God had more in store for him than your average Joe. He was shown partiality by his father, being the son of Jacob's old age. And the Bible says that Jacob loved Joseph more than all his children (see Gen. 37:3). Wrong thing to do, Dad!

Ironically, most of Joseph's troubles stemmed from the special relationship he had with his father. Joseph's life was anything but ordinary. His inspiring story reveals intense episodes of jealousy, conspiracy and betrayal, and depicts the terrible price Joseph paid for his brothers' dastardly behavior. Their father's favoritism toward Joseph more than anything else explains the terrible injustice Joseph suffered when he was sold into slavery. Joseph would relive this painful memory for years until God orchestrated the restoration of his entire family (the whole story is told in Genesis 37–50).

"LITTLE JOE"

If you didn't come from a large family, you can't possibly relate to the magnitude of the domestic squabbles that continue on a daily basis as children learn to adjust to their environment while growing up. In Joseph's time, surrogacy and polygamy were cultural customs where blended families lived together under one or more tents. Each time another child was added to the clan, the sibling rivalry, infighting and tensions of adjustment to one another eventually gave way to a "normal" life. But, from the time Rachel gave birth to Joseph, life at home with the Jacob clan forever changed.

A background check of these two parents will reveal why they favored Joseph over the others. Jacob loved Rachel more than Leah, which incited rivalry between them. Rachel was barren for many years; and after Leah's boys were born, Rachel finally got pregnant with Joseph. Needless to say, Jacob and Rachel were elated. Joseph was not only a "momma's boy," but he was also daddy's delight. Rachel and Jacob became doting and overprotective parents. By the time Joseph came along, most of his brothers were budding teenagers. Later on, Rachel died at childbirth when her second son, Benjamin, was born.

Can you imagine how Joseph's brothers felt when all their father's attention was given to him? Let's lend some credence to the ongoing jealousy these brothers had over the "favored" boy of the family. Jacob was obsessed with Joseph; and now at 17, his dad made him a coat of many colors. It was a garment such as was worn by children of nobles. You can just see Joseph sporting that coat everywhere he went. His brothers were furious, and the Bible says they could not speak peaceably to him. In his naiveté, Joseph clearly enjoyed the lavish attention of his father.

To add insult to injury, Joseph began to have prophetic dreams about his brothers in which they would someday bow down to him. Proudly sharing his dreams with his brothers was like a goad, reminding them of their inferior place to their younger brother. The brothers believed that the dreams were the product of Joseph's arrogance rather than a divine plan of destiny. Their father didn't appear gullible, nor did he reject the possible significance the dreams had. Instead, these dreams caused Jacob to wonder inwardly about their meaning. If you are one given to dreams, take a lesson here: Be careful who you share them with.

THE PRICE IS RIGHT

One day, while his older sons were out tending the flocks, Jacob sent Joseph to check on them. His brothers noticed Joseph coming from a long way off because he was wearing that coat of many colors. "Here comes the dreamer," they sarcastically chided. They devised a plan to kill this thorn in their side. They had had enough. Some of the brothers felt the plot was too extreme, and so instead of killing him, they all decided to toss him into a nearby pit and leave him there. Alone in their presence, and without his father's protection, Joseph's brothers ganged up on him, stripped him of his coat and, in the altercation, they threw him into a dark pit nearby just as they had planned.

Afterward they sat and ate a meal together near the pit they cast Joseph in, but they were haunted by Joseph's wailing cries to be rescued. The brothers soon noticed a band of Ishmaelite merchants coming down the dusty road, headed in their direction. The merchants were loaded down with wares to sell and trade in the Egyptian market. The brothers pulled Joseph out of the pit and negotiated with the traders to sell him into slavery for 20 shekels of silver. This act to spare his life was certainly meant to ease their consciences as well as rid Joseph from their lives forever. Joseph got a bitter taste of his brothers' jealousy and anger, and he never saw it coming.

As a cover-up, the brothers slaughtered a goat and smeared Joseph's coat with its blood. When they returned to their father, they gave him the bloody coat, telling him that they had found it. They led their father to believe that his beloved son had been killed by a wild animal. His own children deceived him, just as he had deceived his brother, Esau, out of his birthright blessing. Jacob was deeply grieved and overwhelmed by the loss of Joseph.

Meanwhile, Joseph, bound for Egypt, was convinced that he would never see his family again, much less the fulfillment of the dreams he had about his future.

"Now the Midianites had sold him in Egypt to Potiphar, an officer of Pharaoh and captain of the guard" (Gen. 37:36, *NKJV*). Joseph was now the exclusive property of Potiphar in Pharaoh's court.

It didn't take long for Joseph the "dreamer" to be favored by his owner, because the Lord was with him. Everything Joseph did prospered, and that benefited Potiphar too. Later, Joseph was given control over Potiphar's estate, managing his affairs with utmost respect and integrity. Not only was Joseph successful, but the Bible says that he was handsome in form and appearance.

I smell trouble.

Potiphar's wife was on the lookout! While her husband was away, she made an attempt to seduce Joseph. He kindly refused her sexual advances, explaining, "How then could I do such a wicked thing and sin against God?" (Gen. 39:9, *NLT*). That was like dangling a carrot in her face and encouraged her to continue chasing after Joseph, ignoring his godly convictions. "For the lips of a loose woman drip honey as a honeycomb, and her mouth is smoother than oil" (Prov. 5:3, *AMP*).

She continued in hot pursuit of Joseph until he fled the scene to avoid her insistent advances, leaving his cloak behind. This encounter reveals the misuse of power by some in high positions.

Angry, and disgraced by a subordinate, Potiphar's wife summoned her husband to tell him about his slave. Acting as a damsel in distress who was taken advantage of, Potiphar's wife attempted to destroy Joseph's credibility by accusing him of seducing her. "I have his cloak to prove it," she whined. In spite of Joseph's impeccable reputation, Potiphar ordered that he be imprisoned. Although he was unjustly accused, prison was Joseph's next place of testing.

PRISON PIETY

Now the dreamer was sitting in prison amongst the inmate population with none other than Pharaoh's butler and baker. Although Joseph had long been abandoned by his family, he was not abandoned by God. Notice how God's presence didn't prevent Joseph from being sent to prison. Rather, God was with him in it. God works through our lives while we are in the depths of despair. He will comfort us but not remove us from our circumstances, so that our character can be refined in that place of testing.

God revealed Himself to Joseph with two unique gifts: the interpretation of dreams and the gift of administration. How does God want to reveal Himself in your "prison"? If you continue to focus on what you don't have, or on the pain someone has inflicted on you, you will be unable to recognize God in that place. As long as we live we will have trials, but the real issue is how we handle them.

Once again, Joseph earned favor with a superior. This one saw fit to promote him to keeper of the prison without anyone questioning Joseph's authority. Joseph's talent to administer the prison would prove to be key later on. His fellow inmate the butler had a dream that he could not interpret. But when the dream was told to Joseph, he interpreted it, telling the butler that in three days he would be restored to Pharaoh's court. When he finished speaking with the butler, Joseph asked the butler to remember him when he was restored to his position.

The baker, who anxiously listened to Joseph interpret the butler's dream, also inquired of Joseph to interpret his dream. Joseph told the baker that he would be executed by Pharaoh in three days' time. Those dreams came to pass. Soon Joseph's fame as an interpreter of dreams spread. Yet the butler, when he returned to his position in Pharaoh's household, forgot all about Joseph.

Two years later, it was Pharaoh who was having troubling dreams. He called in the best magicians and wise men of Egypt, but none could interpret his dreams. Suddenly the butler's memory was jogged and he remembered Joseph. He explained to Pharaoh that he had met a young Hebrew man while in prison who was pretty good at interpreting dreams. Pharaoh quickly summoned Joseph, who was shaven, clothed and presented to the king.

The pharaoh said, "I have had a dream, and there is no one who can interpret it. I have heard it said of you that when you hear a dream you can interpret it" (Gen. 41:15, *NRSV*). Joseph's immediate reply was that God was the source of his ability to interpret dreams.

As Pharaoh recounted his two dreams, God revealed to Joseph their meaning, and he began to interpret them with great clarity and instruction to Pharaoh. Joseph explained that Egypt would experience seven years of abundant harvest followed by seven years of drought and famine. He then advised Pharaoh to appoint officers over the land to prepare for the famine by storing grain during the seven good years so that they would have plenty during the famine. After all was said, Pharaoh told his servants, "We will never find a better man than Joseph, a man who has God's spirit in him" (Gen. 41:38, *GNB*).

"LITTLE JOE" TURNED EXTRAORDINARY RULER

"You're hired, Joseph," Pharaoh declared. Deeply impressed by Joseph's discernment, Pharaoh promptly elevated Joseph to second in command in Egypt. Pharaoh took off his personal signet ring and gave it to Joseph, along with fine linen robes and a gold chain. Wow, talk about promotion! The favor lavished on Joseph was a clear indication that God was still in covenant with Joseph and that Joseph's posterity would be preserved. This type of favor was also lavished upon Mordecai, Esther's uncle, when he found covenant favor in the sight of the king (see Esther 8:15).

Joseph was also given his own chariot and trusted advisors to work alongside him. The wisdom God gave Joseph during this time far exceeded anyone's expectations. So much more grain was produced during the prosperous years that they eventually stopped keeping track of it. Joseph built large storehouses in all the surrounding cities. This saved Egypt's people from the famine years.

Meanwhile, Pharaoh gave his daughter in marriage to Joseph and they had two children, Manassah and Ephraim. Joseph was 30 years old by this time. Let's examine the meaning of the names of these two children. "Manassah" means "to forget." God was helping Joseph forget the injustices of his past. "Ephraim" means "to be fruitful." God had blessed Joseph richly in Egypt.

After seven years of abundance, a severe famine hit, just as Joseph had foretold. The famine wasn't isolated to Egypt. It hit every country, but only Egypt had grain. Joseph opened up his storehouses and began to sell the grain. The grain was not given away, but sold, enabling Egypt to become the breadbasket for all the world.

Joseph's forlorn family in Canaan were beginning to run out of food when they got word that they could purchase grain in Egypt. So Jacob sent his 10 older sons to Egypt to purchase grain so that they might survive the famine. He kept Benjamin, his youngest, home with him.

Twenty years had passed since Joseph's brothers had sold him into slavery. When they arrived in Egypt, they waited in line like everyone else to purchase grain. When Joseph called them forward, all the brothers bowed before him, but they did not recognize him. Joseph knew who they were but didn't let on that he did.

Instead, Joseph accused them of being spies and put them in custody for three days. This left them totally bewildered. Panic set in and they began to tell Joseph the whole story about how they were 12 brothers, referring to one brother that was "no more." He then demanded that one of them stay in Egypt while the others returned and fetched the younger Benjamin who remained in Canaan with their father. Joseph wanted to see his little brother.

Convinced that God was finally punishing them for abandoning their brother Joseph years earlier, they reasoned amongst themselves in their native tongue in front of Joseph. Overcome by what he was hearing, Joseph left the room and wept. Regaining his composure, he returned and instructed Simeon to remain behind while the others returned to Canaan.

While Simeon was held prisoner, Joseph supplied the brothers with provisions for their journey back and had his servants fill the bags of grain they had purchased. Joseph also instructed his servants to hide the money they had paid for the purchase in one of the sacks of grain.

Imagine the look on their faces when they opened up the sacks of grain at home and found the money. Angry at his sons, Jacob was unwilling to let go of Benjamin; after all, he had never gotten over the fact that Joseph was gone . . . and now Simeon was taken captive. After much coaxing, Jacob's son Judah was able to convince his father to let them take Benjamin to Egypt. Jacob made sure the sons carried with them double the silver to return the first payment and pay for the new supply of grain.

DINING EGYPTIAN STYLE

When Joseph saw Benjamin with his brothers, waiting in the courtyard of the palace, he had them all taken to his house where a meal was prepared. They nervously followed Joseph's servant to be seated in the dining room according to their ages as Joseph had earlier instructed. This was a strange sign at which the brothers were astonished. When Joseph walked in, he inquired about the welfare of their aged father. Joseph then shifted his attention to his younger brother, Benjamin, and asked about his identity.

The encounter with Benjamin, for whom Joseph had much affection, so moved Joseph that he excused himself and wept privately.

Afterwards, Joseph returned and directed the meal to begin. When the meal came, Joseph made sure that Benjamin's share was five times more than the others received. This was designed to test the brothers' reaction toward his favoritism. For good reason, Joseph wasn't ready to trust his brothers with his true identity.

Joseph's servants loaded the donkeys with grain and prepared to send the brothers away; but Joseph gave one final instruction to his servant: "Then put my cup, the silver one, in the mouth of the youngest one's sack, along with the silver for his grain" (Gen. 44:2, *NIV*). The next morning, they rode off early. No sooner did they leave than Joseph's steward chased them down. The steward asked why they had stolen Joseph's cup after he had been so kind to them.

The brothers denied any wrongdoing and told the steward that if it was found on them, he could kill whoever had it and the rest of them would become his slaves. A search was conducted, beginning with the oldest brother. But as Benjamin's sack was opened, out tumbled Joseph's cup. They were all dumbfounded by the discovery. In the end, they had to pack up the donkeys and return to Joseph's palace where they were once again brought before Joseph's presence.

Judah begged, "Master, what can we say? And how can we show we are not guilty? God has uncovered our guilt, so all of us will be your slaves, not just Benjamin" (Gen. 44:16, *NCV*). But Joseph wasn't willing to yield so easily. All were free to go, but Benjamin had to stay. This was the moment of truth. Would they abandon their youngest brother to become a slave in Egypt, just like they did Joseph?

Recalling the grief they put their father through when Joseph disappeared, they had a change of heart and were willing to take Benjamin's place. Humbly, Judah pleaded with Joseph for his little brother, telling of their father's special love for Benjamin and how he had already lost one beloved son.

"He alone is left of his mother's children, and his father loves him" (Gen. 44:20, *NKJV*). In fact, Judah was the one who earlier convinced his brothers not to kill Joseph, but instead sell him into slavery. The loss of this youngest son would surely kill their father. It was a burden none of them could bear. "Take me instead," Judah pleaded.

"I AM YOUR BROTHER"

No longer able to contain himself, Joseph ordered his Egyptian servants to leave the room so that he could be alone with his brothers. Then Joseph wept aloud so that the entire house of Pharaoh heard him. A tearful Joseph said, "I am Joseph. Does my father still live?" The brothers were terrified and could not answer.

Joseph could have sold them, imprisoned them for the rest of their lives or killed them and no one would have stopped him. Instead, Joseph now embraced them and instructed his brothers to bring his father and the entire family to Egypt to settle nearby.

There were still five years of famine left; it was better for them to relocate to Egypt rather than continue to travel back and forth. In the end, Joseph wasn't angry or vengeful. He realized that God had brought about these events to save the region from starvation. After 20 years, the family was finally reunited.

Pharaoh was touched by Joseph's story and agreed to pick up the tab for his entire family's move to Egypt, including giving them the best land in the area to settle in—Goshen.

Later, Jacob was in disbelief to discover that his son Joseph was not only alive but was also second in command over all of Egypt. He was eager to see his son and temporarily move his family with the promise from Jehovah that He would eventually return his family to Canaan.

Upon their arrival in Egypt, Jacob's reunion with his beloved Joseph was nothing short of extraordinary as they embraced for the first time in 20 years.

When Jacob had lived in the land of Egypt for 17 years, he approached Joseph, asking him to swear that he would not bury him in Egypt. He wanted to be buried with his fathers in Canaan. Joseph willingly agreed and would follow through on his father's wishes when the time came.

BREAKING TRADITION

One day, Joseph was informed that his father was sick, so he wanted to pay him a visit and bring his two sons, Ephraim and Manasseh, with him. Joseph wanted to check up on his father and see if perhaps Jacob would bless him and his sons. When Jacob heard that Joseph was coming for a visit, he strengthened himself and sat up on his bed as though he had plans of his own for this visit—some unfinished business to take care of before his death.

In their private moments together, Jacob repeated to Joseph the covenant spoken to him when he was in Canaan. "Behold I will make you fruitful, and multiply you, and I will make of you a multitude of people, and give this land to your descendants after you as an everlasting possession" (Gen. 48:4, *NKJV*). God spoke these same words to Jacob when his name was changed to Israel. Among Jacob's last words to Joseph were recollections of the death of his beloved wife Rachel, although it had been 40 years since the event took place.

Jacob then embraced Joseph's sons, saying, "I had not thought to see your face; but in fact, God has also shown me your offspring!" (Gen. 48:11, *NKJV*). In that intimate embrace, Jacob blessed Joseph and his sons.

God, before whom my fathers Abraham and Isaac walked, The God who has fed me all my life long to this day, The Angel who has redeemed me from all evil, Bless the lads; Let my name be named upon them, And the name of my fathers Abraham and Isaac; And let them grow into a multitude in the midst of the earth (Gen. 48:15-16, *NKJV*).

Before their private meeting was over, Jacob told Joseph, prior to blessing all of his sons publicly, "Moreover I have given to you one portion above your brothers, which I took from the hand of the Amorite with my sword and my bow" (Gen. 48:22, *NKJV*).

You would have thought that Jacob would have summoned Reuben, his firstborn, to declare these blessings over him and his family; but neither protocol nor tradition were considered in the overall design of God's plan for this family. In fact, when Jacob pronounced the blessings on his sons, he did not repeat the covenant to any of them as he did to Joseph. Joseph clearly was the next in line to inherit the covenant of his fathers Abraham, Isaac and Jacob.

After the family blessings were over, Jacob died. Then Joseph fell on his father's face, wept over him and kissed him. When the days of mourning came, everyone gathered to pay his or her respects to Jacob in Egypt. Afterward, Joseph requested of Pharaoh that he bury his father in Canaan, and they all made the journey together.

After they laid Jacob to rest, they all returned to Egypt. Joseph's brothers were still bothered by what they had done to Joseph and feared he would hate them and would be eager to repay them for their evil deeds against him now that Dad was gone. Joseph again reassured them, "Don't be afraid. Am I in the place of God? You intended to harm me, but God intended it for good to accomplish what is now being done, the saving of many lives" (Gen. 50:19-20, *NIV*).

CONCLUSION

The actions of Joseph's brothers against him, however reprehensible, were a means for sustaining the life of Jacob's family. As he affirmed to his brothers, Joseph's path was chosen by God.

Suffering mistreatment at the hands of another is a part of life; it may not be as extreme as what Joseph suffered, yet it is easy to grow bitter and weary at the injustices of life. But all it takes is one person in the family to influence the salvation of an entire family. I am the pioneer of the Bernal family. When I surrendered my life to Christ, my sisters, nieces, nephews, sons and daughter followed. So it only takes one believer to totally obey God in order to have that kind of impact on a family.

What God's people say and do makes a difference regarding the welfare of others; Joseph's destiny included saving from starvation not just his family, but an entire nation. Even though Joseph went into a place of hardship, he ended up in a place of blessing.

The story's climactic ending reveals that God truly enables the past to be forgiven—the outcome of Joseph's story was nothing short of incredible. Despite the sinful behaviors and injustices that attempted to stymie the divine destinies of God's patriarchs, God continued to remain faithful to His covenant.

Life Lines

- Joseph spent most of his life trying to overcome the consequences of being his father's favorite.

- Joseph's slavery could not hinder God's plan of reconciliation and covenant blessing.

- Joseph did not yield to the temptations offered by Potiphar's wife, even though she had power and authority over him. Will you pass this same test when you are tempted?

- Praying for others in the depth of your hardship can take your thoughts off of yourself and put them on others.

- Promotion and favor are essential elements that pave the way to fulfilling God's covenant in your life.

- "Joseph teaches us to maintain a positive attitude when treated unfairly. Others often abused Joseph, but he never gave in to despair. He continued to do his best in every circumstance, and in so doing, he prepared himself for the future God had in mind."[1]

- Our relationship with God will never be meaningful to us unless we go through tests and trials, for which the Scriptures give insight.

- Joseph reminds us of the wonder of forgiveness and its healing power. As God has forgiven us, so are we to forgive others, freely and completely.

- Viewing life from God's perspective will lead us to a lasting legacy. We, too, can declare such statements of faith as are declared by the names "Manasseh" ("For God has made me forget the injustices of my past") and "Ephraim" ("For God has caused me to be fruitful in the land of Egypt").

CHAPTER SEVEN

Covenant with Moses

And God spoke with Moses face-to-face, as neighbors speak to one another.
Exodus 33:11, *THE MESSAGE*

The Bible is the most useful tool we have to know God and His ways; it can speak profound truths into our life and provide the encouragement and instruction necessary to motivate us to action. As you review some of the events of Moses' life, you will gain insight and understanding into the heart of this ordinary man whom God chose to covenant with, and it will also reveal the ongoing covenant of God with mankind.

Moses was a towering figure in biblical history who cooperated with God's master plan to pave the way to redeem mankind to God. There are many miraculous events that occurred in the life of this patriarch that demonstrated to God's people His undying love and forgiveness toward them, even in the midst of their hardheartedness.

MOSES, THE MAN

All that the average person knows about Moses is through Cecil B. DeMille's popular 1956 movie *The Ten Commandments*. While Charlton Heston portrays the character somewhat accurately to the biblical text, the ignorant are inspired but unable to decipher many important lessons the movie conveys.

Moses' life begins in the book of Exodus with his birth into a family of Hebrew slaves living in Egypt. Pharaoh was in power, and like his famous predecessors, his rulership was diabolical, oppressive and controlling. The pharaohs of Egypt have always represented Israel's enemy. However, God's people continued to flourish there and grew exceedingly mighty, populating Egypt to the degree that Pharaoh began to take notice. To control the population, a fearful and intolerant Pharaoh attemped to severely limit the Hebrew population by ordering the midwives to kill any male child born to the Israelites. The God-fearing Egyptian midwives weren't able to fulfill his order because the Hebrew women were giving birth in record time—before the midwives arrived.

Pharaoh feared that in the event of war, the Hebrews would join their enemies and fight against them to destroy Egypt. Determined to complete his plan, Pharaoh commanded "all his people" to see that every male Hebrew infant be thrown into the Nile River. Sound familiar? The Gospels record King Herod's attempt to slay all the male children two years and under when he heard rumors that the Christ child was born (see Matt. 2:16).

Moses' parents partially obeyed Pharaoh's command by putting their son into a woven basket and sending him down the Nile. The basket divinely headed in the direction of Pharaoh's daughter, as she prepared to bathe in the Nile.

As providence would have it, Moses was discovered floating near the riverbank. When the princess saw him, she had compassion and took him in, even though she recognized that he was one of the Hebrew babies her father had ordered thrown into the Nile. Unknowingly, she hired Moses' mother as his wet nurse, paying her to care for him.

Those tender years that his own mother bonded with him were critical to Moses' future. She wasn't about to pass up the opportunity to teach him the significance of who Yahweh was, where Moses came from and his future. After all, God had earlier reminded Moses' parents that their child would be concealed from those who sought to destroy him and that He would use their son to deliver the Hebrew nation.

As a result, Moses grew up knowing that he was a Hebrew in the Egyptian monarchy. Pharaoh's daughter gave Moses his name, which means "drawn out." As his people's redeemer, Moses would later draw Israel out of slavery, redeeming them from the waters of the Red Sea.

During his tenure in Pharaoh's court, the Bible refers to Moses as "the son of Pharaoh's daughter," and as such, Moses had the privilege of the best Egypt had to offer. But he also had a divine mandate on his life. The apparent limitations Moses faced at birth and throughout his young life would become steppingstones God would use to redefine him later.

Not everyone has a picture-perfect upbringing; many are born into conflict and uncertainty. None of us has a choice in the matter, and because of this, God is the One who works everything out for good. He is a Master at overturning failure, taking the most dreadful and painful past, and redeeming it for His use.

Raised as Pharaoh's adopted grandson, Moses assisted in the construction of the giant pyramids. A major turning point came in Moses' life as a result of continually witnessing the cruelty done to his people; he struggled with his inability to do anything for them. Though Moses' outer garment displayed the finest of Egypt, his inner heart was seething with anger.

One day, Moses killed an Egyptian taskmaster for brutalizing a Hebrew slave. Thinking no one would find out, Moses hid the body. This unlawful deed was later discovered, and a terrified Moses fled from Egypt. Soon there was rumbling in the Hebrew camp after this incident. God's people were now fully convinced that Moses couldn't possibly be their deliverer, although he was sovereignly preserved from death as an infant and taken into Egypt for grooming and instruction.

Did God make a serious mistake by diverting the infant Moses' basket down the river and into the enemy's palace?

Fearing for his life, Moses wandered in the Sinai desert as a shepherd, surviving the brutal winters and enduring the long, hot summers. Roaming in the desert with no real direction was a far cry from the lap of luxury he had known in the courts of Egypt. With a death sentence looming over him, Moses was certain he wouldn't be returning to Egypt anytime soon.

In time, he married Zipporah, the daughter of Jethro, and for the next 40 years he was content to live in Midian (see Exod. 2:21). By this time, Moses' dream of delivering his people had died.

A BURNING BUSH

At this time in his life, Moses can best be described as a reluctant recruit. But he was now on heaven's MOST WANTED list because the circumstances were right for a supernatural intervention.

> The humility that Moses learned during the forty years he had been in the desert would enable him to remain completely dependent on God. That dependence on the Lord would be the key to Moses' greatness.[1]

As God is wont to do whenever He is looking to reveal Himself in impossible situations, He sent a messenger to pay the aging Moses a visit while he was tending his father-in-law's flock. The element of surprise is always present when God decides to show up; heaven doesn't need to schedule an appointment, even for a much needed mass deliverance in Egypt.

The angel of the Lord appeared in the most peculiar and least likely place—a burning bush. This was no ordinary bush; the Bible says that the bush burned but was not consumed, a phenomenon that for millennia has been symbolic of God's eternal presence and miraculous power for the Jews.

"So God heard their groaning; and God remembered His covenant with Abraham, Isaac, and Jacob" (Exod. 2:24, *NASB*). It was time for Moses to return to Egypt to liberate God's people. Attempting to put Egypt behind him, Moses' dialogue with God suggested that He use another vessel. "'But who am I to appear before Pharaoh?' Moses asked God. 'How can you expect me to lead the Israelites out of Egypt?'" (Exod. 3:11, *NLT*). Rather than being unwilling, Moses was uncertain. Even though God had an answer for every excuse this 80-year-old Hebrew outcast had, he still begged God to use someone else to deliver His people.

Have you been reluctant to step out and obey God because of past failures or mistakes? Are you looking at your weaknesses and making a litany of excuses for not obeying God? Obedience apart from a relationship ends in futility.[2] We need to rely on God in everything we do in life. "We must believe that God is real and that he rewards everyone who searches for him" (Heb. 11:6, CEV). After all, that is what walking by faith is all about.

Moses finally relented, partnering with God for what would be one of the greatest epic battles and displays of God's glory in Jewish history. The dream to deliver the Israelites was awakened in Moses once again. The leaders who sought to kill Moses were all dead by now. After this supernatural encounter with God, Moses returned to his father-in-law, Jethro, and got permission to go to Egypt to help his people. He took his wife, Zipporah, with him; and when they approached the borders of Egypt, his brother Aaron joined them.

The deliverance of God's people began with a series of 10 awful plagues that God released on Egypt in order to induce Pharaoh to let the Israelites go. But then Pharaoh changed his mind and set out to recapture them. By then the Israelites were poised at the foot of the Red Sea; surely Pharaoh's plan to drown them all would be a piece of cake. Not! God had a plan that Pharaoh wasn't privy to—that is, until it was too late. The most incredible visual effects in Cecil B. DeMille's film recorded their deliverance with Moses declaring, "The LORD will fight for you, and you won't have to do a thing" (Exod. 14:14, CEV). As they moved toward the sea, the waters began to part to make a passageway, allowing the entire population of Hebrew slaves to cross the length of the sea to safety. As miraculously as the waters parted, they also closed over Pharaoh and his army in their attempt to capture God's people. The victory achieved at the Red Sea was because Moses was in covenant with the Almighty!

There are several lessons to be learned from this miraculous deliverance:

- God heard the Israelites' groanings and remembered His covenant. They didn't know their covenant rights, yet God intervened and used one man—Moses—who was their covenant connection. *God has heard your groanings and is orchestrating your deliverance for the sake of covenant.*

You may not be privy to every detail of the plan that God has worked out for you, so this is why you will have to trust Him.

- Moses was just as vulnerable as anyone else in his situation. He felt the pressure of the people coming down on him to do something. But he had to trust God for their deliverance. *Your circumstances are temporary and subject to change, depending on your attitude and outlook.*

- Moses could not have done so well in the midst of crisis without a firm belief in God's covenant. No one can truly operate in covenant with a shaky belief system. If your belief system is out of whack, don't discount the Word of God when things don't go your way. There are many promises of victory in the Bible that you can stand on and believe in until the answer comes! God will see you through that hard place. *It may be time to "get a checkup from the neck up." What are you thinking or believing while in your crisis?*

- Moses waited in the desert 40 years before God called on him, in covenant, to deliver the Israelites from slavery. *Too often, when we are in crisis, our impatience doesn't allow God to intervene. Plan for victory and not defeat. Quit trying to change things that only God can change. Replace worry, frustration and the need to be in control with prayer and preparation.*

To operate in covenant with great confidence and faith, your relationship with God is key. You don't have to wait for some "spiritual giant" in the faith to come along and rescue you before you see victory. You have a right as a child of God to go after God for yourself and see the power of your covenant realized—especially in the midst of a crisis.

God will not allow you to be defeated by your enemies if He is fighting your battle. So put your faith in God!

"No faith is so precious as that which lives and triumphs in adversity," wrote the prince of preachers, Charles Spurgeon.

OUT OF EGYPT

Now that God's people were out of the clutches of the Egyptians, having just experienced God's miraculous saving power, they were rejoicing, all 2.5 million of them. But as human nature would have it, their shouts of victory soon turned into whining and complaining. Their behavior was reminiscent of the mental bondages they were accustomed to in Egypt and had yet to overcome.

Recall that God's people had been slaves all their lives and had developed a slave mentality. They never had to make decisions or solve their own problems; their Egyptian overseers had done that for them. They were physically removed from Egypt but were still mentally and emotionally reliving their old tapes (memories) of how life used to be. Confronted with the real world of freedom, they became Moses' strong-willed, rebellious children who required firm yet patient parenting.

The saga continued as they journeyed through the desert with God's miracles of provision: namely, turning bitter waters sweet and providing a daily supply of manna and quail to eat.

THE TEN COMMANDMENTS

It was now time to instruct these former slaves on how they were to live in their newfound freedom.

Moses was to gather the people at Mount Sinai at the sound of the trumpet. This would become the means of summoning the people to solemn assembly for worship, for war and for renewal of the covenant with God. The Israelites prepared themselves for three days and were forbidden to touch even the foot of the mountain. The mountain, surrounded by clouds and a "consuming fire," was shaken by a violent thunderstorm and earthquake.

A captive yet fearful Israelite audience stood riveted outside their tents, listening to Moses deliver the Ten Commandments that God had given him on the mount. Consider the picture here. The Israelites didn't know God as a loving Father and had no relationship with Him; all they knew of Him up to that point were the "acts" or miracles He performed. "The people were more captured by the phenomena of God than the Person," wrote early twentieth-century faith healer John G. Lake.

As incredible and spectacular as these events were, God knew that the Israelites still needed to form a meaningful relationship with Him. History proved this to be true when they erected a golden calf while Moses was atop the mountain receiving the Ten Commandments. The golden calf symbolized strength, loyalty and courage to their former masters, the Egyptians, and was worshiped as a god.

Along with the Ten Commandments, Moses was given other laws to help the Israelites govern their relationships, possessions, social interaction and every other area of life.

Sinai represented the making of a covenant with Israel: "And he declared unto you his covenant, which he commanded you to perform, even the ten commandments, and he wrote them upon two tables of stone" (Deut. 4:13, *ASV*). The covenant was a pledge based on national obedience to God's laws. Included in the covenant were provisions for the failure of sinners to live up to God's perfect demands. The priesthood, the tabernacle and the Levitical sacrificial system were all a part of this covenant. God provided the way of access to His throne room through the shed blood of sacrificed lambs.

Moses' role in giving the Law, a covenant document, is so significant that both the Old and New Testaments frequently refer to this Sinai revelation as the Law of Moses.

The solemn assembly that gathered at Mount Sinai was a prototype of the Church seen in the New Testament:

> You have not come to a physical mountain, to a place of flaming fire, darkness, gloom, and whirlwind, as the Israelites did at Mount Sinai when God gave them his laws. . . . No, you have come to Mount Zion, to the city of the living God, the heavenly Jerusalem, and to thousands of angels in joyful assembly. You have come to the assembly of God's firstborn children, whose names are

written in heaven. You have come to God himself, who is the judge of all people (Heb. 12:18,22-23, *NLT*).

THE ARK OF THE COVENANT

Among the Israelites, perhaps no symbol was more powerful than the Ark of the Covenant. God instructed Moses to build a tabernacle to house the Ark of the Covenant, which was nothing less than a portable temple. The commandments were placed into the gold-lined Ark, along with Aaron's rod and manna. When Israel went to war, they did so with the Ark of the Covenant before them. The Covenant was the power source against their enemies; God Himself was their ally in battle. When they crossed the Jordan on their return to Canaan, the Ark of the Covenant rested on the shoulders of the priests. Indeed, the power of Israel was in its covenant with God. Israel's religion might be called a "pup-tent" religion, in that Israel followed a God-on-the-move. They were His "movable treasure."[3]

When God chose Moses to lead the children of Israel through the exodus from Egypt, through the wilderness and, finally, into their promised land, Moses had no clue what the job required. Like anyone else who is called to lead, you don't begin by knowing all there is to know about leadership. With a staff in hand, Moses led this fledgling flock of former slaves on a journey for 40 years that included some of his greatest life lessons. It was in the wilderness where the nation and its religion were formed, free from the seduction of foreign gods. When the prophet Elijah wanted to escape the power of Baal and meet God, he returned to Sinai in the wilderness (see 1 Kings 19:3-18).

Despite his special status as God's confidant and Israel's national leader, Moses was a man of extraordinary humility.

> It was by faith that Moses, when he grew up, refused to be treated as the son of Pharaoh's daughter. He chose to share the oppression of God's people instead of enjoying the fleeting pleasures of sin. He thought it was better to suffer for the sake of the Messiah than to own the treasures of

Egypt, for he was looking ahead to the great reward that God would give him (Heb. 11:24-26, *NLT*).

God continued to engage Israel in its divine destiny through covenant, revealing His nature and will for them in the Law—the moral principles and ritual observances designed to emphasize and maintain Israel's distinctive status from a tribe of slaves into that of a sovereign nation under God. Not only was Israel established as a kingdom of priests unto God, but it was also called "son" by God: "Israel is my son, even my firstborn" (Exod. 4:22, *AMP*).

All of these extraordinary events would prove to be a precursor to the unveiling of a plan much greater than God's people would understand in their lifetime.

Life Lines

- When God sovereignly directed the infant Moses into the arms of Pharaoh's daughter, it proved to be strategic in sparing Moses' life. Never underestimate who God chooses to use in your life.

- Don't look at your weaknesses or failures as excuses for not obeying God. If you need to be affirmed each step of the way, there is no room for your faith to grow. As a child learns to walk, so you, too, will learn to walk this life of faith.

- The children of Israel had no idea that Pharaoh and his army would chase them down, leaving them stuck on the banks of the Red Sea. You may be facing your own crisis with nowhere to turn. Defying the odds requires determination and a paradigm shift in your thinking. Tough times don't last; tough people do!

- God works everything out for good, even if you can't see it at this present time.

- Though the children of Israel were physically removed from Egypt, they were still mentally enslaved to the memories of the past. In hardship they complained of how life was better in Egypt. There will always be a temptation to look back whenever the mind isn't renewed to what the Word of God says about your situation. Until they mature, God's children often murmur and complain and are impatient.

- Moses experienced the death of a vision. Called by God from his mother's womb, his first 40 years of life revealed an unusual upbringing in Pharaoh's court—no place for a rising deliverer. His next 40 years in a desert, tending sheep, appeared even worse. Would God forget this Hebrew outcast? The desert was Moses' incubator. The next 40 years were God's seal of approval on a humble man who learned how to rely on Him. You may be in a place where you feel God will never use you. Moses' experience proves otherwise.

CHAPTER EIGHT

Covenant with David
Part 1: Inward Development

> *I have made a solemn agreement with David, my chosen servant. I have sworn this oath to him: "I will establish your descendants as kings forever; they will sit on your throne from now until eternity."*
> PSALM 89:3, *NLT*

I have made more than my share of mistakes and lost quite a few friends in the mix. There have been plenty of times when I have put my foot in my mouth, hired wrong staff members, offended people and made bad financial decisions. But mistakes are just that: MIS-TAKES. Am I still useful to the kingdom of God? Yes!

Much of this book is written to encourage the layman to identify with high-profile leaders in the Bible by shedding light on who they were "behind their robes," if you will. This approach is by no means intended to dishonor them or remove the highly regarded position they continue to hold before God and man. Getting to know David allows us to get to know ourselves. It is a means by which we can relate to God and our own humanity, even as we contemplate our own usefulness and ultimate calling to service.

My first impression of David, taken from the Bible, was that he was a "man after God's own heart" and beloved of his people. As I continued to delve into his life, I discovered that his many talents and extraordinary achievements distinguished him as Israel's king. At the same time, I also saw the foibles and indiscretions that plagued David's private life.

While David's career can best be described as complex, he was a gifted musician, a writer and a mighty warrior with an ability to wield a slingshot that toppled his enemies. Capable of the highest loyalty and the basest sin, David was still a man in covenant with God. Journey with me as we travel through time to the place where David's life began, the biblical city of Bethlehem.

A PROPHET'S JOURNEY TO BETHLEHEM

When the prophet Samuel was commissioned by God to find and anoint a new king for the nation of Israel among the sons of Jesse, his natural reluctance to obey God's command is well founded. Having returned from a recent, unpleasant visit with King Saul, Samuel was envisioning an angry and outraged man, rejected by God, who was still in power. And now God's mouthpiece was asked to return to Bethlehem to anoint another in his place!

Fearing for his life, Samuel responded to God, "How can I go? If Saul hears it, he will kill me" (1 Sam. 16:2, *NKJV*). I wouldn't have wanted to be in Samuel's sandals! How was this fearful prophet to manage the matter prudently to avoid exposing himself or any other to Saul's wrath?

Samuel made his way to Bethlehem, not in pomp or with an entourage, but as a servant with a heifer that he was to sacrifice. The elders of Bethlehem were in a quandary when Samuel showed up, asking among themselves, "What is Samuel doing here?" It was strange to see him so far from his home. They believed it was an unusual occasion that might bring evil upon their town due to the rift between Samuel and the king.

Samuel's innocuous approach in this troubling situation eased the tension in these anxious leaders. Samuel inquired among the people where he might find Jesse, the Bethlehemite. It was customary that whenever a public sacrifice was made, the offerer was allowed to invite whomever he wanted. Word traveled fast, as Jesse and his sons soon showed up for the occasion. Jesse had no idea what was going on. The elders were present when Samuel approached Jesse and his sons to consecrate them before the sacrifice took place.

It was at that time that Samuel privately informed Jesse of his purpose for coming to Bethlehem—that there was a future king among his sons who was to be anointed on this occasion. Mind you, at this time, the three oldest sons of Jesse were serving in Saul's army.

A peek into this special occasion will reveal covenant lessons that we should consider. The excited and proud father of supposedly seven sons, who were young, handsome and strong, lined his boys up before the prophet for consideration. He started with the oldest, Eliab. As Samuel began to contemplate each one individually, he inquired of the Lord for His decision.

At the outset, the Lord counseled Samuel not to look at the outward appearance of these young men, because they all looked like "kingly" material. The Lord's selection would be based on the young man's character, something Samuel knew nothing about (see 1 Sam. 16:7). When Eliab was rejected, the other six young men were brought before the prophet. Much to their dismay, Samuel asked Jesse if he had any other sons.

"There remains yet the youngest, and behold, he is tending the sheep" (1 Sam. 16:11, *NASB*). Perplexed and in disbelief, these jealous brothers must have thought, *The callow misfit? No way!* The favor of God upon an individual is not predicated upon his or her proven ability to perform the duties of the office or calling. Neither is God interested in one's outward appearance, as He clearly instructed Samuel. You may meet all the qualifications of a leader because you have been educated and groomed for the position, but God's plumb line is much different from ours.

From the farmer to the housewife to the plumber to the engineer, God is no respecter of persons. Promotion comes from God, and it is simply a heart issue and nothing else. You may have a hard time measuring up to God's standards because you compare yourself to others. But it isn't all that complicated. Motive matters! What is the condition of your heart?

AN UNLIKELY KING EMERGES

As the youngest in Jesse's clan, David was assigned the task of guarding his father's sheep, which is probably one of the reasons why he wasn't included in the original lineup.

Few things seem less spiritual than taking care of a bunch of wooly sheep. But during those quiet years tending sheep, alone to fellowship with nature and his Creator, David found himself not only honing his skills on a harp but also learning some of his greatest lessons in life from the Great Shepherd.

During this time, he recognized God's hand upon him, especially when he rose up and slew a lion and a bear to protect the flock. Many of the psalms that David wrote are reminiscent of those early years he spent alone in the fields. Jesse apparently had no idea of David's bravery and wisdom, because he spoke of him as the most unfit among his sons.

As the story continues, David stood before Samuel, ruddy looking and smelling of sheep, when the Lord instructed Samuel, "Arise, anoint him; for this is he" (1 Sam. 16:12, *NASB*). So Samuel took the horn of oil and anointed David in the midst of his brothers. Imagine the tension that must have been felt when this happened; the jealousy and disapproval of his brothers was suppressed before the prophet, but later on it resurfaced.

The young, precocious teenager probably returned to his duties out in his father's fields the moment this special business was done. Because of the anointing on his life on that occasion, David soon found himself inwardly advanced in wisdom, courage and concern for the people, possessing the divine qualifications of a prince, though not at all advanced in his outward circumstances.

A godly anointing is powerful, and this one rested on David. Why weren't any of David's brothers chosen? You will recall that the three oldest brothers were already serving in Saul's army. Surely they felt they would be chosen. After all, hadn't they earned it?

"Wrath is cruel and anger outrageous, but who can stand before envy, especially the envy of a brother, the intensity of which Jacob, Joseph and David experienced?"[1]

A little sibling rivalry never hurt anyone, but let envy and jealousy continue to fester in the heart and you have family feuds that could last for a lifetime. A prideful and jealous older brother, Cain, responded when asked by Yahweh where his brother was after he murdered him, "Am I my brother's keeper?"

Take heed, those of you who have been given a special anointing or grace for leadership. You, too, will most likely be attacked, probably by those within your sphere of influence. Just as King Saul and David's brothers became envious of David, those who are insecure in their positions will feel threatened by anyone getting noticed around them and may attempt to take them down. Mark those who truly rejoice when good things happen to you—they are genuine friends and have no selfish motives to contend with.

Your covenant with God will secure you to your rightful place in the Body of Christ. If you believe that God has passed you by and promoted others around you, examine your heart. Are you really ready to be promoted? If anger and unforgiveness fester inside of you, bring this issue before the Lord so that you can gain a proper perspective on your situation. God is seldom in a hurry to promote His children. Don't get stuck in the "whys" or "what ifs" in life. Trust God!

THE KING'S MINSTREL

After anointing David, Samuel returned home to Ramah. For David, it was back to business as usual—or was it? David, in seclusion and isolation from family and others, had been honing his skills on the harp. He had no idea why. (There are skills God is developing in you that you may have no idea about. He will reveal the bigger picture to you in His timing, and perhaps you, too, will be brought into your promotion by some unknown person who is watching you from afar.)

Because God never sleeps, His business continues to unfold 24 hours a day, 7 days a week. "But the Spirit of the Lord departed from Saul, and a distressing spirit from the LORD troubled him" (1 Sam. 16:14, *NKJV*). Saul began reflecting on God's disapproval and rejection of him as king. This, coupled with the loss of his dynasty, made him jealous, irritable, vindictive and subject to bouts of rage.

Saul was in desperate need of help. One of his servants suggested that Jesse's son David come and minister to him on the harp. "Behold, I have seen a son of Jesse the Bethlehemite, who is a skillful musician, a mighty man of valor, a warrior, one prudent in speech, and a handsome man; and the LORD is with him" (1 Sam. 16:18, *NASB*). With that kind of résumé, who needs a recommendation to be Israel's next king?

Do you suppose Saul's servant had been watching David from afar when he slayed the lion and the bear? Or perhaps while playing his harp? David's victory over Goliath hadn't yet occurred for this servant to draw any conclusions about David's prowess there. But David, even as a common shepherd, had become an oracle and a champion. So Saul sent for the minstrel who was out tending his father's sheep. It never ceases to amaze me how God goes to great lengths to fulfill His will in the earth as it relates to man.

Later, Saul made David his armor bearer. David's first face-to-face interaction with Saul was through his musical talent—not just any talent, though. The anointing of God rested upon David and caused the sound of that harp to soothe and refresh a tormented Saul. (Elisha, God's prophet, also called for a musician when he was troubled, and when that musician ministered to him, the hand of the Lord came upon Elisha [see 2 Kings 3:15].)

Saul found that even with his growing enmity toward David, nothing else could remedy his ailments like the shepherd boy's harp. What a set-up by God! In his obscurity as a shepherd, God had been preparing David to face some of his fiercest battles. He was now anchored in his relationship to his Lord, knowing that Jehovah God would protect him regardless of what test came his way.

DAVID'S DUEL WITH THE TITAN

In ancient warfare, instead of armies rallying and then fighting each other, it was very common for a champion from one army to take on the champion from the opposing army. Whoever won the contest, at that point, the battle was considered over and the winning army was the one who fielded the winning soldier.

In our story, the Philistines presented Goliath; but Israel had no champion, because everyone from Saul on down was scared to death at the sight of Goliath. The Philistine warrior measured six cubits, equivalent to nine feet, eight inches in height. He would trudge around each morning taunting the Israelites to send out a champion to fight him. King Saul, the tallest and most powerful man in Israel's army, cowered in his tent and promised to reward anyone who would venture out to do battle with Goliath.

Goliath was in his line of sight when David came to the camp to bring provisions to his brothers at the instruction of his father. Hearing the taunting shouts of the titan, David was shocked that no one was willing to challenge Goliath, so he volunteered. His eldest brother quickly intervened and criticized David in front of everyone, ignorantly insinuating that he was a careless and unfaithful shepherd (see 1 Sam. 17:28-29). Eliab was one angry and jealous brother, yet David bore the provocation in an admirable way.

With David, being the youngest, and Eliab, the oldest, perhaps it was customary for the older to trample upon the younger and take every occasion possible to reprimand him. Eliab would rather that Goliath triumph over Israel than that David be the man for the job. This is the nature of jealousy. But those who attempt to exalt themselves over their juniors may live to see themselves, by providence, humbled: "The older shall serve the younger" (Rom. 9:12, *NKJV*).

There was no time for David to quarrel with his brother Eliab. In David's eyes, Goliath's challenge demeaned the living God who would surely give victory to anyone who stepped out to represent Him and His people. David explained to skeptical King Saul about his adventures in his youth, how he slew the lion and the bear and how he was going to dispatch the Philistine. The cowardly king acquiesced to let David do what no soldier in Saul's army was willing to do.

David's recollection of the invaluable counsels of Yahweh while tending sheep began to surface. "If my memory serves me correctly, God had a covenant with father Abraham. And part of that covenant included the curse that would befall those who cursed Abraham" (see Gen. 12:3). Furthermore, Goliath was not circumcised, which meant he didn't have a covenant with God. This gave David hope!

David was not moved by the giant, but by what he believed. David's covenant with God also brought with it the understanding that if God was for them, who could be against them? It had nothing to do with Goliath's size, but with the size of David's faith.

There was no way that young David should have been in the same theater of operation with this Philistine. But David confidently declared to a fearful Saul, "this Philistine shouldn't turn us into cowards. I'll go out and fight him myself" (1 Sam. 17:32, *CEV*). There were thousands of good soldiers in Israel's divisions, but not one rose to the challenge. They could see how big Goliath was, but no one could see the anointing on David.

Someday, you will face a huge problem the size of Goliath, and you will have to face it alone. Your faith in God will be tested. But the size of your problem shouldn't affect your ability to solve it as long as the Greater One lives inside of you. People will try to give you advice and opinions while you are in the intensity of the battle. Some may declare, "Well, you deserve it. There must be sin in your life." Those are religious people acting carnally.

Sadly, there are others in the Body of Christ who are weak and fearful like Saul and the rest of the Israelites. They are moved by what they see, doubting what the Word of God says about their circumstances, and they never attempt to slay their Goliath.

My dear friend Oral Roberts puts it this way, "When you see the invisible, you can do the impossible," and he has been doing the impossible nearly all of his life.

King Saul attempted to give his armor to David. But when David reluctantly donned Saul's armor, it was too heavy and restricting. "I'll just stick with what works," young David might have said. "I know what works for me; I have my own flow; I've had much practice with my weapons."

David loaded his leather pouch with a few smooth stones for his sling and advanced toward his enemy. There was only one Goliath, but David gathered five stones. Why? Goliath had four brothers. David chose the perfect stone to sling at Goliath, but perhaps he mused, *Hmm, I wonder if his brothers are out there? I'll be ready just in case!*

There is an important lesson to be learned here. If you do not practice on your small problems, forget about overcoming big ones. You see, David had practiced defeating the lion and the bear, so now he was ready for Goliath! You don't move directly from the basement to the penthouse in your Christian faith; you must move methodically, one floor at a time.

David was now face to face with Goliath. The fearless Goliath taunted, "I will give your flesh to the birds of the air and the beasts of the field." David accepted the challenge, shouting to high heaven his covenant rights before Israel's greatest enemy:

> You come to me with sword, spear, and javelin, but I come to you in the name of the LORD Almighty—the God of the armies of Israel, whom you have defied. Today the LORD will conquer you, and I will kill you and cut off your head. And then I will give the dead bodies of your men to the birds and wild animals, and the whole world will know that there is a God in Israel! And everyone will know that the LORD does not need weapons to rescue his people. It is his battle, not ours. The LORD will give you to us! (1 Sam. 17:45-47, *NLT*).

Notice how David replied to Goliath in covenant lingo? David's weapon was a sword—the Word of God in his mouth! David's confidence was displayed by his covenant rebuke to Goliath.

Facing your Goliath will also require times when you meditate on the Word of God and confess it, reminding the devil that you aren't moving until the victory comes. His taunting will have to cease because you are in covenant with Almighty God!

Jesus said to His disciples, "Have faith in God. I assure you: If anyone says to this mountain, 'Be lifted up and thrown into the sea,' and does not doubt in his heart, but believes that what he says will happen, it will be done for him. Therefore, I tell you, all the things you pray and ask for—believe that you have received them, and you will have them" (Mark 11:22-24, *CSB*). You may feel foolish when you first start speaking to your mountain of a Goliath, but remember that you are going to have to be willing to do something that perhaps you've never done before. And, of course, you may have to take this stand of faith for a season until you know you have the victory inside of you. Desperate times call for desperate measures!

When I returned home from Bible school, I was ready to conquer the world. I had my sermon notes in tow and I was going somewhere to make things happen. I had a whole lot of zeal without temperance or experience. It wasn't until I started a church that what was inside of me began to be revealed. I was greatly challenged as to what I really believed in my head versus in my heart—there is a big difference! One motivates you to action and gets results because faith is involved, and the other falls by the wayside and becomes ineffective. After a while, I learned how to stand on God's Word, and my faith matured. Today, I can believe for things unimagined when I first got out of Bible school.

Don't despise the testings of the Lord; learn to embrace the Lord in the midst of them. This is where your character is shaped and your life becomes anchored in God. This is a time for your faith to mature.

> You know that under pressure, your faith-life is forced into the open and shows its true colors. So don't try to get out of anything prematurely. Let it do its work so you become mature and well-developed, not deficient in any way (Jas. 1:3-4, *THE MESSAGE*).

The late John F. Kennedy wrote, "When written in Chinese, the word 'crisis' is composed of two characters—one represents danger and the other opportunity." It all depends upon how you perceive your Goliath.

David was a mere youth, without armor or even a shield. Goliath towered menacingly over him and was protected by an impressive array of armor, including a shield bearer. Yet, when the Philistine was a stone's throw away, David slung his slingshot and hit him on the forehead with a smooth stone. Running forward, David drew the Philistine's sword and lopped off his head. So

David prevailed over the Philistine with a sling and a stone!

One day, I was watching *Animal Planet*, a television program underscoring the relationship between humans and animals. The program featured a story about an old lion that was too old to keep his pride of females—younger, stronger males ran him off—and he could not hunt either. He was an old lion, and he was hungry. So he concealed himself by crawling up in some weeds about 30 to 40 yards from a pen of goats. All night long he would growl in a low, deep rumble.

What the lion wanted to do was to instill such fear in the goats that the goats would bolt, jump over the fence and hopefully scatter in his direction. The old lion couldn't hunt for his prey. His only chance to get a meal was to use intimidation, fear and isolation.

This is how the Bible describes Satan's modus operandi—he goes about as a roaring lion seeking whom he may devour. He's not a roaring lion, but he roars and hopes that he can intimidate, isolate and get you and me to run away from the house of God, or run away from God altogether—and run right into his clutches. The devil doesn't have the strength to take you out. In reality, the devil is no match for you. You have power and authority at your disposal to overcome him because of your blood covenant with Yahweh.

DAVID AND JONATHAN— COVENANT PARTNERS

Our story continues with the children of Israel plundering the tents of the Philistines immediately after Goliath was taken out. Don't you know that Saul's son Jonathan probably had a ringside seat in the outdoor local amphitheater when the battle of all battles took place between the underdog, David, and the heavyweight champion, Goliath?

A warrior in his daddy's army, Jonathan was stunned at how David attacked and slew Goliath with a measly slingshot and stone. Saul was just as stunned, and now he really wanted to know about this young lad; so he summoned David. With the bloody head of the Philistine in hand, David approached the king, telling him he was the son of Jesse, the Bethlehemite. Prince Jonathan, who was about 30 years old and King Saul's firstborn, soon latched onto David, impressed by his heroism and modest demeanor. "When David finished talking with Saul, Jonathan felt very close to David. He loved David as much as he loved himself" (1 Sam. 18:1, *NCV*).

Jonathan's heart was knit to the soul of David, who was about 17. We have two men: one of royal descent, a prince; the other a pauper and a simple shepherd. In ancient times, shepherds were so low in social status that they could not even testify in a court of law. These two should have had nothing in common, and yet they formed a covenant of friendship.

Such covenants of brotherhood were frequent in the Near East. They were ratified by certain ceremonies that, for the most part, took place in the presence of witnesses and required blood sacrifice; the persons covenanting would be sworn brothers for life.

JONATHAN AND DAVID CUT A COVENANT

"I pledge my oath to you, David, that everything I have is yours, my name is yours, my robe is yours, my weapons are yours, my family is yours," declared Jonathan. David in turn recited to Jonathan the same solemn oath. This was one of several covenants made between Jonathan and David. Even though David was insignificant and didn't have any gifts to exchange with Jonathan, the oath guaranteed that the terms outlined would be fulfilled throughout their lifetime, and to successive generations.

Once the covenant vows were declared, Jonathan doffed his clothing and his weapons and placed them on David. Jonathan gave all that he had to protect David from harm and to ensure his position as future king. He verbalized his solemn oath by pledging, at great personal risk, to protect David from harm (see 1 Sam. 20:13). Men like Jonathan were a rarity. Indeed, only God could motivate a man to do something like this.

Compared to Jonathan, David was unimportant and insignificant. Yet the young 17-year-old was suddenly wearing Prince

Jonathan's robe. From this point on, whenever David went out wearing that robe, doors opened and people moved out of the way, because the name of Jonathan now preceded young David.

It amazes me how God brings people together. What brought these two—the prince and the pauper—together? It was a crisis! Israel was again on the brink of destruction at the hands of the Philistines. All Israel was fearful of Goliath—he was like three Mike Tysons on steroids. All of his life the only thing Goliath studied was how to be a man of war. He was a trained killer. By contrast, David was a shepherd boy who played his harp and sang. Yet Jonathan saw something in David that he wanted to be associated with and gave himself to David in a covenant that would bind them together as one. They had separate lives but inseparable bonds. Jonathan was an important part of God's plan for David.

When I was growing up, I enjoyed listening to Smokey Robinson's music and watching Jim Brown play football and star in movies. Like David and Jonathan, there is no bigger contrast in social status than between Smokey, Jim Brown and me; yet they are now two of my best friends! When it comes to friendships, the strongest bond in the universe that keeps them together is the covenant of love.

A FUGITIVE ON THE RUN

King Saul now regarded David as the ultimate threat. "Saul has killed thousands of his enemies, but David his tens of thousands" (1 Sam. 18:7, *NCV*). The praise of the people directed at David incited jealousy and resentment in Saul. Get ready for adversity! As your destiny makes way for itself, coupled with God's favor, you will make some people jealous, very jealous. Some will believe that you are out to replace them, and your best efforts will not convince them otherwise. As others begin to sing your praises, look out for the one who isn't singing.

As reward for the head of Goliath, Saul promised his daughter to the champion. He offered his oldest daughter, Merab, to David. But Saul's second daughter, Michal, was in love with David. So

Saul offered Michal, thinking he could use her as a pawn to destroy David.

It wasn't long after the Goliath incident and his marriage to Michal that David realized he could no longer remain in the palace with the king. A paranoid and irrational King Saul was breathing threats of David's demise to his servants, and Jonathan immediately sought David to advise him to leave. Fearing for his life, David fled from Saul; but soon a band of admirers joined David while he lived as a fugitive in the wilderness of Judah.

On one occasion, the king was pursuing David and fell providentially within David's reach. David took the opportunity to secretly cut a piece of the hem of Saul's garment. When at a safe distance, David called out to Saul and dangled the piece of his garment before him, revealing to Saul just how close to death he had come. David pleaded with Saul for his life, trying to persuade him to have a change of heart. Even though David's subordinates egged him on to do away with Saul, David was later convicted that he was coming against his master, and thus ordered his men not to touch the king. David had the rarest of qualities: a love and respect for his enemy. Saul was still king, and he was Jonathan's father.

Recognizing that his intentions to kill David were wrong, a remorseful Saul pleaded, "You have declared today that you have done good to me, that the LORD delivered me into your hand and yet you did not kill me. For if a man finds his enemy, will he let him go away safely?" (1 Sam. 24:18-19, *NASB*). During the course of their conversation, Saul blessed David and pleaded with him not to cut off his descendants and destroy his name. David swore to Saul that he would not, but returned to his hiding place.

Godly authority is given to the trustworthy. Many disqualify themselves from receiving more authority from God because of the way they disrespect authority, even in the workplace. Remember, it was because of David's high calling that he was subjected to such a great test with a cruel, demented king like Saul.

Nowhere in the Bible does it say to only be in subjection to righteous and just authorities, but rather to "all" authority. If you want God to promote you, learn to pass this test. Only God knows why certain people hurt others. Leave them to Him. Vengeance belongs only to God.

The covenant rites that Jonathan and David declared to each other would be tested time and again. Jonathan's willingness to submit to David, even though Jonathan was rightful heir to the throne, is amazing. Jonathan recognized that David would eventually be king over Israel.

ZIKLAG: PURSUIT AND RECOVERY

David was in a bad season of his life. A demon-possessed King Saul was still trying to kill him. David had to continually hide from Saul. Things were so bad that he even went to the camp of the Philistines and asked for their protection but was rejected by the Philistine king.

David, a man without a country, was temporarily lodging in a little place called Ziklag. As he and his 600 men approached the town, they noticed that it had gone up in smoke and everything burned to the ground (see 1 Sam. 30:1-2).

David had carelessly left his family unprotected. Imagine his dilemma. He was already depressed and wondering what was going to happen to him. But approaching this horrific scene, David and his men expected to find dead bodies all over the place. Instead they found the place abandoned because all of their families had been captured. Facing Goliath was one thing, but dealing with 600 angry, grief-stricken men was another story altogether.

What was this fugitive on the run, who was in covenant with the Almighty God, going to do? The Bible says that when the thief is caught, he must restore sevenfold what he has stolen (see Prov. 6:31).

Let's examine David's journey to recover all.

1. HE CRIED UNTIL THERE WERE NO MORE TEARS

"Then David and the men with him lifted up their voices and wept until they had no more strength to weep" (1 Sam. 30:4). Imagine 600 men crying in agony for their families. Not only did David have to deal with his own personal loss, but he also had to deal with the combined losses of his men who were now looking for someone to blame. David's own army wanted to kill him. David felt alone and overwhelmed. His situation looked hopeless. It would have been easy for David to argue with God about this matter, complaining that he didn't deserve to be in this place. All that David had experienced was trouble from the time Samuel secretly anointed him king. He had spent years running from Saul, and now he had lost everything.

When you have had a major loss, the first thing you should do is just cry until there are no more tears. Crying is healthy because it releases toxic emotions inside you so that you can begin to heal. If you suppress your true feelings and don't release them in grief, physical or mental problems can occur.

2. HE ENCOURAGED HIMSELF IN THE LORD

The very next thing David did was to encourage himself in the Lord and refuse the temptation to blame others. He had enough of a disciplined prayer life to make his top priority seeking God's will in the matter. He then found a man of God (a priest) and sought guidance for their next move.

If you don't have a pastor or a church to support you spiritually, your life will be a disaster. When the pressure builds up in my life, I have a pastor, Dr. David Yonggi Cho, to reach out to. I can pick up the phone and call him and ask for advice and help. Everyone needs a man or woman of God, or a church, for spiritual guidance.

3. HE RECEIVED SPECIFIC INSTRUCTIONS

God instructed David, "Pursue them . . . you will certainly overtake them and succeed in the rescue" (1 Sam. 30:8, *NIV*). Immediately preparing to implement God's plan, David and his men met an Egyptian soldier from the Amalekite army. He had been left behind three days earlier by his superior because he fell ill. His army could not bring him along because he was a liability to them. So David's men fed him. The soldier told David that he got sick right after they had burned Ziklag to the ground. Being the military strategist that David was, he asked the Egyptian soldier, "Can you take me down to this troop?" David wanted to find out where their wives and children were holed up. The Egyptian soldier agreed to divulge the whereabouts on condition that David would not kill him or deliver him into the hands of his master (see 1 Sam. 30:11-15).

When you're in a crisis, stay open to some strange and out-of-the-ordinary help. David got assistance from his enemies in the form of an abandoned Egyptian soldier. With the Egyptian's sword in hand, David led his men as they followed this soldier to the enemy's camp. They then settled in a nearby foxhole in order to spy out the land. What they discovered sent David's heart racing as he watched the Amalekites celebrating their great victory over Ziklag and all the spoils they had gathered. David was about to rain on their victory party in a big way.

4. HE AND HIS ARMY WERE GIVEN THE VICTORY

"And David smote them from twilight even unto the evening of the next day: and there escaped not a man of them, save four hundred young men, who rode upon camels and fled. And David recovered all that the Amalekites had taken; and David rescued his two wives. And there was nothing lacking to them, neither small nor great, neither spoil, nor anything that they had taken to them: David brought back all" (1 Sam. 30:17-19, *ASV*).

On that day, David turned tragedy into triumph. In God's eyes, David's kingship was demonstrated in the rubble of Ziklag, where he had learned to encourage himself in the Lord his God.

You may be experiencing your own "Ziklag." Never give up! Ziklag is not your destiny, but a steppingstone along the way.

If you've lost your joy, it's coming back sevenfold.

If you've lost your money, it's coming back sevenfold.

If you've lost family, they're coming back sevenfold.

But how, one may ask, could this be? Losing something is one thing, but just giving it away out of foolishness, ignorance or sin is another. The ignorant might add, "Surely God will not return what I have lost. God is going to teach me a lesson."

The fact of the matter is that God isn't leaning over the banister of heaven watching you like a tyrant. The lesson He wants to teach you is about His unconditional love. David made a mistake by leaving his family unprotected. But this mistake wasn't going to destroy him. We all make mistakes. But God is a good Father. All He knows is that you're His child and His covenant with you includes complete restoration of all things. And do you know why He does it? For His own glory.

Close your eyes and think of a great loss you've suffered—a friend, a marriage, a dream, a vision, a business or maybe your health. I want you take a step of faith and picture your loss being restored and bringing a sevenfold blessing with it. It may take time, but thank God in advance. Receive a revelation of the covenant of recovery, because it's all coming back to you and your family, in Jesus' name.

The battle that ended the lives of Saul and his three sons was a battle lost to the Philistines in the Jezreel Valley. Wounded and about to die, Saul witnessed his sons slaughtered and immediately entreated his armor bearer to kill him. But his armor bearer refused, so Saul fell on his own sword, knowing the Philistines would make a mockery of him had they captured him alive. When they located his body, the Philistines dismembered him, cutting off his head, surely in memory of their own slain Goliath. They hung his blood-soaked torso and those of his sons from the city wall of Beth Shan as public trophies. What a terrible ending.

It was Jonathan who had gone searching for David several times during the heat of his daddy's unending jealous rage to renew their vow of covenant friendship. They swore an oath to watch over each other's families in generations to come should anything unfortunate happen to either one. At his death, do you suppose Jonathan wondered if David would keep the covenant they had made together?

CHAPTER 9

Covenant with David
Part 2: A Time of Transition

> *I have made a solemn agreement with David, my chosen servant.*
> *I have sworn this oath to him: "I will establish your descendants as*
> *kings forever; they will sit on your throne from now until eternity."*
> PSALM 89:3, NLT

When a runner appeared to David from Saul's camp to announce the defeat at Jezreel, he carried the crown and armband of Saul, telling David that Saul and his sons were dead. In shock, David and his men mourned, wept and fasted until evening for their loss: "How I weep for you, my brother Jonathan! Oh, how much I loved you! And your love for me was deep, deeper than the love of women" (2 Sam. 1:26, *NLT*).

When the season of mourning was over, David began to transition into his kingship role. This would not be without the disapproval of some. Periods of transition are seldom easy. Whether it's a new job, getting married, having a baby, moving—you name it—transition is challenging.

The workplace can be a source of great testing and stress, especially when you get used to working for one boss and then have to work for another who is perhaps a tyrant or less than reasonable. Transitioning into full-time ministry can bring uncertainty and stress. The right heart attitude will work to your favor.

Saul's body probably hadn't even grown cold when Abner, Saul's nephew and commander-in-chief, enthroned Saul's surviving son, Ishbosheth, over Israel. With the exception of the tribe of Judah, all the others had chosen David to be their king. Did Abner have a legitimate right to do this, or were the evils of nepotism continuing to rule the family roost? The immediate consequence of Ishbosheth's coronation brought a war that Abner and his men lost. Eventually the kingdom came under David's rulership.

A KING'S EXAMPLE

As soon as David was crowned king over the entire nation, he made Jerusalem the capital of a united Israel and had the Ark of the Covenant returned to the city. This was a symbolic gesture that David wasn't going to allow worship of the Lord to get lost in the daily grind of life. He was setting an example before the people of the value of the presence of the Lord. It was time to celebrate!

David put on a tremendous feast and led the celebration, dancing before the Lord with all his might. David didn't care what people thought. He was honoring his God. This was no old-fashioned jig or twist. He was leaping and whirling before the Lord in a linen ephod (an undergarment)—apparently without regard for the dignity of a king. Having the presence of the Lord with him was enough to bring the child out of the king. However, proud of her royal lineage, David's wife Michal upbraided him for disregarding the dignity of the crown and, in her eyes, acting more like a buffoon than a king. David wasn't moved by his wife's reaction; instead he was glad to abase himself before the lowliest handmaids in Israel in the service of Yahweh. As a result of her prideful actions, Michal was justly put under a curse of barrenness.

After years of military feats and continued political success, David was both hailed and feared for being the foremost example of God's king to Israel.

Years after the death of Saul and his sons, David began to think about his friend Jonathan. People had come and gone in his life since Jonathan's death, but none compared to the genuine friendship and undying commitment both had for each other. David felt indebted to him, remembering the covenant they had made together. So he began to inquire whether there was anyone remaining from the house of Saul to whom he could show kindness for Jonathan's sake.

"Saul's servant Ziba is still alive, perhaps we can inquire of him," David's servant respectfully suggested as he bowed before the presence of his master. Ziba had been living a quiet and rather peaceful existence in the city, his days no longer filled with the constant demands and responsibilities of a courtier. This once popular and sought-after servant had blended into the landscape of his surroundings, tending to his family, when he heard about King David's request.

Summoned to the palace by one of David's servants, Ziba entered the presence of the king, and after exchanging pleasantries, he informed him that Jonathan did in fact have a son who was lame in his feet.

"His name is Mephibosheth," Ziba offered.

"Tell me about this Mephibosheth," the king said.

"When the child was five years old, news of the death of his father and grandfather reached Jezreel, and his nurse grabbed him and fled, fearing that you would take him captive. In flight, she dropped the child, seriously injuring him, and he became a cripple. What spooked the young boy's nurse was her misguided notion that you would kill all of Saul's seed so that there would never be cause for a political coup by someone who might believe that the throne belonged to him," Ziba said.

The young lad's nurse had no idea that Jonathan and David were in covenant!

An important reminder about covenant should be stressed here. When Jonathan sought David, it was the greater seeking out the lesser. As David came into his kingdom, he sought out Mephibosheth, the lesser. What could Mephibosheth have to offer David? Absolutely nothing! After 20 years, David now had the power to bless Mephibosheth and was seeking him out.

LORD MEPHIBOSHETH

The little 5-year-old cripple was now 25. For 20 years he had been brainwashed into thinking that because he was the seed of Jonathan, he would automatically be a threat to David; and if David ever got hold of him, Mephibosheth would be dead. After inquiring of his whereabouts, Ziba informed King David that Mephibosheth lived in Lo Debar. Only about 25 miles from Jerusalem, Lo Debar was an utterly desolate place where nothing grew. Not surprisingly, Lo Debar means "absence of God."

A son of Jonathan was living in Lo Debar! King David must have been incredulous. This little band of people loyal to Saul went and hid in a place so foul and unpleasant that if David knew of their whereabouts earlier, he probably would have just let them be.

"Send for him," King David ordered Ziba.

When they returned from Lo Debar, and as they entered the king's palace, Mephibosheth began to tremble with fear, keeping Ziba by his side. As was customary, Ziba and Mephibosheth were escorted into a small chamber so that Mephibosheth could be bathed and groomed before entering the king's presence for the most important encounter of his life.

Uncertain of King David's reaction toward him, Mephibosheth fell on his face in great reverence and fear when the king entered the room. Can you picture this poor crippled man trying to pay homage to King David?

To Mephibosheth's surprise, King David approached him with an intimate embrace, greeting him with great tenderness and compassion. The king's greeting quickly turned into a conversation.

"Mephibosheth, don't be afraid. I would like to show you kindness. You know, son, I was a good friend of your daddy's. In fact, we were in covenant together when he was alive, and I've been thinking about the oath we swore together.

"And now that your daddy's gone, I want to make good on my end of the promise. Tell you what, son, I will return to you all the land that belonged to your grandfather Saul, and you will always be welcome at my table" (see 2 Sam. 9:7).

Mephibosheth could hardly believe what he was hearing. The king took Mephibosheth in and made him one of his family. Mephibosheth suddenly become wealthy. The grant of his grandfather's estate was confirmed to him and the management of the estate was committed to Ziba. Once King Saul was David's sworn enemy, but now David showed kindness to his house and was delighted to do so.

Not understanding covenant, Mephibosheth's natural reaction was predictable: "I am no better than a dead dog, sir! Why should you be so good to me?" (2 Sam. 9:8, *GNB*). You see, Lo Debar had become Mephibosheth's prison of shame and isolation. Though he was the son of a prince and the grandson of a king, he saw himself as a dog before King David. While Mephibosheth had resigned himself to a meager life, his true inheritance was secured in a covenant blessing that promised an abundant life.

However, Mephibosheth had to move from Lo Debar to King David's palace in order to claim his blessing!

Have you ever felt like Mephibosheth? It is hard for many of us to believe that God loves us unconditionally.

I was crippled emotionally, spiritually and even mentally in my perception of God. I never wrapped my mind around God the Father—I never really had a father growing up—so God as Father never really meant much to me. Many of you don't know what real love is either. So it's hard for you to believe that a holy God would love you—a weak and sinful creature (as you see yourself). Instead of feasting at the Master's table, you are abandoned at Lo Debar, carrying a paralyzing burden or affliction that overwhelms you with shame and guilt.

For most of my life, I was living in "Lo Debar"—as a matter of fact, I frequented most of the local bars! If they had a jukebox and a pool table, I was there. Me, go to church on Sunday? No way! But one day, God called the Holy Ghost—"Ziba" represents the Holy Ghost in our narrative—and said, "Go, fetch Bernal. I need him. I have a plan for San Jose. There's a church that is going to be birthed there. There are people he's going to reach that no one else is going to reach with My gospel."

When I surrendered my life to God, all I heard was "Welcome home, son. You're the apple of My eye. I'm going to prosper you. I'm going to give you everything your daddy didn't give you. And, everything the devil has stolen from the Bernal family, I'm going to give back a hundredfold."

Then God revealed to me that His love and blessings were not conditional on how bad or how good I was. God doesn't love everything we do; but we can't stop Him from loving *us*, because God is in covenant with us!

In order to receive his inheritance, Mephibosheth had to leave Lo Debar. He had to leave his familiar surroundings, his family, his friends and everything that meant anything to him back there. However, there was no future in Lo Debar. As uncomfortable as he was at first, Mephibosheth embraced what belonged to him and, no doubt, was mindful of what family he had left, and rescued them out of Lo Debar as well. They, too, were shocked to hear about King David's kindness.

There are many reasons why people don't abandon their personal Lo Debars. Here are a few:

1. FEAR

Mephibosheth was royalty, yet the memory of his father, Jonathan, faded into nothingness as the years passed, and he was content to eat the crumbs from the table of apathy. If you will recall, his greatest fear was that David would have him executed as a survivor of Saul's regime. The physical circumstances of his daily life were constant reminders of the shame and inferiority he had grown accustomed to. For Mephibosheth to believe otherwise wasn't possible outside of divine intervention. His physical condition didn't help either. Thinking about his future didn't cross his mind. What future? His self-worth was reduced to a dead-dog persona that also had a crippling effect on him. Mephibosheth had an identity crisis!

Like poverty and illiteracy, a physical disability can challenge a person's sense of self-worth. A disabled person might feel useless to society, much less to God. A handicap could cause anyone to become bitter at God, and at life.

What is your greatest fear? Failure? A handicap? The Bible says that "fear has torment," incapacitating its victims. God wants to give you a new identity in Christ that will remove the stronghold of fear. You are worth more to God believing in His Word than believing the lies of the devil. You belong at His table. Don't forget,

God is interested in helping you succeed and prosper in this life, not only when you get to heaven.

2. BELIEF SYSTEMS

What was Mephibosheth's response to David when he welcomed him into his family? "I am no better than a dead dog! Why should you be good to me?" What does that tell you about Mephibosheth's thinking? His mind could not fathom the goodness King David showered upon him, especially since his perception of the king was already skewed. Rejection was his automatic reaction. Lo Debar created a defeated mindset that didn't allow him to think about another life; he couldn't imagine freedom outside of his daily grind. He was living the rat race created by a mind filled with hopelessness.

I cannot stress enough the importance of meditating on the Word of God and being changed by it. Throughout this book I have mentioned the subject of renewing the mind, because without this critical process you will be unable to confidently walk in your covenant with God. God is faithful to keep His end of the covenant; it is man that doesn't always believe what is written. The sin of unbelief is a great barrier to accessing covenant.

If your belief system is contrary to the Word of God, the truths or convictions you live by today may contribute to your frustration and disappointment concerning God's intervention in the affairs of your life. "For as he thinks in his heart, so is he" (Prov. 23:7, *NKJV*). Gaining a godly perspective on the struggles of your life doesn't happen overnight. A close examination of what you believe about God and His Word will provide clues. That exam isn't hard to do: "For the mouth speaks from the overflow of the heart" (Matt. 12:34, *CSB*).

Your world is shaped by what you believe and has a profound effect on how you live. The opinions others have of you may be more important to you than God's opinion of you. What you speak out of your mouth is connected with what you believe. Is it defeat? Cynicism? Unbelief? If you are always saying what you don't have, then you will never have what rightfully belongs to you, because what rightfully belongs to you doesn't exist in a "don't-have" mindset. Conversely, covenant lingo is faith speaking those things that are not as though they are.

If you have lived most of your life in defeat, you are going to have to think differently. In order to do that, the Word of God must become a priority in your life. The life of faith isn't automatic. Yet the more you ponder the Scriptures and allow the Holy Spirit to illuminate your understanding about your covenant rights, the more you will walk in them. Old mindsets, religious traditions and wrong doctrines create false patterns of thinking that keep you from true freedom in Christ. They must be dismantled to make way for a new way of life. "My people are destroyed for lack of knowledge" (Hos. 4:6, *NRSV*).

When you surrendered your life to Christ, the eternal seed of salvation was deposited within you, and that spiritual seed is what allows you to believe and hope for things that would otherwise be impossible or out of your reach. If you will recall, believing was the entrance into your spiritual life. "When you pray and ask for something, believe that you have received it, and you will be given whatever you ask for" (Mark 11:24, *GNB*). You believed that Christ's death for you was real and that He forgave you of your sins, right? The same holds true for the rest of the spiritual truths noted in the Bible. You will never realize your place at God's table without changing your thought life.

3. RESISTANCE TO CHANGE

Mephibosheth wasn't looking for change. He was comfortable where he was living, under a cloud of fear brought on by a lie. His environment committed him to a lifestyle of defeat with no possible hope for his future. His lack of understanding kept him from strong faith to believe for a different future. Even though he was the beneficiary of a covenant through his daddy, Jonathan, he was totally oblivious of its power to raise him up from his poverty.

Living in the status quo is a dangerous position to be in because it creates a false sense of security that doesn't allow for spiritual growth. Stagnant waters are not drinkable; they attract all kinds of insects and give off a putrid odor. But if you don't understand the reality of your condition, you will see no need for change. Old habits produce a litany of excuses and die hard. The current that keeps you flowing in the wrong direction will have to be exposed for what it is. Then you can make a conscious effort, like the salmon, to swim upstream and go against that current. As the nature of the salmon is to go against the current to spawn new life, so the believer has been given a new nature, or a supernatural ability to resist the current of the status quo in order to change.

Believe it or not, some people would rather remain stuck in a rut than explore the possibilities of a higher life. You see, Mephibosheth possessed the covenant privileges when he was in Lo Debar, even though he probably wasn't aware of them. There are many Mephibosheths in the Body of Christ today who do not access their covenant rights and are even unaware that royal blood is flowing through their veins.

Laziness, apathy or indifference can be hindrances that some folks aren't willing to overcome. For them, comfort is more appealing than intestinal fortitude. There may be a hidden, troubling sin that you don't want to deal with. Or you may think that it's too difficult to rise up and be different against social and peer pressure, even when your own spiritual sanity and well-being are at stake.

After the children of Israel were delivered from Egypt, it took time to get Egypt out of their collective thinking. Most of the generation that started out in the wilderness died off because they murmured and complained and longed for the way things were in Egypt.

Are you afflicted with spiritual cataracts and unable to see what God is doing? Salvation is free, but the spiritual discipline to maintain that freedom will require effort.

DINING AT THE MASTER'S TABLE

Picture with me the moment when Mephibosheth came to sit at the dinner table next to King David. David's sons must have stared, wondering, "Who is this guy?"

"Hey, that's Saul's grandson. What's he doing at our table?"

"What's he doing sitting next to our dad?"
"Why is our dad calling him 'son'?"
"And why is he calling our dad 'father'?"
"He's no relative of ours!"

You see, King David had some knuckleheads for sons, especially Absalom. This is the way a lot of church people act when you try to worship at their church! If you don't measure up to their standards, you're not welcome in their church. So Mephibosheth, wiping his mouth from a rich kingly meal, the likes of which he hadn't tasted in 20 years, replied to King David's sons, "I agree with you guys. In fact, I hated you guys all my life. And truthfully, I didn't really feel at home with all of this pomp and splendor—that is, until your daddy told me a story.

"Before we were born, my daddy, Jonathan, and your daddy made a covenant. They vowed to each other, 'I'll take care of you and your family, and your family's family to a thousand generations.' So, I'll tell you something right now. I don't deserve to be here but I'm here because of that covenant."

The reality that Mephibosheth had done nothing to merit King David's favor and mercy is something to meditate on. He didn't eat in the servant's quarters; he was sitting next to the king. Promotion positions you where Christ covers your sins, failures and weaknesses.

"I'll call nobodies and make them somebodies; I'll call the unloved and make them beloved. In the place where they yelled out, 'You're nobody!' they're calling you 'God's living children'" (Rom. 9:25-26, *THE MESSAGE*).

Dining at the Master's table has its privileges and blessings. From healing to favor, to honor to provision, no matter what the need, there is an abundant supply at His table. The restoration of all things is an integral part of covenant. Although restoration is a process that requires renewing your mind to your covenant rights, it is attainable!

You might be interested to know that Mephibosheth means "shame-destroyer" or "image-breaker." What a picture of our Lord! Jesus became our shame-breaker and has made us in His image and likeness. A covenant blessing awaited Mephibosheth beyond his wildest dreams. He had been born to royalty, and it was providence that brought him into his rightful place at the king's table!

AN UNGUARDED HEART

Rising to great prominence in his life and career, King David appeared invincible. Goliath and the hostile Philistine armies that surrounded them hadn't been able to defeat Israel. He was 55 years old, and up to this point, his life appeared to be spotless. To have had that type of notoriety and success was certain to fill David's heart with pride if he had no accountability.

To set the stage for this often quoted historical episode, the Bible makes a brief note that David took more concubines and wives in Jerusalem prior to Bathsheba (see 2 Sam. 5:13). So, it is safe to assume that King David wasn't lacking for sexual fulfillment.

"One evening David got up from his bed and walked around on the roof of the palace. From the roof he saw a woman bathing. The woman was very beautiful, and David sent someone to find out about her" (2 Sam. 11:2-3, *NIV*).

Evidently, in a moment of weakness, one woman bathing on a rooftop was all it took for David to succumb to adultery and a cover-up. Can you imagine the tabloids of David's day? The Bethlehem *Enquirer* would have run amuck, ad nauseum, with the juicy gossip of David's clandestine affair with Bathsheba. Were the people of David's day as "forgiving" as we are? Did this serious blunder destroy David's political career and life? A closer look at the events surrounding this grievous sin will reveal some interesting yet provocative insights.

At one time in his early life, David was sensitive to the conviction of God, having been remorseful for cutting the hem of King Saul's garment. He sought the counsel of prophets and allowed himself to be held accountable. He now answered to no one. You can be sure that the enemy stalked his prey and pounced on him when he least expected it. This proved to be a most dangerous place for King David to be.

All Satan had to do was appeal to David's flesh by dangling Bathsheba before his eyes, and he grabbed the bait. Why? King David took for granted the divine favor and approval of his actions to that point, leaving his heart unguarded, and his heart began to deceive him. He took what didn't belong to him and found himself head over heels with a married woman, Bathsheba. Then, when David heard the news that she was pregnant, he tried to cover up his sin.

Adultery was bad enough, but when he had arranged to have his mistress's husband killed, it displeased the Lord. After a period of mourning for her husband, Bathsheba soon bore David a son. The birth of the child, so soon after the marriage, broadcast the crime.

A year later, God sent Nathan the prophet to confront David about his sin. His actions were detestable. Yet in God's mercy, David would be forgiven if he repented. David confessed his sin, and though he received forgiveness, his moral failure had a terrible impact on his family.

After his repentance, Nathan prophesied, "The sword will never depart from your house, because you despised me and took the wife of Uriah the Hittite to be your own" (2 Sam. 12:10, *NIV*). Along with its consequences, sin carries the stain of guilt and shame. When David's son Amnon followed his father's similar example and raped his half-sister, Tamar, David did nothing. Later, Absalom, David's son, murdered Amnon and fled the country. Robbed of his moral authority because of his own sins, King David seemed strangely silent over the crimes committed by his children. David would reap the same sin he had committed against Uriah, as an "intimate" would sleep with his wives in public. And worst yet, the illegitimate child conceived through this illicit affair with Bathsheba would die.

When Absalom finally returned home, his outright rebellion and attempted coup brought many problems to David's reign. David endured many trials and great sorrows, but his own son's attempt to dethrone him must have been the worst nightmare of his life. Needless to say, Nathan's prophecy of turmoil in David's family didn't take long to come to pass. God never winks at sin, ever. Sexual sin is a major tool Satan has used through the centuries to destroy lives, ministries and anything else in its path.

WEAKNESSES THAT NEED A SAFEGUARD

1. BEING IN THE WRONG PLACE AT THE WRONG TIME

The adultery with Bathsheba happened when all the men were at war. What was David doing home? Kings were supposed to be with the army. David neglected his business, delegating his position to Joab, his commander-in-chief. If you find yourself in the wrong place at the wrong time, flee. Otherwise, you, too, may find yourself reaping a host of problems.

"No temptation has overtaken you except such as is common to man; but God is faithful, who will not allow you to be tempted beyond what you are able, but with the temptation will also make the way of escape, that you may be able to bear it" (1 Cor. 10:13, *NKJV*).

When the apostle Paul was referring to God making a "way of escape," that is exactly what he meant. Some things don't need to be spiritually discerned. David could have cried out to God for a way out and it would have been granted to him. You can be sure that God would have provided a way of escape when you consider all the lives damaged by David's sin. Remember, when entertaining the idea of sexual sin, it isn't likely that such a person is going to run to the Bible or refer to a book like this for serious solutions—that thought won't come to mind until it is too late.

2. IDLENESS AND ISOLATION

King David dozed away the afternoon, which he should have spent in more constructive ways. There was a time when he prayed not only in the morning and evening but also at noontime. The bed of sloth can often prove to be the bed of lust.

Do you have too much time on your hands? Beware! When you isolate yourself, you become vulnerable. Isolation often stems from impure motives and signals an unwillingness to be held accountable for one's actions. A divine grace is given to every believer when he is facing temptation; whether the believer takes the way of escape determines who is in control.

3. LACK OF ACCOUNTABILITY

Believing himself above scrutiny was King David's greatest downfall. Never think that you don't need others to speak into your life. If you had had a chance to interview King David before this grievous sin, he probably would have been unwilling to admit that his heart was full of pride.

Pride is like bad breath. You are the last to know you have it. Preventative measures are always the best solution to ward off any kind of scheme of the devil.

Examine yourself to see if there is any pride or arrogance in an area you haven't considered, before it's too late. Accountability is a safety net that protects you in times of trouble. Pure motives stem from a pure heart with nothing to hide. A pure heart is God's most valuable possession.

4. THE PROGRESSIVE NATURE OF SIN

Satan appealed to David's flesh at the height of his career. After seeing Bathsheba bathing, he saw that she was very beautiful. Sight turned into desire. Desire turned to possession, regardless of her marital status. To compromise our biblical convictions is a sure sign that we are headed in the wrong direction.

How did Satan tempt Jesus? "If you are God's Son, order this stone to turn into bread" (Luke 4:3, *GNB*). Satan's attack on Jesus was an attack on His physical weakness. There was nothing wrong with Jesus wanting to eat. The point is that Satan was trying to gain a foothold in His life so that Jesus would start listening to him. Jesus responded with the Word of God. Because Satan is so perverted, wicked, greedy and manipulative, he assumed that Jesus must be like that too. Not so! Satan missed it by projecting his own character onto Jesus.

If the circumstances at home or in your marriage are sour and you aren't willing to covenant with God to stand for the marriage, you will start fantasizing about another way of life, and Satan will accommodate you. If you do not cast down those thoughts and bring them into subjection to Christ, you'll find yourself in the same predicament as David.

Sin left unchecked grows like a weed, having a life of its own. Satan probably won't use the word "adultery" as much as he will entangle your heart with the other person and you will begin to reason that you are in love. "Adultery" is too harsh of a word when you are trying to ease your conscience about the sin you are about to commit. "It couldn't be that bad. After all, we love each other and we will eventually make things right," clamors the heart of reason.

"There is a way that seems right to a man, But its end is the way of death" (Prov. 14:12, *NKJV*). Jealousy, lust and revenge may also consume one's thought life without any conscious regard that these actions go against establishing a covenant with God and are in fact sin.

5. CLOSING YOUR EAR TO THE HOLY SPIRIT'S VOICE

While it was a year before Nathan the prophet confronted David about his sin, David had other opportunities to make things right. You can't get away with murder. You can be sure that the Spirit of God was convicting him; but after a while, that conviction began to wane and David's heart began to harden in his sin. Conviction of sin is as necessary to the believer as the air he breathes.

We all have experienced seasons like David's where we weren't willing to listen to the Holy Spirit's leading when He was trying to warn us of potential wrongdoing. The bitter consequences David reaped are reminders for us to pay attention to those yellow blinking lights. Whatever David's motives for having Bathsheba's husband killed on the battlefield, he did so without restraint. He continued in a downward spiral that led to an evil shadow being cast over him, staining his character. This also revealed the awful lengths to which the best of men will go when they ignore God's grace to abstain from sin. Remember David's lesson: What we do in secret, if left unchecked, will become public.

6. COVER-UP LEADS TO FURTHER DEVASTATION

Some immediate measures to conceal David and Bathsheba's sin were necessary. The king's honor was at stake, as well as Bathsheba's safety; the sin of adultery was grounds for her death.

"When David bravely slew Goliath it was done publicly, and he gloried in it; but, when he basely slew Uriah, it was arranged in secret, for he was ashamed of it. Many were the aggravations of this murder. It was deliberate. He took time to consider it."[1]

It never pays to run from the truth of the Word of God concerning your actions, because keeping your actions covered always requires an ongoing hidden agenda. To think that no one will ever know is a lie.

God is acquainted with the most intimate details of your life—every thought, motive and action. This could be the very reason that many believers keep their distance from the Lord. On the other hand, some people don't believe that God knows every deep, dark secret about them. Otherwise they wouldn't do some of the crazy things they do. If David tried to get away with his sin, what makes you think that you wouldn't do the same? Yet the Bible says, "He reveals deep and hidden things; he knows what is in the darkness, and light dwells with him" (Dan. 2:22, *NRSV*). God is omniscient, yet it's amazing that He still wants our companionship.

TIMES OF REFRESHING

The grievous sin that King David committed had to torment him. After all, he was known as a man after God's own heart. Does a person suddenly dismiss God while he is in sin? "Excuse me, God, but I will be back when I'm finished." Does God just turn a blind eye to sin, waiting for His kids to return to His loving arms? How did David reconcile his blatant actions, knowing that he had an extraordinary relationship with a holy and righteous God? He couldn't.

When the relationship between God and man has been marred by sin, man's tendency is to turn away from God. However, at this point, it is wise for man to pursue God for personal repentance and reconciliation. Otherwise, his actions will only continue to escalate. When a wild horse has been tamed, it is said to have been "broken." That means the horse has been brought under the control of its master. A person who has been broken over his sin isn't likely to return to that sin, because his actions have been brought under the control of the Lord. This is what God is after.

When all was said and done, David found himself pursuing God. His contrite heart expressed the emotional battle he fought in his sin:

> Have mercy on me, O God, according to your unfailing love; according to your great compassion blot out my transgressions. Wash away all my iniquity and cleanse me from my sin. For I know my transgressions, and my sin is always before me. Against you, you only, have I sinned and done this evil in your sight . . . Cleanse me with hyssop, and I will be clean; wash me, and I will be whiter than snow. Let me hear joy and gladness; let the bones you have crushed rejoice. Hide your face from my sins and blot out all my iniquity. Create in me a pure heart, O God, and renew a steadfast spirit within me. Do not cast me away from your presence or take your Holy Spirit from me. Restore to me the joy of your salvation and grant me a willing spirit, to sustain me (Ps. 51:1-4,7-12, *NIV*).

I meditate on this psalm from time to time. You don't have to be deep in sin to appreciate David's transparency and insatiable longing for God. It's contagious. David had a way to capture the heart of God.

There is one final point on the matter of David's repentance. There is a major difference between godly sorrow and worldly or fleshly sorrow. When a believer has committed sin and seeks forgiveness based on the fear of the consequences of his actions, the focus of that repentance is on self and often leads to deception. True godly sorrow comes when the individual realizes that the sin he committed is against God first, and then he is able to gain a godly perspective on the person violated. The individual doesn't consider himself in the matter.

"Against you only have I sinned and done this evil in your sight." That is how you will know that genuine forgiveness and restoration can be realized.

When you begin to climb the ladder of success, you are bound to run into temptation now and then. Don't be caught off guard. Take heed! You could be a person of character and integrity and without warning fall into sin to gratify the lust of your flesh, just like David.

A little fatherly advice: "For whom the LORD loves, He chastens . . ." (Heb. 12:6, *NKJV*).

Father in heaven, lead us not into temptation but deliver us from evil.

THE END OF AN ERA

The passion and intensity of King David's personal relationship with God was once again restored and we can read about this restoration expressed in many of the psalms where David revealed his vulnerability and weaknesses, his hopes and desires and, most of all, his confidence in God!

King David had a powerful impact on the political life of the Hebrew people, even though he fell short in many ways. The covenant God made with David brought out the idea of kingship and kingdom. The fact that David's kingdom was not just an earthly kingdom but was to be eternally established is shown from many of the New Testament passages announcing the coming of the Messiah as King. From David is a royal line of kings, whose descendant would be the Messiah, also known as the Son of David. In short, King David has become a timeless symbol of Israel's past glory and future hope.

LIFE LINES

- David's eldest brother, Eliab, had a wrong attitude toward David when David was chosen to become Israel's next king. What can be said about your attitude when others are promoted over you? Allow God to open the right doors at the right time. Promotion does not come from the east or the west, but from God.

- When approaching your Goliath, stick to what works for you. Others may try to change your style, personality and natural instincts. Politely refuse. You are unique. Nobody does you better than you.

- What appears impossible may just have your name on it. When "they" say it can't be done; for them, it can't. Refuse to become another "they"!

- David credited his covenant with God as the power behind his ability to slay the lion, the bear and the giant.

- Big victories come with plenty of practice on little ones. Before you challenge Goliath, make sure the lion and the bear are dead. Keep slinging your slingshot. You'll get the hang of it.

- Everyone loves a winner. Fame can be intoxicating. Stay transparent, humble and teachable. You can be destroyed faster than you can achieve success.

- King Saul was one of the tools God used to fashion David into the great king that he became. David honored Saul to the end, refusing to lift his own hand against him. How do you react to unjust authority in your life? Are you angry and wish you were somewhere else, or is God using your current situation to fashion you just as He did David?

- It would take approximately 13 years for David to become king after he was chosen in his youth. Be careful in the transition stage from conception to fulfillment. Most pitfalls occur because of our lack of patience. *Testing always precedes promotion.*

- The soul of Jonathan was knit to the soul of David. Everyone needs a best friend. Being successful, yet lonely, is no success at all. Good friends are hard to find, especially when there are no strings attached. We get few opportunities to develop lifelong friendships, so take the time.

- We were all like Mephibosheth when we entered God's kingdom—crippled, dysfunctional and without a thing to offer Him but our broken life. Yet we are allowed the privilege of dining at the Master's table where we have been freely given all things that pertain to life and godliness. Are you still eating the crumbs at God's table? Jesus made us worthy through covenant, so we can enjoy His blessings.

- Adultery is a sin that is forgivable. Don't wallow in shame and guilt. It is not the end of the world. If David hadn't moved on to be reconciled to God after his grievous sin, he would never have completed the task God had given him to do. There are consequences to sin, but God doesn't condemn you. God wants you to learn from it and get beyond this experience. You can't change what happened, but you can choose to make the most of your life in spite of it. Seek forgiveness as you meditate upon Psalm 51.

- Even though David knew his conflicts were a result of his own sin, he was able to say, "It is good for me that

I was afflicted, That I may learn Your statutes" (Ps. 119:71, *NASB*).

- David, so brilliant in building the nation, was strangely helpless to guide or govern his family. David was a failure as a father; he proved unable to control, guide or discipline his children. How tragic when our sins impact our children. We need to learn from David's mistakes and guard our hearts against the alluring attractions of sin.[2]

CHAPTER TEN

Covenant with Isaiah

For unto us a child is born, Unto us a Son is given; And the government will be upon His shoulder. And His name will be called Wonderful, Counselor, Mighty God, Everlasting Father, Prince of Peace. Of the increase of His government and peace There will be no end, Upon the throne of David and over His kingdom, To order it and establish it with judgment and justice From that time forward, even forever. The zeal of the Lord of hosts will perform this.

Isaiah 9:6-7, NKJV

Have you noticed the common thread in the reaction of God's patriarchs when God recruited them for His service? Most were reluctant and looked at the weakness of their flesh to justify excluding themselves from becoming His mouthpiece. Isaiah was no exception.

This Old Testament patriarch could best be described as a fiery prophet, bold and uncompromising in fulfilling his role to the nation of Judah in his day. Isaiah was fearless and straightforward in the presence of kings and was known to bring scorn to the aspirations of state officials. Yet Isaiah was noted for his deep reverence toward "the Holy One of Israel." He didn't start out that way. He was a highly educated statesman, poet and prolific writer, with a masterful command of the Hebrew language, before God called him to be His spokesman. And although Isaiah was a very public figure, he was a very private man.

Isaiah's key role was to prophesy the future coming of the Messiah who would become the Mediator of the New Covenant. Some of Isaiah's prophecies detailed a vivid portrayal of Christ and His suffering for the healing and redemption of mankind, while others made reference to Him as the soon coming King. Isaiah's New Testament counterpart was John the Baptist, who also declared the coming of the Messiah. Furthermore, Isaiah's influence and upbringing were like that of the apostle Paul.

Much of the book of Isaiah is a prophetic dialogue between the prophet and Yahweh that contains detailed messages to His people, their enemies and about their future. It's amazing to learn that God revealed the message of the coming Messiah through Isaiah some 700 years prior to His coming. The sovereign connection between the Old and New Covenants is clearly outlined throughout the book of Isaiah, which, in the grand scheme of things, is the blessed hope of the Church.

There is no doubt in my mind that this connection with the Old and New Covenants has convinced many Jews, who at one time did not embrace the New Testament, to reconsider the reality of the deity of Christ. Had there been no New Testament, we might have concluded that the prophet's messages had little foundation to sustain them.

God raised up prophets to be His voice on earth, especially in times of crisis, battle or impending judgment. The office of an Old Testament prophet was an impressive but dangerous occupation. Gifted with profound wisdom and an exceptional display of powers, it was common for kings and other national leaders to call upon prophets to seek their counsel in their demanding and stressful roles as leaders.

The prophet's message often challenged the people and their leaders with God's commands and promises. Because of this confrontational stance and the continuing tendency of people to rebel against God, true prophets were not popular.

Since the prophets of Israel had no "official" standing comparable to that of, say, priests, their right to speak in the name of the Lord was open to criticism. I suppose that is why God used them in such dramatic ways; there was no way that anyone could deny their messages were from Yahweh. Nevertheless, their positions as God's appointed seers brought great persecution and consternation upon them.

Noah cried out, "Repent!" prior to the catastrophic flood that covered the earth in his day, while Moses declared judgment against God's people in the golden-calf debacle. The high priest, as representative of the king, accused the prophet Amos of sedition and prohibited the prophet from speaking in Israel. In another case, Jeremiah's conflicts with the king got him incarcerated and hauled into court by authorities who asked for the death penalty. When Jeremiah sent a scroll to the king, the king burned it. In spite of the prophets' trials and persecutions, they continued to faithfully herald God's truth as they were receiving it.

As we explore the life of this extraordinary prophet Isaiah, his inspiring and convicting messages will challenge you to "believe His prophets, and you shall prosper" (2 Chron. 20:20, *NKJV*).

JUDAH'S FIERY PROPHET

Isaiah was born in Judah to his father, Amoz, who was a descendant of Jacob. He married an unnamed prophetess and had two children. Isaiah was established as a scribe in the royal palace in Jerusalem. It was a respectable career, but God had other plans for His servant. Like all great poets, Isaiah must have been born with an ability to skillfully convey the heavenly messages he was receiving after he yielded his life to Yahweh.

As God frequently does when He recruits a man to represent Him on earth, He made a dramatic entrance into Isaiah's rather mundane life through a vision. Isaiah described this awe-inspiring vision as follows: He saw Yahweh as King on the throne in the setting of a majestic heavenly temple. Six-winged seraphim encircled Yahweh. The pillars of the heavenly temple shook from the shouts of these seraphim declaring, "Holy, holy, holy is the Lord of hosts; the whole earth is full of His glory! And the foundations of the thresholds shook at the voice of him who cried, and the house was filled with smoke." Isaiah cried out in terror, "Woe is me! For I am undone and ruined, because I am a man of unclean lips, and I dwell in the midst of people of unclean lips." What happened next would have sent anyone running from the presence of Yahweh. An angel then approached Isaiah and took a live coal from the altar and touched it to Isaiah's lips, declaring, "Your iniquity and guilt are taken away, and your sin is completely atoned for and forgiven" (Isa. 6:3-5,7, *AMP*).

The Bible speaks about the untamable tongue: "Even so the tongue is a little member and boasts great things. See how great a forest a little fire kindles! And the tongue is a fire, a world of iniquity. The tongue is so set among our members that it defiles the whole body, and sets on fire the course of nature; and it is set on fire by hell" (Jas. 3:5-6, *NKJV*). I suppose that is why God used a hot coal off the altar to deliver the prophet from his sin. The words that he would utter would now be from the throne of Yahweh, not from an uncontrollable fleshly nature.

Immediately following that supernatural episode, Isaiah declared, "Here am I! Send me" (Isa. 6:8, *NKJV*). Isaiah's prophetic career was launched.

Many of Isaiah's fiery prophetic utterances addressed Judah's sin and indifference toward Yahweh. Isaiah's messages also revealed how desperately spiritual renewal was needed in his day. Sin continued to fill the land because both the northern kingdom of Israel and the southern kingdom of Judah embraced Canaanite Baal worship. Even God's people were neither hot nor cold, but lukewarm, in their spirituality. Zion's worship had become conventional and formal, and their hearts were detached from their God.

The prophet confronted their rebellion and unwillingness to listen to the Lord's instructions. In response, the people lashed out at Isaiah, saying, "Do not prophesy to us what is right; speak to us smooth things, prophesy illusions, leave the way, turn aside from the path, let us hear no more about the Holy One of Israel" (Isa. 30:10-11, *NRSV*).

Many in rebellion do the same thing today. They speak out against the righteous—they want to be left alone in their sin. Rebellion is deep in the heart of a man or woman who is set against the Lord's ways. When you have gone wayward in life and don't want to listen to the godly counsel of others, you are in danger of

God's judgment. Return to the place of repentance and forgiveness and into right standing with God.

"An unfriendly man pursues selfish ends; he defies all sound judgment" (Prov. 18:1, *NIV*).

With equal importance, Isaiah tempered his words of judgment with powerful prophecies of God's comfort and encouragement. Isaiah prophesied Yahweh's intervention to bring His people back to a true knowledge of Him. God was determined to redeem Israel by His grace, blotting out their sins for His own sake. A new era would come where the people would be regenerated; and it would start with those in authority over God's people. An outpouring of Yahweh's spirit would also be part of this new era.

Isaiah's tenure as prophet spanned the reign of four kings— Uzziah, Jotham, Ahaz and Hezekiah.

NATIONS, KINGDOMS AND PEOPLE IN CONFLICT

As a young man, Isaiah witnessed the rapid development of Judah into a strong commercial and military state under the leadership of King Uzziah. Judah attained a degree of prosperity and strength never before enjoyed since the days of Solomon. King Uzziah had a long and prosperous reign of 52 years. Although the prosperity of Uzziah's kingdom was still being felt in the days of his son Jotham's reign, along with it came social, political and religious corruption.

In Judah's society, abuse of the Mosaic Law was graphically illustrated by the sins of the elite against the poor. These affluent and influential men illegally appropriated the property of the less fortunate and sold off their holdings, such as livestock, for unpaid debts. Judges took bribes, and as a result, the corrupt power brokers began to control the legal system, stripping the poor of their rights. And no one spoke out against these injustices except the prophets of Judah. Isaiah called these rich rulers to account for how they oppressed the downtrodden, perverted justice and tore down the moral and social fabric of their nation.

These landlords, Isaiah prophesied, would reap the same treatment they inflicted on the poor. As a result, they were permanently cut off from any inheritance within Judah and would have no part in the future restoration to the land (see Isa. 10:13-19; 14:22).

Isaiah was considered a dangerous agitator because his direct prophecies disgraced these landlords and also embarrassed the false prophets who foretold only peace and prosperity. They commanded Isaiah to stop prophesying because he preached truth that revealed their corruption. There is nothing more dangerous than the false sense of security that arises when one thinks God condones sinful actions.

Isaiah's messages also included prophetic judgments and warnings against the enemies of Israel and Judah. Having been reared in Jerusalem, he was well fitted to become a political and religious counselor who would speak the most critical truth in the face of opposition. He contended with God on many occasions concerning Judah's enemy, Sennacherib, king of Assyria. The ever-menacing Assyrians had a mad lust for conquest and attacked Judah unceasingly.

God still uses prophets today, whether in public or private office. When a calling is as strong as Isaiah's, there is no doubt that persecution and judgment will follow the prophet who is unwilling to compromise the message God has given him.

Ahaz succeeded Jotham as king of Judah. He was one of Judah's evil kings and his wickedness brought God's judgment on the nation. Isaiah was completely opposed to King Ahaz's plan to ally with Israel's enemy, Assyria, for protection, and he warned the king against it. The prophet believed that faith in Yahweh was a sufficient guarantee of divine protection.

At this time, Isaiah began to prophesy the coming of the Messiah as deliverer. Well, King Ahaz wouldn't hear of it. At one point, Isaiah's conflict with the king's public policy caused him to withdraw from speaking. His contemporaries said that his messages were contrary to the law. Later, when God raised up another king, Isaiah had more freedom to elaborate on the matters of heavenly concern. Not surprisingly, Ahaz's reign proved to be the worst in Judah's history.

A COVENANT PRINCIPLE—CLEANSING THE TEMPLE

After the reign of King Ahaz, his son Hezekiah became king. The young 25-year-old king inherited a heavy burden from his father. While his father was one of the wickedest kings in ancient Israel, quite surprisingly, his son was totally different. King Hezekiah became a reformer during his reign.

"Now it is in my heart to make a covenant with the Lord God of Israel, that His fierce wrath may turn away from us" (2 Chron. 29:10, *NKJV*). The king abolished the high places, tore down the sacred pillars and even smashed the bronze serpent that Moses had made because the Israelites offered sacrifices to it, calling it Nehushtan. Talk about a cleanup!

After purifying the temple, King Hezekiah placed emphasis on worship and called for a celebration of the Lord's Passover, which was an important annual religious festival that had not been kept for decades. But what was supposed to be a seven-day celebration turned into a two-week glorious turn of events. Once the celebration was over, everyone returned home to destroy their idols and shrines, purging the land of idolatry.

In my book *Living Under an Open Heaven*, I wrote about the demise of idolatrous nations. Where there is idolatry you'll also find the spirit or principality of confusion affecting governments, militaries and even economies. Many nations in the world today are consumed in idol worship and they, too, suffer the same plight the nations of Judah and Israel suffered. The prophet declared, "Their molded images are wind and confusion" (Isa. 41:29, *NKJV*).

In the United States, all religions are tolerated—Islam, Buddhism, satanic worship, secular humanism, all—except Christianity! Our twenty-first-century society is highly intolerant of Catholic and Protestant Christians. Why? Fundamentally, Christianity teaches societies regarding right and wrong behavior while many other religions are based on Satan's lie that salvation can be found through other means than Jesus Christ. This is the greatest deception. I believe that the most critical front in America's spiritual battle, as well as in any other nation, is the battle for the hearts and minds of its people. This, of course, was the prophetic thrust of Isaiah's ministry.

In the fourteenth year of King Hezekiah's reign, the Assyrians attacked Judah. While the border fortresses were taken, King Hezekiah pleaded with the Lord for intervention. Hezekiah's prayers were answered as God miraculously threw back the Assyrians and prevented them from overtaking Judah. This was a turning point in the history of Judah. The nation was preserved and the people were shown a powerful example of the effect prayer has when offered by a godly ruler! Hezekiah proved to be one of the best kings in Judah's history.

"Blessed is the nation whose God is the LORD . . ." (Ps. 33:12, RSV).

Later, the Bible says that Isaiah visited the king, informing him to get his house in order because he was about to die. In response, King Hezekiah pleaded with the Lord to intervene and God graciously extended his life another 15 years.

Although King Hezekiah was one of the great kings of Judah, there is no question that God used Isaiah to help Hezekiah rule Judah.

PECULIAR ACTS OF OBEDIENCE

God often required strange and unusual displays of His prophets, illustrated sermons if you will, in order to convey a message to His people. Without explanation, the Lord told Isaiah to remove his clothes and sandals, and for three years he was to live barefoot and naked among the people (see Isa. 20:2-3). To the untrained eye, that was an unreasonable request that surely cast great embarrassment on the prophet among the people.

It is easy for us today to miss the power of prophetic symbolism in antiquity. Prophetic messages can be difficult to interpret because they often have dual meanings. Isaiah's strange public nakedness was more than a visual device to communicate a message; it was a "sign" that would predict a future event. In the prophet's understanding, such acts set events into motion.

God had a much greater purpose for Isaiah's extremely unusual prophetic behavior. Isaiah was predicting the fate that awaited Egypt and Ethiopia—whose people would be carried off as prisoners, "naked and barefoot," humiliated and exiled. The message was a further warning against relying on Egypt and Ethiopia in the face of Assyrian threats. The performance of symbolic acts was deeply rooted in the established practices of prophecy and not in the prophets.

Since Isaiah's primary role was to prophesy the future Messiah, the relevance of the messages spoken in this prophetic book provides a bridge connecting the Old and New Testaments. Therefore, I have included some of those prophecies as compelling evidence of God's continued plan to restore covenant to mankind. Remember, what Isaiah is prophesying in the Scriptures that follow would not take place for 700 years.

A BIRTH ANNOUNCEMENT— "IT'S A KING"

"Therefore the Lord himself will give you a sign. Look, the young woman is with child and shall bear a son, and shall name him Immanuel" (Isa. 7:14, *NRSV*).

"For unto us a Child is born, Unto us a Son is given; And the government will be upon His shoulder. And His name will be called Wonderful, Counselor, Mighty God, Everlasting Father, Prince of Peace. Of the increase of His government and peace There will be no end" (Isa. 9:6-7, *NKJV*).

> Who has believed our message? To whom will the Lord reveal his saving power? . . . He was despised and rejected—a man of sorrows, acquainted with bitterest grief. We turned our backs on him and looked the other way when he went by. He was despised and we did not care. But he was wounded and crushed for our sins. He was

beaten that we might have peace. He was whipped, and we were healed! All of us have strayed away like sheep. We have left God's paths to follow our own. Yet the LORD laid on him the guilt and sins of us all. He was oppressed and treated harshly, yet he never said a word. He was led as a lamb to the slaughter. And as a sheep before the shearers, he did not open his mouth. . . . But it was the LORD's good plan to crush him and fill him with grief. Yet when his life is made an offering for sin, he will have a multitude of children, many heirs. . . . I will give him the honors of one who is mighty and great, because he has exposed himself to death. He was counted among those who were sinners. He bore the sins of many and interceded for sinners (Isa. 53:1,3,5-7,10,12, *NLT*).

Eons later, I am sure that many were puzzled by the idea of a virgin birth. The prophetic description would require God's illumination to lift it right out of the realm of incredible and into the realm of the saving grace of God. Otherwise it would become another birth followed by another death among deaths and another life unjustly taken at the hands of a cruel justice system.

"Who will listen?" the prophet asked.

With great clarity and heavenly unction, Isaiah described the suffering of the Messiah. He would be disfigured beyond all human appearance as the sin of the world was heaped upon Him. The Savior would become, for those who looked on Him, the source of their healing and redemption.

Isaiah not only spoke of Christ's suffering and redemption but of the glories of a kingdom that would have no end. (This wasn't a message of doom and gloom.) It was a message of the Messiah's resurrection and the worldwide influence of His Church. The Messiah's death would provide so much more for mankind than escaping hell. Man would not be relegated to crawling on his hands and knees to get God's attention. The blood of the Messiah shed on the cross would be the seal of a new and everlasting covenant between God and man.

The people in Isaiah's day must have scratched their heads, wondering, *What is he talking about? He's a dreamer, a storyteller.* It was of no relevance to them since the prophecy would not occur in their lifetime. However, God didn't flinch at the thought. Rather, His mind was on the future, so the eventual birth of the people's Redeemer was destined to arrive.

Isaiah's prophetic messages in the last half of his book mostly speak of comfort and salvation and also the future glory awaiting Israel. We who are not of Jewish descent are considered privileged Gentiles or "spiritual Israel." Speaking of the Jewish race, the Bible says, "Branches were broken off so that I might be grafted in. That is true. They were broken off because of their unbelief, but you stand only through faith" (Rom. 11:19-20, *NRSV*). In other words, we Gentiles are included in Israel's glorious future.

Along the lines of critical relevance, I have also included pertinent verses that continue to resonate from the heart of God regarding what His intentions are for His people.

> Do you not know? Have you not heard? The Lord is the everlasting God, the Creator of the ends of the earth. He will not grow tired or weary, and His understanding no one can fathom. He gives strength to the weary and increases the power of the weak. Even youths grow tired and weary, and young men stumble and fall; but those who hope in the Lord will renew their strength. They will soar on wings like eagles; they will run and not grow weary, they will walk and not be faint (Isa. 40:28-31, *NIV*).

Yahweh reminds His people of His immutability and intimate care for them. Though the righteous may face dark valleys of anguish and despair, God's Word should remain the anchor of their faith. The phrase "renew their strength" means literally to "change strength" as one might change into fresh clothes.

> Forget about what's happened; don't keep going over old history. Be alert, be present. I am about to do something

brand-new. It's bursting out! Don't you see it? There it is! I am making a road through the desert, rivers in the badlands. . . . the people I made especially for myself, a people custom-made to praise me (Isa. 43:18-19,21, *THE MESSAGE*).

The future restoration of Israel is plainly understood. Being instructed not to "remember the former things" emphasizes the radical newness of what God is up to. The former things of the world have a way of distracting God's people and keeping them from the genuine relationship God is after. "I will do a new thing" signals the freshness of God's ways and the continual possibility of a sudden, unexpected turn of events. The challenge for the Church is to remain open to the radical freedom of God to "do a new thing" in the context of God's mercies. For His mercies are new every morning.

A GLORIOUS FUTURE

"Arise, shine, for your light has come, and the glory of the LORD rises upon you. See, darkness covers the earth and thick darkness is over the peoples, but the LORD rises upon you and his glory appears over you. Nations will come to your light, and kings to the brightness of your dawn" (Isa. 60:1-3, *NIV*).

Isaiah is clearly painting a picture of the redeemed—the Church. He declares that there is coming a time when deep darkness will come to the people, yet the glory of the Lord is imminent. As the prophet prophesied, we are supposed to be the light of the world, illuminating Christ's gospel to the ends of the earth.

> The Spirit of the Lord God is on Me, because the Lord has anointed Me to bring good news to the poor. He has sent Me to heal the brokenhearted, to proclaim liberty to the captives, and freedom to the prisoners; to proclaim the year of the LORD's favor, and the day of our God's vengeance; to comfort all who mourn, to provide for those who mourn in

Zion; to give them a crown of beauty instead of ashes, festive oil instead of mourning, and splendid clothes instead of despair. And they will be called righteous trees, planted by the Lord, to glorify Him (Isa. 61:1-3, *CSB*).

The time within which these events would occur was left intentionally unspecific (that is prophecy) and therefore resonates well with an open-ended promise. Relief is promised to the oppressed, the brokenhearted and the captive.

CONCLUSION

God gave the Jewish people the land of Canaan as an everlasting inheritance. However, their uninterrupted possession of it was conditioned on the nation walking in God's ways and keeping His commandments. Throughout her journey, Israel broke all of God's commandments, and both Judah and Israel temporarily lost the land of their inheritance. Ultimately, God had mercy on His people.

The book of Isaiah is a story of the future. It goes beyond Isaiah and the difficulty he faced as God's messenger. Most of Isaiah's prophecies are as relevant today as they were in the late eighth century B.C. They all had their purpose in Isaiah's day, but they would also serve a larger purpose in setting the stage for the dramatic finale of all time: *Jesus' death before Israel, her kings and the nations.* While individual prophets do not live forever, God's Word spoken to them and through them has power to outlive them, to survive and speak to succeeding generations. Prophecy is forever reliable and forever alive.

"Surely the Lord God will do nothing, without revealing His secret to His servants the prophets. The lion has roared; who will not fear? The Lord God has spoken; who can but prophesy?" (Amos 3:7-8, *AMP*).

Life Lines

- Isaiah portrayed the Messiah as God and man, teacher and founder of the kingdom of peace and love. This book gives a manifold presentation of Christ.

- Christ's perfect sacrifice for sin was foretold by Isaiah some 700 years before it occurred.

- Trees and prophets share one important characteristic—both are planted for the future. Seedlings are often overlooked and prophets are often ignored. Isaiah is one of the best examples of this.[1]

- The famous preacher D. L. Moody spoke of idols: "You don't have to go to heathen lands today to find false gods. America is full of them. Whatever you love more than God is your idol."

- Do you have idols in your life, whether work, pleasure, family or ministry? Seek first the kingdom of God and those things you consider most precious to you will be put into proper perspective so that nothing comes between you and God (see Matt. 6:33).

CHAPTER ELEVEN

Covenant of Redemption

For if that first covenant had been faultless, there would have been no occasion sought for a second.
HEBREWS 8:7, *NASB*

THE NEW COVENANT

When God made the human race, its diversity was as unique as it was fascinating. We met some pretty interesting people in the Old Testament!

While Adam's relationship with God prior to the Fall revealed his and Eve's unique unbroken fellowship, Noah's life revealed the patient mercies of God toward a wicked and perverse generation.

Father Abraham taught us about faith through his willing obedience to sacrifice his son of promise to God. Jacob, the cunning and crafty patriarch was transformed and, amazingly enough, fathered the 12 tribes of Israel.

Joseph patiently suffered injustice at the hands of his jealous brothers, yet God faithfully delivered his family from a famine and restored Joseph to them.

Moses, God's chosen deliverer, led a conglomeration of Hebrew slaves through the Red Sea and into the wilderness. The patient yet persecuted leader taught God's people how to relate to Yahweh and was used to establish the Law and social order.

David's valiant victory over an uncircumcised Philistine brought mixed reviews. On one hand the people celebrated his victory, followed his conquests and sang songs heralding his success in the battlefield. On the other hand, the jealous and uncontrollable rage of King Saul sent David fleeing for his life. And when an opportunity arose, David refused to kill his archenemy.

Covenant friendship between David and Jonathan spared David's life on many occasions. Who can forget the kindness that King David showed to Jonathan's son, Mephibosheth, all because of covenant? If you ever doubt God's covenant blessings for your life, return to this story. It is sure to encourage you to believe once again for your rightful place dining at the Master's table.

We concluded our examination of the Old Testament patriarchs with Isaiah, God's messenger—an unpopular, fiery prophet who declared the coming Messiah. Now we transition from the Old Covenant to the New Covenant.

THE COVENANT OF ALL COVENANTS

As we examine the New Testament era, our sights turn toward the village of Nazareth in Bethlehem where two people met and fell in love.

Joseph was a typical hard-working young man, a carpenter by trade. He desired to get married, raise a family and live a rather normal life, blending into the local landscape of Jewish society. Mary was an excited young teenager looking forward to marriage and preparing for the occasion like any other young bride-to-be. That is, until the picture-perfect scenario suddenly changed.

When God was ready to reveal another part of His plan to mankind, He dispatched the angel Gabriel to visit Mary. Gabriel wasn't some chubby, winged cherub who came floating into her room like one you might see sitting on a mantle over a fireplace, guarding the home. The Bible states that angels take on the form of man. Evidently these emissaries are around us often, because we are admonished to entertain "strangers," for by doing so, some have unwittingly entertained angels (see Heb. 13:2).

"[T]he angel Gabriel was sent by God to a city of Galilee, named Nazareth, to a virgin betrothed to a man whose name was Joseph, of the house of David. The virgin's name was Mary" (Luke 1:26-27, *NKJV*).

When Gabriel appeared to Mary, he told her that she would bear a son and call His name "Jesus." Her natural reaction was predictable: "But how can I have a baby? I am a virgin." Understanding Mary's perplexity and confusion, the angel reassured her, "The Holy Spirit will come upon you, and the power of the Most High will overshadow you. So the baby born to you will be holy, and he will be called the Son of God" (Luke 1:34-35, *NLT*).

By faith Mary agreed, saying, "Let it be unto me." Before Gabriel left her presence, he surprised Mary, informing her that her aging barren cousin, Elizabeth, would conceive a child. Imagine Mary's mixed emotions after this heavenly visitation. She was fearful and cautious yet joyful and full of faith.

She had been given a divine assignment to bring the Messiah into the world. She must have pondered, "What about Joseph? How will I tell him?" Pregnancy out of wedlock was grounds for stoning in those days. Her mind was reeling as she prepared herself to address this difficult situation based on her upcoming marriage.

Joseph's first reaction to Mary's pregnancy was to put her away secretly to protect her from public scorn and release himself from the betrothal. That is, until the angel of the Lord appeared to him in a dream and confirmed all that was told to Mary. As a result, they married and Joseph did not have sexual relations with her until after Jesus was born. This was in order to protect the virginity of the mother and Jesus' divine Sonship, as predicted by the prophet Isaiah.

Mary immediately made her way to her cousin Elizabeth's house to tell her about the angelic visitation. When Mary arrived and entered the house, Elizabeth heard her voice from another room and the babe in her womb leaped; immediately she was filled with the Holy Spirit.

Elizabeth's miracle pregnancy with her son, John, would be a much greater part of God's plan than either of them imagined. John would become a divine cog in the wheel toward redemption, as he would introduce the Messiah to the world.

Later, when Jesus was born, Mary and Joseph were in Bethlehem to register for the census ordered by Caesar Augustus. Because there was no room for them in the local inn, Mary gave birth to her Son in a nearby stable, wrapped Him in a blanket and placed Him in a manger.

Afterward, wise men from the East came to Bethlehem to see the "King of the Jews" and brought gifts to Him.

According to Hebrew custom, when Jesus was eight days old, He was circumcised so that He might become the legal seed of Abraham.

Recall that circumcision was a sign of God's covenant with Abraham. Because of Jesus' supernatural conception, He had no human, biological father. Jesus' adopted father, Joseph, traced his lineage to David through Solomon, which Jesus legally inherited, and as a result fulfilled prophecy concerning Messiah's lineage (see Matt. 1:17).

Although Joseph and Mary did not join together to conceive Jesus, Joseph is the one through whom Jesus is begotten as the "son of David," and Mary is the one through whom He is begotten as the "Son of God."

As with Moses, Jesus' infancy was at risk of death at the hands of jealous King Herod. The powers of darkness were constantly trying to thwart the plan of God by attempting to do away with God's generals. Satan was more aware of this birth than of any other. In the end, the religious rulers of the day would be used as pawns to exterminate the Son of God.

Very little is known or recorded about Jesus' early years. Mention is made about Jesus as a 12-year-old boy going with His parents to the Temple in Jerusalem to celebrate the Passover. There in the Temple, Jesus was talking among the priests, scribes, teachers and locals. They were all astonished at His knowledge and understanding. He was called "a son of the law" by the Jews. When it was time for them to return home during that visit to Jerusalem, Jesus remained behind. When His parents realized that He was not with them, like any concerned parents, they returned to find Him.

When they found Jesus, Mary and Joseph questioned their young Son sternly. His response reminded them of His divine calling: "Did you not know that I must be about my Father's business?" Jesus was tending to His Father's business even at that young age.

"And Jesus advanced in wisdom and stature, and in favor with God and men" (Luke 2:52, *ASV*).

JOHN THE BAPTIST

The miracle births recorded in the Bible were of individuals who would not live normal, run-of-the-mill lives; they would be given fully to the service of God, as we have seen thus far. John the Baptist's parents, Elizabeth and Zacharias, were beyond childbearing years, with no hope of conceiving children, until their lives were divinely interrupted by the angel Gabriel who later visited Mary.

Zacharias was performing his priestly duties in the Temple when suddenly the angel Gabriel appeared to him next to the altar. Terrified, Zacharias stopped what he was doing and listened intently. "Elizabeth, your wife, will bear a son by you . . . He'll achieve great stature with God" were the glad tidings to the priest.

Gabriel continued, "He will herald God's arrival in the style and strength of Elijah, soften the hearts of parents to children, and kindle devout understanding among hardened skeptics—he'll get the people ready for God" (Isa. 1:13,15,17, *THE MESSAGE*).

Fearful, and in disbelief, Zacharias inquired, "How shall I know this? For I am an old man, and my wife is well advanced in years." Because of his disbelief, the angel of the Lord told Zacharias that his vocal cords would be shut off to prevent him from speaking because of his disbelief. The Lord brought reproof to Zacharias's doubtful heart. His speech was finally restored to him on the day of his son's circumcision.

John was born six months prior to the birth of Jesus. His life's mission was the subject of prophecy: "For this is he who was spoken of by the prophet Isaiah when he said, 'The voice of one crying in the wilderness: Prepare the way of the Lord, make His paths straight'" (Matt. 3:3, *RSV*).

John's youth was spent in the wilderness, away from his culture and religion, so that he was not contaminated by these strong influences. His service as forerunner to the Savior didn't need anyone's persuasive assistance. Like King David, whose formative years were spent tending sheep, the wilderness was John's classroom. Without culture, tradition or religion to distract him, John, who ate a steady diet of locusts and honey, was by religious standards a reject.

John began his ministry in the wilderness of Judea. The sum of John's preaching was the need for repentance. He called the Pharisees, who were constant critics standing at a distance, a "generation of vipers." His message to the people was blunt and to the point! His voice was unstoppable because it carried with it a clarion call: "Produce fruit worthy of your repentance."

His warnings were more than suggestions: "Every tree that does not produce fruit will be cut down." He baptized multitudes upon the confession of their sins in the river Jordan. John's baptism was for repentance only, preparing the people to embrace their Messiah. Repentance in the New Testament is not remorse or even a change of heart. It is a radical about-face from one's former life.

Many questioned whether John was the Christ. However, John cleared up that confusion straightaway: "I baptize you with water; but one who is more powerful than I is coming; I am not worthy to untie the thong of his sandals. He will baptize you with the Holy Spirit and fire" (Luke 3:16, *NRSV*).

John did not make himself the center of his ministry to attract others to himself. He realized that he was a messenger sent by God to bring people to Jesus Christ to exalt Him.

COVENANT BAPTISM

In order to accomplish His mission on earth, Jesus set aside His deity. Among other things, He submitted to the baptism of repentance before launching His public ministry.

When John's fame reached Jesus in Nazareth, He came from Galilee to the Jordan River to be baptized by John. It was providence that John the Baptist would be selected to baptize Jesus. However, this was more than a ceremonial observance.

The baptism Jesus submitted to inferred a change of heart, forsaking sin and living a new life. John baptizing Jesus was the first public declaration of Jesus' ministry. Instead of going to Jerusalem and identifying with the established religious leaders, Jesus went to a river and identified Himself with those who were repenting of sin. Even at the age of 12, when Jesus visited the Temple, He understood His mission. Eighteen years later, at His baptism, He began fulfilling it. And as Jesus prayed, God spoke to Him and confirmed that it was time to act.

During Jesus' baptism, the Bible says that heaven opened and the Holy Spirit descended in bodily form like a dove upon Him, and a voice came from heaven, saying, "You are My own dear Son, and I am pleased with You" (see Luke 3:22). After Jesus' baptism, He lived and ministered in "resurrection" power before His actual death and resurrection three-and-a-half years later.

Why would the Lord Jesus, who was conceived of the Holy Spirit, need the Spirit to descend upon Him at His baptism? Since there is only one Spirit, how could this one Spirit both indwell the Lord Jesus and descend upon Him?

The answer lies with understanding that there are two functions of the Spirit. When we are baptized in the Holy Spirit, the Spirit lives within us to lead us and guide us in life. But then there comes a time when we must be empowered for service, whatever our calling in life is. That empowering should manifest as it did with Jesus.

Another important point to make about Jesus' baptism: If baptism was a sign of repentance from sin to live a new life, and Jesus was without sin, why did He instruct John to baptize Him?

As one commentator noted, "Jesus' mission on earth was to identify with our humanness and sin, thus He was prophetically portraying His upcoming death and resurrection for our salvation. Jesus was also giving us an example to follow by endorsing the act of baptism."[1]

Before Jesus left earth, He instructed His disciples to practice the sacrament of baptism. Baptism shows submission to Christ and a willingness to live God's way. To be baptized simply means to be put aside, to be terminated, so that we may live not by ourselves, but by God's power.

We were buried in baptism as Christ was buried in death. As Christ was raised from the dead by the great power of God, so we will have new life also. If we have become one with Christ in His death, we will be one with Him in being raised from the dead to new life. We know that our old life, our old sinful self, was nailed to the cross with Christ. And so the power of sin that held us was destroyed. Sin is no longer our boss (Rom. 6:4-6, *NLV*).

Circumcision in the Old Covenant and baptism in the New Covenant serve as demonstrations of the believer's commitment to this covenant with God. Both circumcision and baptism are also descriptive of the regenerating work of the Holy Spirit in the life of the believer.

Water baptism and Spirit baptism are two foundational rites the believer should submit to. Understanding these important baptisms will make a difference in your life.

JESUS' PUBLIC LIFE AND MINISTRY

Jesus often referred to Himself as the Son of man. He wanted the people to relate to His humanity. Jesus didn't minister under the New Covenant; He operated under the Mosaic Law and Abrahamic covenant. A better covenant would become available only through His death and resurrection.

The four Gospels—Matthew, Mark, Luke and John—contain detailed accounts of the words and works of Jesus written by different authors with varying perspectives. At times, the Gospels appear to be contradictory, but the overall gist of the accounts we will focus on won't detract from the message being conveyed.

After Jesus' commissioning by the Spirit at His baptism, He underwent a time of testing in the wilderness, which He successfully overcame. He then began His public ministry. This occurred when He was 30 years old and lasted about three-and-one-half years.

It was a Sabbath morning when Jesus made His way to the synagogue in His hometown of Nazareth. Empowered by the Holy

Spirit, He stood before His own townspeople and picked up the book of Isaiah to read a familiar passage of Scripture.

> The Sovereign LORD has filled me with his Spirit. He has chosen me and sent me To bring good news to the poor, To heal the broken-hearted, to announce release to captives And freedom to those in prison. He has sent me to proclaim That the time has come when the LORD will save his people and defeat their enemies (Luke 4:16-19; Isa. 61:1-2, *GNB*).

Before He sat down, Jesus informed His curious audience that Isaiah's prophecy was fulfilled and was standing before them. They all marveled at Him, saying, "Is this not Joseph's son?"

They could not understand such a dramatic and controversial claim at this time.

A first order of business, as Jesus officially began His ministry, was to choose 12 disciples. He would pour His life into them and train them to do the ministry when His task was completed on earth. His first recruits, James and John, were known as the "sons of thunder." Then there was impetuous Peter, who always stuck his foot in his mouth. Jesus also selected Judas, the money-hungry disciple who was in charge of the treasury, who also betrayed Christ. His crew also included Matthew, a despised tax collector. There were others, but the most prominent were these. Most were fishermen by trade except, of course, Matthew.

Associating with tax collectors to the extent of including one in His inner core of followers was abhorrent to Jews of traditional piety. This evoked hostility toward Jesus from the religious leaders.

Jesus' warnings that His disciples would deny, betray and abandon Him were challenged but were proved to be accurate, especially with regards to Judas and Peter. Even after Jesus' resurrection, doubting Thomas's cynicism spoke volumes: "Except I shall see in his hands the print of the nails, and put my finger into the print of nails, and thrust my hand into his side, I will not believe" (John 20:25, *KJV*).

Jesus' disciples were unable to grasp the role God had assigned to Him, with its emphasis on suffering and death. They expected Jesus to usurp Roman authority and form an earthly kingdom. This faulty understanding led them to dream of various kinds of power roles for themselves in this kingdom, which incited strong rebukes from Jesus.

In choosing the 12, Jesus did not act alone. His selection was solely by the authority and choice of God, including the appointment of Judas, the betrayer. Jesus didn't choose them for their talents and abilities; rather, He chose them in order to build them. Most important, all of His disciples, empowered by the Holy Spirit, would eventually make an impact on the world.

THOSE PESKY RELIGIOUS VIPERS

Now there is the matter of the Pharisees and Sadducees that followed Jesus wherever He went and confronted Him for violating the religious laws and customs of Judaism. There were other religious sects that gave Jesus a hard time, but those two were the most prominent.

Who were those pesky critters?

PHARISEES

The Pharisees were a devout subgroup within Judaism and were experts in the Jewish Law. They were an active political interest group who sought power and ways to exercise their influence. They read, studied and memorized the Scriptures more than most churchgoing people today will ever do. They tended to despise Galileans, whom they regarded as ignorant. As a result, they were reluctant to view Jesus as the Messiah. The Pharisees were much less hostile to the disciples. Even when the disciples plucked grain on the Sabbath, a wrongful act in the eyes of the Pharisees, it was Jesus they questioned, not His disciples (see Mark 2:23-24).

The Pharisees objected to Jesus' liberal teaching and practice of the Law as they understood and observed it. They were offended most of all by His apparent claim of authority to declare what was binding in the Law and what was not.

SADDUCEES

The Sadducees were an elitist Jewish subgroup connected to the wealth and power of the nation. They were mainly drawn from the governing class and had a small following among the people. Their mission was to establish Judaism's dignity in the eyes of the Gentiles. They differed from the Pharisees on certain theological points, namely in their disbelief in the resurrection and angels.

Even though the religious "vipers" of Jesus' day could be considered His Achilles' heel, they never deterred Him from fulfilling God's ultimate plan of redemption for mankind.

THE ROYAL LAW OF LOVE INCARNATE: JESUS' FIRST MIRACLE

One of Jesus' first sermons to the multitudes included these profound words: "For I have come down from heaven, not to do My own will, but the will of Him who sent Me" (John 6:38, *NKJV*). With that thought in mind, capture a glimpse of the miracle worker in action. Notice the common thread of redemption that runs throughout the New Testament Covenant.

Jesus' ministry was only one week old when He began staffing His ministry and had already chosen five disciples. These were the embryonic days of Jesus' ministry, and they were all getting to know each other. Jesus responded to a wedding invitation and took His first disciples with Him. This wedding was to take place in a hamlet called Cana of Galilee, population of only a few hundred people, about four miles from Nazareth.

The setting of His first miracle was the backdrop of an intimate, personal family setting. Jesus' mother was the catalyst for the miracle in this story. Scholars suspect that Mary was related to the bride or groom and that she was a part of planning the wedding.

Regardless, Jesus was among the invited guests. During the wedding celebration, the unthinkable happened. The party ran out of wine. Running out of wine at a Jewish social event was terribly embarrassing. Probably knowing that their situation needed divine intervention, Mary was happy to offer Jesus' assistance, even though it was not for the guests to remedy the problem (see John 2:1-11).

Jesus' mother said to Him, "They have no wine."

Jesus responded, "Woman, what does your concern have to do with Me? My hour has not yet come."

Ignoring His response, Jesus' mother instructed the servants, "Whatever He says to you, do it."

According to Jewish tradition, one of the biggest occasions of the year was a wedding ceremony, which lasted seven days. The host was expected to have enough food and wine on hand for the entire seven days. They were probably a poor family who therefore had a small budget and couldn't afford to go out and purchase more wine.

Jesus was about to begin His miracle ministry over a social crisis! This was not a life or death situation; they simply ran out of wine. You see, Jesus wasn't saying no to the request, but simply "not yet."

In using "woman" to address His mother, Jesus was cutting the umbilical cord. For 30 years, Mary had been His mother. His words were not an act of rudeness or disrespect toward His mother, but rather an important assertion of Jesus' emancipation from parental control.

Mary's impatient request reflects the fact that she was seeing her son as the Messiah who had been promised by the prophets for thousands of years. She knew that the promised Messiah could do miracles.

At the wedding, there was a set of six water pots of stone used for purification of the Jews. The water pots were symbolic of the old religion out of which new faith would spring forth—Christianity. These water pots were 20 to 30 gallons apiece in capacity, potentially holding up to 180 gallons. Jesus instructed the servants to fill the water pots with water. And they filled them to the brim. This was a miracle about to happen.

Jesus further instructed the servants to draw some water out of the water pots and take it to the master of the feast. They immediately followed His instructions. The master of the feast tasted the water turned into wine and did not know where it came from, but the servants who had drawn the water knew.

The master of the feast then called the bridegroom and said, "Every man at the beginning sets out the good wine, and when the guests have well drunk, then the inferior. You have kept the good wine until now!" (John 2:8-10, *NKJV*).

What does water represent in this story? Water represents the Word of God. What does wine represent? The Holy Spirit. Turning water into wine is an act of turning scarcity into abundance.

In Scripture, we are called vessels (see 2 Tim. 2:20-21). In every house, there are vessels of honor and dishonor. What makes a vessel honorable? The Word of God. Are you filled "to the brim" with the Word of God? That's the only way the new wine will come pouring out of you in abundance.

Some folks come to church once a month and get frustrated because they're not experiencing a powerful, prosperous Christian life. They live in scarcity. Well, no wonder! There is a miniscule amount of the Word of God in them! The law of sowing and reaping, the law of reciprocity, is always at work. The more water that is in you, the more wine that comes out of you. I tell people all the time—"Get your blessed assurance to church!" Sadly, most people only go to God when they are in a critical crisis—cancer, a terrible car accident, or something else just as deadly.

Have you ever run out of something? Money? Time? Patience? Ideas? Jesus is not going to move because we're anxious or fretting—He doesn't work that way. The voice of impatience believes that God doesn't care.

This event at the wedding of Cana is instructive for us because it was a social gathering amongst family and friends. The beginning of Jesus' ministry shows that the miraculous, life-giving power of God is at work, even (and perhaps, especially) in the intimate daily needs of our life. This means that you and I can go to God about anything!

SIMON PETER

No discussion of Jesus' public ministry is complete without looking at those He chose as disciples. A primary subject of study and speculation is Simon Bar Jonah, later known as Simon Peter.

Simon was a successful businessman and a natural born leader prior to responding to the call to be a disciple. He was enthusiastic, pretentious and impetuous. He was a genuine Galilean. There were several notable incidents that surrounded Peter's life that are memorable.

Simon's introduction to Jesus occurred when he became a beneficiary of a miracle. Discouraged, Simon, James and John had just spent all night fishing without a bite. They were unloading their boats and cleaning their nets when Jesus approached them.

Do you suppose Jesus knew their predicament? I think so!

Because Simon had not yet become a disciple, I believe that Jesus wanted to put some convincing bait out there in the form of a miracle. (You can't be a good salesman if you don't believe in the product you are promoting.) Jesus' miracles weren't always dramatic physical healings or deliverances. He appealed to the most basic needs of man—this time it was Simon's livelihood.

If Simon, James and John spent the night fishing, this tells me that it wasn't done for sport. Simon was a fisherman by trade, and in order to keep his business thriving, he needed to catch an abundance of fish.

So Jesus instructed the three to throw out their nets for a catch.

Hesitating, they packed their boat again and returned to the water. According to Jesus' command, they threw out their nets in the same area where they had been unsuccessful, and a great multitude of fish were caught, so much so that their nets began to tear.

This miracle event had a profound affect on Simon (see Luke 5:1-11).

It was after this encounter that Simon surrendered his life to become one of Jesus' disciples. Simon's role became more prominent in Jesus' ministry as time went on, and thus his name was changed to Peter. It was Peter who uttered the notable profession of faith at Caesarea Philippi when challenged by Jesus regarding who He was. "You are the Christ, the Son of the living God," Peter declared.

Astounded by Peter's response, Jesus replied, " . . . for this was not revealed to you by man, but my Father in heaven. And I tell you that you are Peter, and on this rock I will build my church, and the gates of Hades will not overcome it" (Matt. 16:17-18, *NIV*).

This exchange with Peter continues to challenge the Church today. As Jesus acknowledged that flesh and blood had not revealed His identity to Peter, the believer must also experience this truth in the same way—by the Holy Spirit. Human reasoning reduces man to religion. When the believer "knows" the Lord inwardly and not in his intellect alone, power is manifested that hell cannot contend with.

Peter's denial of the Messiah, when Jesus had been arrested just before His crucifixion, would prove to be one of the most dreadful moments of his life. Being forewarned by his Lord that his faith would be tested and that he would fail the test, prideful Peter denied it. Confidently he declared, "Lord, I am ready to go with you to prison and to death" (Luke 22:33, *NIV*).

After Jesus was arrested, Peter was in the Temple court, watching at a distance. While he was there, three people on three different occasions came up to him and associated him with Jesus. During each separate occasion, when the pressure was on, Peter emphatically denied knowing Jesus. After the last denial, Peter heard a cock crow. Immediately Jesus' eyes fastened onto Peter's and he then remembered the Lord's words, "Before a cock crows today, you will deny Me three times" (see Luke 22:54-62). Peter went outside and wept bitterly.

Although Peter was fraught with many weaknesses, his usefulness to the Kingdom was extraordinary. After Jesus ascended to heaven, Peter was in the Upper Room on the Day of Pentecost. After this powerful divine encounter, Peter preached the purpose of Christ's death and a mighty outpouring of the Spirit came upon all who were there. Three thousand souls were added to the Church that day.

The events of Pentecost completed the change in Peter's character. He was no longer an unreliable, self-confident, prideful man; but rather a steadfast, trusted and reliable covenant partner of the Lord's, leading the fellowship of believers in Jerusalem and beyond.

RECIPIENTS OF AN UNKNOWN COVENANT

THE CENTURION AND HIS SERVANT

The divine settings in which Jesus walked on a daily basis paint a picture of God's love for the Gentiles, as well as for the Jews.

To appreciate this story, it is important to know something about centurions. The centurions were soldiers who were despised by Jews because they were Gentiles and therefore considered unclean. Centurions were also members of the Roman pagans who had conquered Israel and enforced the Roman rule.

Yet this particular centurion wasn't a reprobate, nor was he a hater of Jews. In fact, the Bible says that he loved his country and built a synagogue for the Jews to worship in. He was a kindhearted, generous man. It is probable that he had some knowledge of the Old Testament, having had some interaction with the Jews. He must have had some prominence in the community, because he had an army under his command.

This centurion had a Jewish servant who was paralyzed and tormented, and as a result, the servant was bedridden. This servant had been in his employ and was highly valued. According to Levitical law, Jews could not enter the home of a Gentile, so the concerned centurion sought out help for his ailing servant among the "elders of the Jews." It is certain that at some point the centurion had heard about Jesus' miracle ministry in his interaction with these religious leaders. Imagine eavesdropping on one of their private moments with the centurion. The elders of the Jews, looking intently at the officer, say of Jesus, "No one ever spoke like this Man."

The Bible notes on many occasions that the multitudes marveled at Jesus' authority. The religious authorities were in a quagmire as to the source of Jesus' ability to control demons. Nonetheless, the centurion anxiously pleaded for help on his servant's behalf, addressing his request with great respect for the authority Jesus held. What right did this officer have to ask for assistance from the Miracle Worker, considering his reputation for suppressing the Jews? None. This plea for mercy tells you something about his relationship with his servant.

When he learned that Jesus was on His way, the centurion sent another message to Jesus, informing Him that it wasn't necessary for Him to come, all he asked was for Jesus' words of authority and his servant would be healed.

The centurion wasn't requesting an audience with Jesus; in fact, he never actually met Jesus or spoke to Him personally.

The centurion understood authority, because he was one in authority and, therefore, under authority. Although an outsider and an alien to the Jews, the centurion still had the faith and courage to plead on his servant's behalf. Furthermore, the centurion had a revelation: Jesus didn't have to defile Himself in order to heal his servant. All he needed was for Jesus to speak a word of healing to him. Jesus marveled at how great the centurion's faith was. His servant was healed that very hour.

There is another centurion in the book of Acts who was a God-fearing, generous man and a recipient of God's grace. The apostle Peter was divinely sent to preach Christ to the centurion whose name was Cornelius, and he and his household were converted (see Acts 10:22).

The centurion Cornelius represents Gentiles who are saved through faith in the Lord's Word. *Faith is the doorway to covenant.* God's power to save or heal works when the believer stands in his authority, knowing heaven's resources are there to back him up. Whether Jew or Gentile, the authority of the covenant rests in the finished work of the Cross.

THE CANAANITE WOMAN—COVENANT MERCY

Traveling to the traditionally pagan regions of Tyre and Sidon, Jesus was accosted by a Canaanite woman. This desperate Gentile woman had problems at home—her daughter was seriously demon possessed.

When you consider the miracles Jesus performed, many of these desperate people were not thinking about the religious prohibitions that kept them bound to the traditions of their day. This woman wasn't the stereotypical religious sort hanging out at the temple, doing her religious duties, praying and believing God for a miracle. No, in fact she was a heathen without a covenant with God.

Nevertheless, she cried out to Jesus for mercy so that her demon-possessed daughter might be delivered. This woman was on a mission of mercy. Jesus didn't respond to her plea at first. The disciples knew she was a Gentile and looked disparagingly at her with an unsympathetic attitude. This didn't stop her though.

This desperate mother all the more insisted that Jesus do something for her. Jesus said to her, "It is not right to take the children's bread and throw it to their dogs" (see Matt. 15:26). The woman struggled with Jesus' reply and with His reluctance to help her.

Why then did Jesus not act immediately?

It was apparent that He wanted to teach His disciples a thing or two. When the disciples looked to Him concerning her need, Jesus said that He had come only for the lost sheep of the house of Israel.

Instead of taking offense at Jesus' innuendo, she conceded to His point that priority in the divine plan of salvation was to the Jews. Yet, she immediately replied, "Even the dogs eat the crumbs which fall from their master's table." Essentially she told Him that she didn't need a whole loaf of bread, that there were enough resources in Him that she only needed a morsel and the demons would flee from her daughter.

Her response of faith amazed Jesus.

This woman's faith was even greater than the centurion's. What did the Canaanite woman do to demonstrate her faith? She didn't take silence for an answer. She was persistent.

Jesus was limited in His demonstration of the covenant to the Jews in His earthly ministry. His death provided an opportunity for Gentiles, or "spiritual Israel," to freely partake of the new and everlasting covenant. Throughout the Gospels, many of the recipients of the covenant were Gentiles with desperate faith in an "unknown God," which reveals God's unfailing love and mercy toward mankind.

Jesus turned to His disciples and asked, "Are you guys listening to any of this? I have not found such great faith in My life until today."

Jesus then answered her, saying, "Woman, you have great faith! Your request is granted." Her daughter was healed from that hour. This miracle took place remotely, as Jesus did not go to her daughter to pray for her but spoke the word only.

There is something to be learned from this woman's persistent faith in light of her child's need for deliverance. This miracle overcame conventional religious thinking because it involved a mother's love for her child. She is the only person said to have had "great faith," contrary to the "little faith" the disciples were known for.

What kind of hurdles or obstacles are you facing in your life? Do you have a child who is in need of healing or deliverance? Allow this woman's testimony of faith to inspire you so that you, too, can believe and receive.

THE WOMAN WITH THE ISSUE OF BLOOD

Interrupted on His journey to Jairus's house to raise his daughter from her death bed, Jesus and His disciples were pursued by a woman identified only as the "woman with the issue of blood."

This woman had an incurable blood disease that had been with her for 12 years. She was weak, lonely, rejected and had endured much at the hands of many physicians. She had spent all that she had and was not helped at all, but rather grew worse, the Bible says (see Mark 5:26).

She did everything she knew to do. Even Luke, the physician, admitted that she could not be healed by a physician. For 12 years she searched for a cure.

She had had the best advice physicians could give and made use of the medicines and methods they prescribed. The financial drain must have left her weary. She had to be a woman of means for it to take her 12 years to empty her bank account. But now that she had spent all that she had, she was desperate.

The diagnosis: There is no cure.

According to ceremonial law, this woman was unclean and restricted in her contact with others. Anyone who touched her would also be defiled and have to undergo purification. A social outcast, she sought to keep her condition a secret. In her desperation, she wasn't thinking about needing to physically touch Jesus; she just wanted to touch the hem of His garment in hopes of somehow being healed.

She reached through the crowd, ducking to avoid the jostling of the crowd, when she fell to her knees in a puff of dust as she grabbed the fringe of Jesus' garment. Immediately, Jesus turned to the crowd and said, "Who touched Me?"

The disciples almost ridiculed His question, "The multitudes throng You, and You are asking who touched You?" as they pushed the crowds away from Jesus.

Ignoring the disciples, Jesus knew someone in the crowd was healed and He wanted to know who. "Someone did touch Me; for I perceived that [healing] power has gone forth from Me" (Luke 8:46, *AMP*).

A calm came over the crowd and soon a lady emerged as she parted the crowd and stood before Jesus. With a glow on her dusty face, she lifted her head and made eye contact with Jesus. As He moved closer, He wiped the dust from her face and gently caressed her as though she was the only one He had come to heal.

Frightened, she began to tremble. Can you imagine how she must have felt? Her uncleanness was discovered and yet she had been healed. As she began to testify, the crowds must have whispered among themselves, "If we had known that she had this disease, we would have cried out, 'She's unclean.'" Their distraction to get to Jesus camouflaged her uncleanness and allowed her the opportunity to receive a blessing from the Master.

Jesus comforted her and sent her on her way completely healed. He did not take credit for making her well, but pointed to her faith as the real source of her healing. Many, like this woman, have gone to physicians and exhausted their efforts, but have not been cured. What did this woman possess in order to receive healing?

She placed a demand upon the virtue that flowed from Jesus' body. She wasn't looking to make physical contact with Jesus because of her condition, but her desperate faith believed that if she could just touch something He was wearing, she would be made whole. That type of faith had corresponding action—her dashing into the crowd in defiance of the social and ritual boundaries set by her condition. She was limited, but she didn't care. What did she have to lose? She had already lost all her money and her confidence in the medical community.

I can see why this woman was healed. Desperate faith brought about desperate measures, which in turn released the mercy of God to bless this woman who was ignorant of her covenant rights.

HEALING AT THE POOL OF BETHESDA

Jesus was headed for Jerusalem on the Sabbath to celebrate one of the Jewish festivals. While walking about the roads of the bustling city, passing local vendors and open air markets, Jesus came upon the Sheep Gate where there was a pool called Bethesda, or "house of mercy." Next to this pool was a great multitude of sick people, the blind, lame and paralyzed, who were waiting for the supernatural moving of the waters: "[A]n angel would go down into the pool from time to time and stir up the water. Then the first one who got in after the water was stirred up recovered from whatever ailment he had" (John 5:4, *CSB*).

What an opportunity for Jesus to exercise His miracle-working power! However, in Jesus' ministry not everyone was healed, so His gaze fell upon the next recipient of the covenant, a man who had an infirmity for 38 years.

What? Working a miracle on the Sabbath?! His disciples were nervous.

Jesus had a captive audience—the sickly weren't going anywhere. Most of all, this was a perfect setting for the next lesson the disciples would learn. "Watch and learn, boys," the Master instructed.

The odors were penetrating and offensive to the passersby, but Jesus wasn't moved. Taking a simple bath wasn't possible unless they had someone to help them. These invalids were the rejects of society. Unable to help themselves, they became beggars and had nothing else to live for but the moving of the waters in hopes that they might be healed.

As Jesus made His way through the crowd, He was careful not to step on any one of them. The disciples followed behind Him, trying not to make too much contact with the untouchables.

Jesus finally reached His man.

He knelt beside the paralytic and leaned into him, asking an obvious question, "Do you want to be made well?"

Unable to move, the paralytic interpreted Jesus' question through his own assumption about how his healing would come. He bemoaned, "I have no man to put me into the pool when the water is stirred up, but while I am coming another steps down before me." He, therefore, was saddened by his predicament. He did not know Jesus, so would not have had faith in Him. I muse at the thought of being in the midst of the conversations that must have taken place among these invalids through the years concerning the mysterious stirring of the waters by an angel.

This paralytic believed in the wrong thing, but he wanted to get into the water and be healed. For 38 years he had fantasies of walking. Jesus was moved with compassion, knowing this paralytic would probably be there for another 38 years if He didn't heal him. So Jesus did the impossible and commanded the paralytic, "Rise, pick up your bed and walk." The man heard the life-giving words of Jesus without the mention of faith, and he was immediately healed. It wasn't his crazy belief system or his weird doctrine that healed him, nor was it the water!

When asked by the religious crowd about his Sabbath healing, he replied, "I don't know who He was. Some stranger came up to me and spoke words of life to me and now I can walk. He had a beard . . ."

Where do you suppose Jesus found the man after he was healed?

Jesus later found the man in the Temple. They struck up a conversation and Jesus confirmed his healing, speaking to him about his sin.

Jesus somehow linked the healing of the paralytic man with forgiveness of sins. Yet initially, sin wasn't addressed when he was healed. Therefore, Jesus urged that the man's healing should be more than physical: "You know better now. Go and sin no more."

It was the Sabbath, and it was not lawful for the man to carry his mat. The religious cared only for the ritual of Sabbath-keeping; they had no concern for the paralytic.

Every Jew respects the law and believes in keeping it. The Jews realize that apart from keeping the law, they have no way to please God, to behave themselves or to protect themselves. A typical Jew will tell you that, next to God, nothing is as great or as important as the law. God is number one and the law is number two. For this reason, they persecuted Jesus, who said He had fulfilled the law, and they sought to kill Him.

BART'S STATION

Concluding His ministry outside of Jerusalem with one final miracle, Jesus was on His way to Jerusalem for His final Passover. He had to pass through the city of Jericho where He would meet up with yet another recipient of God's covenant. By this time, Jesus and His disciples were thronged by the multitudes.

Departing from Jericho, the crowds followed Jesus down the dusty road in the cool of the evening. It was common for the blind, sick and lame to be strewn across His path everywhere He went. Jesus wasn't preoccupied or distracted by every need, but there were those who were on heaven's "hit list" that experienced His miracles. As was His custom, Jesus studied the people to discern which ones were in line for His miracle-working ministry. The Bible doesn't state that Jesus ever did one miracle twice, revealing the uniqueness and ever-present witness of the Spirit. God's next target—blind Bartimeus! (See Mark 10:46-52.)

I call him Bart for short.

Bart could hear the sound of the crowd approaching. Curious, he reached into the crowd as they passed him and grabbed the tunic of one of the passersby, and asked what the commotion was about.

Pushing Bart away as though he were some inanimate object, the follower responded, "It is Jesus of Nazareth."

Realizing the man wasn't going to help him, Bart quickly began crying out, "Jesus, Son of David, have mercy on me!" It is certain that Bart knew something about Jesus by the address of his desperate plea.

The crowds tried to silence Bart.

"Be quiet, beggar. He can't hear you anyway." But Bart would not keep quiet and cried out all the more. Even though Bart had many obstacles in his way, he was desperate and wouldn't allow the crowds to drown him out.

Jesus was apprehended by the desperate plea in the crowd and commanded that the "blind man" be brought to him. Throwing aside his garment, a symbolic gesture of throwing his past away, Bart somehow made his way to Jesus.

As Bart was in the presence of the Miracle Worker, he was asked, "What do you want Me to do for you?"

Bart replied, "Teacher, that I may receive my sight."

In that instance of healing, Jesus did not touch Bart at all. Instead, He sent Bart on his way with the assurance that his faith had healed him. Bart immediately received his sight and then joined the crowd following Jesus to Jerusalem. No more begging and no more poverty; he now had a chance to make his life count for something.

This helpless beggar is depicted as having faith, recognizing that Jesus could help him, even though he didn't know Jesus intimately.

What is the difference between a beggar and a whiner?

Bart, the beggar, was this way because of blindness; he needed transformation and he kept pressing to get it. A whiner complains about everything, not necessarily looking for a solution.

No one wants to be bothered with someone who is stuck on the side of the road. Life is passing them by. Did you know that you can be stuck on the side of the road with an academic degree? Some people like being in that condition. The most common excuse for people who are stuck is, "How do I know it will work this time?"

Bart's story illustrates our own need to be healed of spiritual blindness. Blindness was a metaphor frequently used for lack of knowledge and understanding, especially about one's future. When we are healed of spiritual blindness, there is no more begging or poverty; and we, too, have a chance to make our life count for Christ.

"I was once blind, but now I see."

THE SAMARITAN WOMAN

Jesus was thirsty and it was high noon.

An unidentified Samaritan woman was trudging along a familiar road in the midsummer Judean heat when she made her way to a local water well to draw water because she was thirsty. Carrying her water pot upon her shoulder, I imagine that this lonely woman wasn't thinking about her future; she wanted to take care of business and return home. Tired of being the talk of the town, she probably chose the noon hour to go to the well to avoid the public scorn of her immoral lifestyle.

But on this particular day, she was on the heart of God!

Having deliberately chosen the Samaritan road, an unpopular road for a Jew to travel, the Bible says, "He needed to go through Samaria" (John 4:4, *NKJV*). According to Jewish custom, Jesus could have crossed the Jordan and passed through Perea instead, a bit out of the way but still feasible. I believe this need to go there was prompted by the Holy Spirit.

Jesus sent His disciples away to buy food so that He could have an intimate conversation with this "promiscuous woman." He knew that the disciples might want to demean her about her lifestyle. Even though Jesus was free from the limitations of race, sex and religion, He knew that the disciples still struggled with His motives and ministry.

The Messiah's encounter with the Samaritan woman began with a simple request: "Give Me a drink."

She replied, "How is it that You being a Jew ask a drink from me, a Samaritan woman? For Jews have no dealings with Samaritans."

The historic ethnicity and background of the Samaritans is worth noting. The Samaritans were "mongrel" Jews, both in blood and religion. The Jews had deep resentment toward the Samaritans dating back several centuries. When the Assyrians conquered Samaria, they deported the local Israelite population and imported alien nations to resettle Samaria. These people brought their own pagan religions with them but were later instructed in the worship of Jehovah.

There was no love lost between Jews and the racially mixed Samaritans. By understanding the animosity between these groups, the Samaritan woman's question to Jesus makes more sense.

Jesus simply ignored her objection and immediately began divine instruction. Some issues are best left alone—quarreling about religion is usually the most unproductive of all quarrels for sure.

Jesus instructed the Samaritan woman, "Go get your husband."

Perplexed, the woman responded, "I have no husband."

"You have well said, 'I have no husband,' for you have had five husbands, and the one whom you now have is not your husband," Jesus replied (John 4:17-18, *NKJV*).

With a word of knowledge, her scandalous past was exposed, not to embarrass her but to bring conviction to her heart. Jesus' innocuous approach was gentle and nondegrading. He didn't tell her to straighten her life out or she would go to hell. *Love* identified her weakness in order to gain her confidence so that she could receive the message of freedom He was presenting her. All Jesus had to do was pinpoint one aspect of her life and He had her full attention. A few words under the guidance of the Holy Spirit can do far more than the best sermon ever could.

The word that Jesus spoke to this woman was truth known only by the Spirit. This kind of approach is a great evangelistic tool to win the lost because it removes the believer from interfering with God's agenda. Knowledge of the truth inspired by the Spirit makes one free.

Jesus had no prior knowledge of her condition. Thus, she fully embraced the message He was offering her and left His presence a free woman.

After their conversation, the Samaritan woman immediately ran and told the people in her home town what had happened to her. With exuberance in her newfound freedom, she said, "Come and meet a man who has told me everything about my life." Jesus didn't tell her everything about her life, only one very important aspect of her life that had kept her bound.

Revival broke out in the city and many of the Samaritans of that city believed in Jesus because of the encounter of this unlikely individual. One preacher and one lonely and despised woman impacted an entire city.

THE PRODIGAL SON

The setting for this particular story is a family with two sons and a wealthy father. The brothers weren't close, probably due to sibling rivalry. The younger, a restless young man, was tired of the mundane life tending his father's fields. He wanted to get out and see the world. The older son, well, he was the goody-two-shoes of the family.

So this young and irresponsible son had the notion to ask his father for his share of his father's inheritance that was customarily due to him after his father's death. Uneasy about the request, his father nevertheless consented and divided the monies amongst the brothers.

With his share of the inheritance, the younger headed off into the sunset with his money bag in tow and a satchel stuffed with his belongings. The Bible says that he went to a far country. I suppose he wanted to get as far away from home as possible.

This proud little prodigal was footloose and fancy-free, living a carefree life removed from the clutches of his family's influence. It didn't take long before he squandered his entire inheritance on wild living. Sin was pleasurable for a season, but when the funds ran dry, all his friends abandoned him and he began to long for home.

A famine hit the land where the prodigal was living and he was in desperate need. He went searching for a way to make ends meet and ran into a Gentile man who was willing to take him into his employ. The young lad was reduced to caring for the man's pigs. This was not a good job for a Jew, considering the fact that swine were unclean. It was the greatest imaginable insult, but he was desperate. The Bible says that he was so hungry that he would gladly have filled his stomach with the pods that the swine ate. The swine were eating better than he was.

By this time, he began to sober up. Realizing the condition he was in, the prodigal pondered, "How many of my father's hired servants have bread enough to spare, and I perish with hunger. I will arise and go to my father and will say to him, 'Father, I have sinned against heaven and am no longer worthy to be called your son. Make me one of your hired servants.'"

He was beginning to take full responsibility for his wrong actions. So this dishonored and remorseful son rose up, dusted himself off and made the long and contemplative journey home.

Much to his surprise, he was met by his elated father who, when he saw his son from afar, ran to meet him. If that greeting wasn't shocking enough, his father fell on his neck and kissed him. Looking like a beggar and smelling like a swine's meal of pods, the prodigal in turn sheepishly hugged his father, relieved to be home.

The boy's father instructed his servants, "Quickly bring out the best robe and put it on him. Put a ring on his hand and sandals on his feet." His father extended unconditional love toward his son to restore their broken relationship. The son was in disbelief at all the hoopla; he was grateful just to be home and eat with his father's hired servants.

This story is symbolic of the covenant God has with His children. It is an exchanged life—one coming from the world and resting in covenant partnership with God. Mephibosheth was rescued from Lo Debar and found himself dining in King David's palace because of a covenant.

Although the Bible doesn't specifically mention the prodigal son finding God, it is an allegory about being restored to a father. Remember that the image one has of one's father is the image one will have of his or her heavenly Father.

This story is rich with symbolism.

1. *The Robe:* Symbolic of God's (the father's) righteousness, or the prodigal's restored position to his father.

Placing a robe on him conferred his rightful place as a son. It was given to the boy without merit, simply because of whose he was! At salvation, believers are draped with a robe of righteousness. In other words, this robe covers our sins and elevates us in right standing with God. The intimate embrace of his father revealed his forgiveness toward his son.

2. *The Ring:* Symbolic of God's (the father's) unending love for his son. The ring sealed the covenant between the boy and his father. Consequently, this restored son was instantly given family authority! How we are loved by God when we return home to the Father's house! The seal that keeps the covenant alive in us is love.

3. *The Sandals:* Symbolic of God's salvation and the new walk of faith the returning son would come to realize. Our salvation in Christ initiates a new walk, a new lifestyle, that leads us to embrace our covenant with God in a fresh and living way. "The life which I now live in the flesh I live by the faith of the Son of God, who loved me, and gave himself for me" (Gal. 2:20, *KJV*).

4. *The Fatted Calf:* The celebration, which included a fatted calf, not only satisfied this starving lad's hunger but signifies Christ who fills all believers with divine life to enjoy. "My son was dead and is alive again; he was lost and is found," a relieved father declared (Luke 15:24, *NKJV*). For all practical purposes, all prodigals are dead in a parent's eyes; but upon returning home, it is as if they have literally come back to life. When you come to salvation, you are made alive in Christ (see Eph. 2:1,5).

An interesting point to this story. When the prodigal hit rock bottom, he "came to himself." Boy, isn't rock bottom when reality finally hits and you come to yourself? You wake up and discover why you had to go through what you went through to get to where you are today.

Finding God in your journey will give you direction. Without the love of God to anchor your life, you are vulnerable to anybody's influence, because you don't know what you were created for.

The road back to God for each prodigal is different. Parents, there are no guarantees in life's journey. No matter how hard we strive to teach our children about God, or how often we pray for them to discover Christ in their life, some decide to reject it all for a season. Even in families where God is glorified, children sometimes rebel.

However difficult the circumstances, we should never give up on our kids, no matter how far away they may seem to be. Pray for them. Your prayers may spare them from destruction that the devil has plotted for them.

There were many prodigals in the Bible.

We've already learned how King Hezekiah, more than any other king in Judah's history, trusted the Lord. You would think that his son, Manasseh, would have come to love and trust Yahweh, too. However, when Manasseh became king at the age of 12, he immediately turned against God and did evil in the sight of the Lord (see 2 Chron. 33:2).

Later, after Manasseh and the people of Judah had been captured and taken in chains to Babylon, he finally turned back to the God of his fathers. After years of rebellion, God was still merciful to Manasseh.

The prophet Samuel's sons were evil in the sight of the Lord, even though Samuel was consecrated to the Lord by his mother, Hannah. Israel's first prophet proved to be one of their greatest, yet his seed proved otherwise.

Do you think the prodigal son ever imagined himself eating pig's food in a faraway land? He wanted to spread his wings and was looking for adventure to get away from his self-righteous brother. Many of us can relate to being young, foolish and impetuous. How many of us have done crazy things out of peer pressure?

The world is full of prodigals. There isn't anything you've done that will keep God from accepting you.

GOING AGAINST THE GRAIN

Jesus' ministry to the multitudes was a ministry of undeniable miracles that altered the course of history, even before His death on the cross. Jesus' life was a prophetic message of the kingdom that was to come.

Much of His time and energy was spent reaching those outside the synagogue—the "unchurched." These folks made little or no effort to observe the Jewish law. Many were engaged in occupations that were thought to be immoral or dishonest. Jesus repeatedly ate with tax collectors, harlots and sinners. In His culture, eating with someone was a sign of acceptance, reconciliation, mutual trust and sharing of life. Therefore, when Jesus ate with these outcasts, His actions were viewed by the religious community as blasphemous. The meals Jesus ate with the common folk illustrated a prophetic message. There would be a day when they would feast together at the Master's table. Much of Jesus' teachings were in defense of His calling "sinners" to God's table (see Luke 18:9-14).

Jesus offered the multitudes a spiritual inheritance that included forgiveness, membership in God's family and a share of the blessings of the coming age, things the religious denied He had the power to grant. Jesus repeatedly embraced the unclean, a violation of the purity laws. Therefore, the direct contact Jesus had with the dead and those possessed with unclean spirits violated Jewish law.

Jesus' message of free access to God's kingdom appealed to the poor and the powerless, which included women, who were not fully embraced in the sacred system of Judaism. The nameless and the faceless had no future in the "system." Jesus' popularity grew simply because He valued people. His message of good news was the hope they needed to believe in a better way of life. Society's elite and religious were self-sufficient; they had no need of a Savior.

The gospel that Jesus preached sent shock waves through the religious community. They were offended by the miracles Jesus performed on the Sabbath or on Jewish holidays and observances.

Society's boundaries were no longer to be drawn by the observance of ritual law.

Jesus did not condemn the religious community's allegiance to the law, but the abuses of their positions as teachers, priests, scribes and leaders. Legalism and hypocrisy were an ineffective witness. Although there was much good in Judaism, the burdens imposed on common people were intolerable. For these traditionalists, Jesus' life was indeed an enigma.

A friend and well-known author, Dr. Jack Deere, explains:

> The Pharisees claimed to be looking for the coming Messiah, but they never really expected the Old Testament examples of supernatural phenomena to be repeated in their lifetime. They had a theoretical belief in the supernatural—they believed in angels and the resurrection of the body—but expected nothing supernatural in their lives. They did not listen to God's voice apart from the Scriptures, and they never heard his voice in the Scriptures.[2]

Their only hope of keeping the sanctity of their Jewish piety intact was to kill the Messiah! How ironic is that!

THE DEATH OF A KING

Few episodes in history have been dramatized and portrayed more than the final and dreadful hours of Jesus' life, commonly known as His Passion.

The road to Jesus' death began at a grove of olive trees known as the Garden of Gethsemane. It was the night watch and the disciples were sound asleep. Jesus knelt and began to pray, experiencing the weight of His soon death, agonizing to the point of sweating great drops of blood. In prayer, Jesus submitted His will to the Father, consenting to partake of the cup of suffering. Suddenly, He heard the sound of clanging armor and the rustling of bushes when a posse of armed men appeared before Him. A lantern in the posse quickly cast illumination over Judas who accompanied them. The other disciples were startled by the commotion and woke up.

Simon Peter impulsively drew his sword and hacked off the right ear of one of the temple guards, trying to prevent the arrest. Exercising His divine power, Jesus took the bloody ear and positioned it back where it belonged, making His captor whole. It is remarkable to me that Jesus demonstrated such compassion toward one of His enemies.

One of the authorities gestured to Judas to identify the accused. Judas then leaned over to kiss Jesus as though greeting Him with a friendly salutation. Jesus whispered to Judas, "Are you betraying the Son of Man with a kiss?" (Luke 22:48, *NASB*). Jesus wanted Judas to know that He was aware of the deadly consequences of his actions. His betrayal was complete, and 30 pieces of silver were handed over to Judas. Jesus offered no resistance to His arrest.

In the intimate moments of the Last Supper the previous night, Jesus had washed His disciples' feet before they ate their last meal with Him. A somber mood had fallen over the entire event when His disciples professed their loyalty to Him. The greed-driven Judas quietly withdrew from the meal in order to inform the priests of the proper location for the arrest.

Matthew's Gospel says that once the arrest was over, "All the disciples forsook Him and fled." This fulfilled the prophecy that He would be rejected and forsaken.

Jesus was left alone with His captors and taken to the authorities, who brought Him before a Sanhedrin tribunal court to be judged. Realizing that according to Roman law they did not have the power to execute anyone, the religious leaders assessed Him guilty of heresy and transferred Jesus to Pilate.

Pilate was the Roman procurator, a politician and an agent of Caesar Tiberias in Judea. When Pilate realized that Jesus was from Galilee, the jurisdiction of Herod, he sent Him up to Herod who was himself in Jerusalem in those days.

Pilate, Herod and the soldiers tossed Jesus around like children kicking a ball back and forth. When Pilate explained to the people that he would discipline and release Jesus, the people vehemently cried out for the release of Barabbas. They wanted Jesus put to death.

The name Barabbas means "the favorite son of the Father." By choosing a man with that name, they were prophesying what they really needed; they just didn't know it. And they said, "Let His blood be upon us."

When Jesus was officially condemned to death, Judas was overwhelmed with remorse and attempted to undo his evil by returning the money, only to be contemptuously rejected by the high priest. Feeling helpless, Judas committed suicide by hanging himself.

Although Jesus was mocked and beaten beyond recognition, He did not open His mouth to defend Himself. The road to Calvary took Him through the city arrayed in a scarlet robe and a crown of thorns.

This was His hour of destiny.

EYEWITNESS NEWS

There were many eyewitnesses to Jesus' crucifixion. There were those who wanted Him crucified and those who agonized in grief during the emotionally charged hours leading to His death.

Mary Magdalene and Jesus' mother were there, embracing each other and trying to find solace in this "senseless" death. The religious community didn't recognize women for their contribution to society, much less for their spiritual life. Yet women were central to Jesus' ministry and closest to Him at His death. Mary Magdalene's undying devotion to Jesus was partly due to the great authority He demonstrated when He exorcised seven demons from her. She became a leading figure amongst those serving Jesus.

Mary Magdalene was the first witness to His resurrection. Not only was Jesus remembered for treating women with respect, but He was also portrayed as a Man who had a genuine concern for them.

As Jesus hung nailed to the cross in unimaginable agony, dark clouds began to gather. Jesus offered healing words to the penitent thief on the cross beside Him when the thief made a request of Jesus: "Lord, remember me when you come into Your kingdom."

Jesus granted his request, promising an imminent rendezvous with him in Paradise.

At around noontime, the sun was darkened. For three hours God extinguished the sun's light, and darkness came over the land, signifying that God put our sins upon His beloved Son (see Isa. 53:6). He was completely forsaken by His Father. And from noon until 3:00 P.M., Jesus was dying as a substitute for sinners. But the suffering Servant died triumphantly: When Jesus breathed His last breath and said, "It is finished," His work was fully accomplished. In this final declaration, Jesus was not thinking of His mortal life but that He had succeeded in His mission to redeem mankind to the Father.

This was no ordinary death, as many perceived. Jesus' death sent a message to the principalities and powers that God's kingdom was about to give way to the souls of men; a spiritual population explosion was imminent. As Isaiah had prophesied 700 years earlier, this supernatural turn of events released God's everlasting covenant in a new and a living way.

At Jesus' death, the veil of the Temple was torn in two "from top to bottom," signifying that the separation between God and man was no more. The veil had been necessitated by man's sin. Christ had taken on the sins of all (see Rom. 8:3). This act was impossible to perform without God's intervention.

When Jesus was removed from the cross, He was wrapped in a linen cloth and buried in a rich man's tomb. On the third day, when Mary Magdalene, Salome and Mary, the mother of Jesus, went to the tomb, they brought with them some spices to anoint His body. To their amazement, the griefstricken women found the tomb empty. In their despair, an angel appeared to them with words of comfort: "He is not here. He is risen."

They rushed to tell Peter, John and the other disciples about this miraculous turn of events. In almost disbelief the disciples returned with the women to the tomb.

MEDIATOR OF A BETTER COVENANT

In the Old Covenant, man's direct approach to God was limited to the priesthood, trespass offerings, blood sacrifices and the many ordinances outlined in the Law.

While God was binding Himself in covenant to Abraham on earth, He was also making covenant with Jesus in heaven. "Now to Abraham and his Seed were the promises made. He does not say, 'And to seeds,' as of many, but as of one, 'And to your Seed,' who is Christ" (Gal. 3:16, *NKJV*). Abraham was the earthly representative; Jesus was the heavenly representative. The covenant was not only between God and Abraham, but between God the Father and God the Son. By making covenant with Jesus, He was making covenant with someone He knew would never break it, and thereby removing the need for a curse.

This New Covenant is better than the old. If you'll read Deuteronomy 28, you'll find the blessings that are promised to those who keep the terms of the agreement. They're fabulous promises. But keep reading and you'll also find the curse that will fall on those who break the agreement. That's where the New Covenant differs. Although we ourselves have been guilty of breaking the terms of the covenant, we've been freed from the penalty of it.

From the time Jesus was born until He died at Calvary, He never broke the terms of the covenant. Yet when He went to the cross, He bore the curse or penalty for breaking it. Why? So that you and I would never have to bear it. Jesus became the sacrificial Lamb that established your covenant with God.

"Christ has redeemed us from the curse of the law, having become a curse for us (for it is written, 'Cursed is everyone who hangs on a tree'), that the blessing of Abraham might come upon the Gentiles in Christ Jesus, that we might receive the promise of the Spirit through faith" (Gal. 3:13-14, *NKJV*).

Redemption means to exchange, to purchase, to buy back, to pay a ransom for. Redemption must bring new life—spirit life—to fallen man. Sinners commit sin because the root of their life is in sin. But for believers, the root of their life is in Christ. So for us, sinning is unnatural. That's why we're instantly convicted when we sin.

The DNA necessary to live the spiritual life is awakened through the born-again experience, because of Christ's indwelling: "For in him we live and move and have our being . . . 'We are his offspring.' Therefore since we are God's offspring, we should not think that the divine being is like gold or silver or stone" (Acts 17:28-29, *NIV*).

Jesus was not only the blood sacrifice, but He also became our representative—the Mediator between God and man! "We have an Advocate with the Father, Jesus Christ the righteous" (1 John 2:1, *NKJV*). He not only sees to our forgiveness when we confess our sins, but He also cleanses us from all unrighteousness.

Just as the covenant with Abraham brought Abraham into an intimate relationship with God, and he was known as a "friend of God," so also the covenant in Christ's blood assures us of this same kind of intimate relationship. It is a new covenant because it not only affords the opportunity for closer fellowship between man and God, but it also includes an inheritance: "And if you are Christ's, then are you Abraham's seed, and heirs according to the promise" (Gal. 3:29, *NKJV*).

This is our covenant of redemption—an everlasting covenant!

Not one leader of any religion has claimed to be the savior of the world. None of them bled and died for the salvation of mankind. Confucius quoted some Solomonic truths, as did others, but he never claimed to be "the way, the truth and the life." Buddhism is a philosophy. Buddhists, Jews and Muslims, all point you upward toward God. That is why Jesus said broad is the way; religion is a broad way. But once you get close to God, in order to gain access, you must proceed through the narrow gate—Christ (see Matt. 7:13).

COVENANT OF GRACE

The Law did not contain the covenant of grace. The Pharisees declared that the Law was given as a means of salvation. When the Law is properly understood, the Christian can then enjoy God as he lives life from the inward witness (see Rom. 7:22).

When the author of Hebrews made a direct comparison of the Old Covenant and the New, the deficiency of the Law was said not to be its legalism but the fact that it called for repeated sacrifices and therefore was but a foreshadowing of what was to come.

Under the New Covenant, we have a better Priest, a better sacrifice, and a better sanctuary. The whole of redemption is free grace to us. I'm so glad that I live in the age of grace, mercy and blessing.

A study of Jesus' life shows how we should walk in the New Covenant. He stripped Himself of God's power. At age 30, Jesus was Spirit-empowered to walk in the covenant. By His death and resurrection, Jesus enabled us to walk in the power of the covenant. Every work done by Jesus was in the authority of the Abrahamic covenant, and that covenant was sealed in His blood at His death.

God always takes the initiative. My responsibility is to respond to God's invitation. The greater approaches the lesser to initiate covenant. You have been saved by grace; it's a gift of God. Blood covenant is the basis for that grace.

No matter where you are or what your circumstances, God will chase you down. He goes after the backslider, just as He went after Adam and Eve. God always seeks the lost. Jesus had to appear and fully pay our debt, because we were spiritually bankrupt. To understand redemption, we must understand grace.

What is common grace? Common grace is for saint and sinner alike; God makes His sun rise on both good and evil and sends rain on the just and the unjust. God is good to everyone; His tender mercies are over all His works. After the Fall, man was no longer in the likeness of God, yet man continues to bear the image of God. "Christian" means "Christ-like," and to get back to God's likeness, one must get God back into his life.

God's ultimate dream is to place us back in right standing with Him. The entire covenant process is something initiated, established, confirmed and fulfilled by an act of divine will.

COVENANT MEAL

Across America it is traditional to celebrate a meal on Thanksgiving Day. This is not a typical meal. It is usually a large feast where family and friends travel far and wide to get together. Thanksgiving is a time to give thanks for our country and for the many blessings we have. Certain meals take us back to fond memories—when I eat chicken, I think of Grandma. When I eat spaghetti, I think of my late brother-in-law, Ed.

Commemorating certain historic events and rites in the Bible are meant to be reminders of powerful truths they originally represented when they were established. Since God is the same yesterday, today and forever, the truths are still pertinent to us and still have the power to impact our lives.

The Lord's Supper, known also as Communion, is a symbolic covenant meal. The purpose of this memorial feast is to draw attention to the main mission of Jesus. He was not only the perfect atoning blood sacrifice and our representative on the Cross, but He was also the covenant meal. "I am the living bread which came down from heaven: if any man eat of this bread, he shall live forever: and the bread that I will give is my flesh, which I will give for the life of the world" (John 6:51, *KJV*).

The elements used in Communion are significant for us today.

The *bread* symbolizes His broken body. Isaiah 53 prophesied the physical mutilating of Jesus' body for our sins, revealing that the stripes (the beating) He endured were for the healing of man's physical body.

The *wine* represents His poured-out blood to redeem man. The blood ultimately sealed the covenant between God and man. When Jesus instituted Communion, He used the expression, "This cup is the new covenant in My blood" (1 Cor. 11:25, *NIV*). The bread and the wine are powerful covenant symbols of the finished work of the Cross.

"As often as you do this," Jesus spoke of Communion, "do it in remembrance of Me."

COVENANT OF HEALING

Isaiah's Old Testament messianic passages are important to understand in order for us to receive everything we need in life, especially the healing of our bodies.

Many people struggle with believing in God's healing power today, even though the Bible clearly states that healing is the children's bread and is always served fresh at God's table. But is it contrary to the principles of faith to use doctors and medicine when you need to be healed? Here are a few points to ponder if you are uncertain regarding your medical condition and need some answers.

Dr. Herold G. Koenig, a Duke University medical researcher, says that faith is good for your health. Dr. Koenig found a clear relationship between faith and health, one that he titled his book after—*The Healing Connection*. "Christians have long believed that faith and health are closely linked but twentieth century medicine has been skeptical or downright scornful of such a notion. The pile of evidence is growing and showing that spiritual faith has a very real, scientifically measurable and positive association with mental and physical well-being." Dr. Koenig has published 25 books and more than 200 professional journal articles detailing his findings.[3]

According to Koenig, the key to the healing connection is having a deep, personal relationship with God and love for your neighbor. In other words, if your faith is strong and you can believe the Word of God without wavering, regardless of your circumstances or symptoms, then you'll be able to receive your healing. But that kind of faith takes more than just hearing a few sermons about healing. It takes a deep personal revelation of God's healing power to combat the fear, doubt, unbelief and everything else that Satan dishes out when you are ill.

For the believer who hasn't yet developed that kind of faith, the doctor may be his best friend.

If you're still uncertain as to whether or not to seek medical attention, and fear rises within you when you think about doing without your medicine or the help of a doctor, then go to the doctor.

Covenant is relationship oriented and releases the faith and confidence to access the healing you need. Your ultimate goal should be to seek the Healer and establish yourself in that divine relationship.

DAWNING OF A NEW KINGDOM

One thousand years before the birth of Jesus, Yahweh cut a covenant in which He promised King David, "You will always have descendants, and I will make your kingdom last forever" (2 Sam. 7:16, *GNB*). The kingdom that Yahweh referred to was no earthly kingdom. It would be an everlasting kingdom.

Well, that kingdom is here!

"How so?" one might ask.

Man lost the original kingdom of heaven on earth through Adam in the Garden. He gave the kingdom to an unemployed cherub, Lucifer, who is now Satan, the prince of the power of the air. Through Jesus' death and resurrection that spiritual kingdom was restored. That is why we can say we live in this world but are not of it. We are not under its dominion or control.

The Bible says that Jesus has delivered us from the power of darkness and translated us into the kingdom of God (see Col. 1:3). The word "translated" means to be taken out of one place and put into another. In other words, our citizenship is not primarily of this earth. For example, we are not primarily American or Indian or Korean; we are first and foremost citizens of the kingdom of God.

A kingdom is defined as a king ruling over his domain or territory. The evidence that God's kingdom has been established is the impact that it has on its inhabitants, as Jesus and His disciples experienced. In this kingdom, the King empowers His people to live and prosper in life by faith. Faith, like the law of gravity, though it cannot be seen, is in force when you apply this kingdom's principles to your life. As you see the effects of the law of gravity at work, so you will see the fruit of your faith. Demonstrating or manifesting healing and the casting out of demons is simply evidence that God's kingdom is present on earth.

Every king is automatically a lord over his domain. If Christ is our King, He should have lordship over us. If He does, then the King's provision includes money, healing and anything else we have need of. Thank God for putting Jesus where we can reach Him. The promise of the coming of the Holy Spirit to awaken us to our covenant follows in the next chapter.

Life Lines

- The 400 years between the Old and New Testaments were a turbulent time for the Jewish people, leading up to their rule by the Roman Empire. However, the Messiah was being prepared to come on the scene.

- Jesus' miracles revealed the amazing faith of non-Jewish recipients to a Jewish covenant.

- Jesus walked in great authority while ministering to the sick and setting the captive free. He frequently drove out spirits and spoke to illnesses with just a word. Many times, Jesus didn't have physical contact with the individuals for whom He performed miracles.

- The greatest resistance to Jesus' ministry came from the religious crowd known as the Pharisees and the Sadducees. It is no different today. Whenever you step out to do the works of Jesus, you will always find the religious trying to explain away miracles and criticizing those who are trying to serve the Lord.

- Jesus had many things to say about the religious leadership, referring to them as "whitewashed tombs . . . full of dead men's bones . . ." (*NIV*).

- Jesus' first miracle wasn't a life-saving one. He turned water into wine, quenching the thirst of the guests at a wedding in Cana. Don't discard His care for you in every area of your life.

- Peter frequently displayed his all-too-human flaws during his years as a disciple. But his relationship with Jesus transformed him from being an ambitious and defensive man to a caring, selfless individual. Has your character had a chance to emerge in Christlikeness since you've come to Christ?

- An in-depth, personal encounter with the Lord at lunchtime by the local well made a believer out of a notorious woman. So powerful was the testimony of her changed life that a whole city in Samaria was influenced by it.

- The royal law of love was the motivating factor in everything Jesus did. That is why the religious couldn't understand Him. He was an enigma to them. Yet to the nonreligious, Jesus was intriguing, likeable and forgiving.

- Our covenant with God is purely on the basis of grace.

CHAPTER 12

Covenant Sealed with the Spirit

That the blessing of Abraham might come upon the Gentiles in Christ Jesus, that we might receive the promise of the Spirit through faith.
GALATIANS 3:14, *NKJV*

The Tent of Meeting, the Tabernacle, the Ark of the Covenant, the Holy of Holies—these visual aids were a necessary tool God used as prototypes of His presence on earth prior to Christ's incarnation. God's relationship with His people under the Old Covenant did not occur apart from the priests, prophets, kings and disciples, with the exception of a few. However limited that relationship, God knew there was a day coming when things would be different.

Jesus gathered His disciples after His resurrection to prepare them for their future without Him. He spoke to them, saying, "All authority has been given to Me in heaven and on earth. Go therefore and make disciples of all the nations, baptizing them in the name of the Father and of the Son and of the Holy Spirit, teaching them to observe all things that I have commanded you; and lo, I am with you always, even to the end of the age" (Matt. 28:18-20, *NKJV*).

Their initial spiritual crisis concerned whether they would be able to follow Jesus' example after He was gone. Jesus' disciples had been in His school of ministry for three years and daily witnessed how He relied upon the Father to fulfill His ministry.

Recalling all that talk about their future while Jesus was with them, these ordinary men were absolutely astonished. They must have questioned among themselves, "How are we going to preach the gospel to the ends of the earth?" Most probably had never been out of the country.

They would be challenged to cultivate a relationship with the Holy Spirit just as Jesus did. They had the basic foundation for their spiritual life in Jesus' example, but their lives would soon be empowered by the Spirit in ways they had never known or experienced. Much of what the disciples had learned and experienced in ministry was going to be accelerated. The Holy Spirit would become the divine instrument for guiding them into the broader reaches of the knowledge of God (see John 16:12-14).

Jesus further instructed the disciples, "Do not leave Jerusalem, but wait for the gift my Father promised, which you have heard me speak about. For John baptized with water, but in a few days you will be baptized with the Holy Spirit" (Acts 1:4-5, *NIV*).

Jesus was preparing them for a new experience, so He used the familiar to introduce the unfamiliar. The disciples witnessed John's followers being submerged in water baptism. Holy Spirit baptism would take on a similar form, but the spiritual after-effects would not evaporate as the water did off of a dripping convert.

These men were to wait for the coming of the Spirit before rushing off to tackle their new assignments. Waiting for this dynamic future to unfold involved a measure of uncertainty and urgency.

Before the Lord's death, the disciples had no interest in praying for spiritual things. Rather, they contended among themselves as to who would be the greater. After the Lord's death and resurrection, their spiritual condition radically changed.

WHEN GOD THROWS A SURPRISE PARTY

The disciples were burdened to persevere in prayer for the promise of the Spirit. So they gathered the people, waited and prayed on the second-floor living room of John Mark's home, the place where Jesus and His disciples had met for their last supper together. It was a great matter for the 120 to pray in one accord for 10 days.

> On the day of Pentecost, seven weeks after Jesus' resurrection, the believers were meeting together in one place.

> Suddenly, there was a sound from heaven like the roaring of a mighty windstorm in the skies above them, and it filled the house where they were meeting. Then, what looked like flames or tongues of fire appeared and settled on each of them. And everyone present was filled with the Holy Spirit and began speaking in other languages, as the Holy Spirit gave them this ability (Acts 2:1-4, *NLT*).

The significance of this encounter occurring in the ancient city of Jerusalem is apparent because this city was known as the "dwelling place of God" among the Jews of the Old Covenant.

The 120 who were gathered in the upper room were suddenly baptized and began to speak in dialects other than their own. The *Life Application Bible* adds, "Why tongues of fire? Tongues symbolize speech and the communication of the gospel. Fire symbolizes God's purifying presence, burning away the undesirable elements of our lives and setting our hearts aflame to ignite the lives of others."[1]

Peter stepped forward, empowered by the Holy Spirit, and explained the experience to the bewildered masses, linking it to the death and resurrection of Jesus. He explained that the fulfillment of the ancient prophecy in the book of Joel had just begun!

> I will pour out My Spirit on all flesh; Your sons and your daughters shall prophesy, Your old men shall dream dreams, Your young men shall see visions. And also on My menservants and on My maidservants I will pour out My Spirit in those days (Joel 2:28-29, *NKJV*).

After Peter finished preaching, 3,000 people from the streets of Jerusalem were added to the fledgling church. All 3,000 immediately submitted to water baptism and joined the community of believers. Dr. Jack Deere comments on this particular event in his book *Surprised by the Voice of God*: "All the supernatural phenomena in the upper room indicated that the proclamation of the church would be divinely inspired by heaven."[2]

This power of Pentecost and the impact it had on Jesus' disciples would inwardly challenge their traditions and religious dogma. The spiritual paradigm was yet to be formed in them. When Jesus faced religious persecution, the disciples saw firsthand how He handled it. His whole life's message went against the Jewish religious structure of the day. Until that time, the disciples could hide behind Jesus and even deny Him without the threat of death; but that "shield" was now removed and they were on their own. Although it was an undeniable spiritual awakening, until that paradigm became a strong reality in them, their faith would be severely tested.

Their greatest challenge after the Resurrection was to emulate Christ to the world. The disciples would have to rely on the Spirit more than they had imagined in order to build the fledgling church. It was not an easy transition, but they had no other option. The spiritual learning curve was about to take shape.

It took years for the disciples to sufficiently internalize Jesus' concept of the kingdom of God in order to be able to teach it to others. The children of Israel faced a transitional dilemma, too, when they crossed the Red Sea into their Promised Land. The exuberance of their miraculous exodus faded into memory when they faced the tough times that followed. Their minds were enslaved to Egypt, unable to grasp the price of liberty ahead.

With time and experience, the disciples became increasingly dependent upon the Spirit's leading to risk it all in order to do what their risen Lord commanded. It took 200 years after the Resurrection before believers began worshiping in buildings constructed specifically for worship. Until then they met in houses or caves—wherever they could gather safely away from official government persecution.

The outpouring of the Holy Spirit did not remain isolated within the four walls of the upper room. It is clear from the text that it was anything but private and hidden from view. The Spirit's arrival was a noisy affair with special effects that attracted an interested public "from every nation."

ANOTHER LOOK AT PENTECOST

Jerusalem's Feast of Pentecost revealed more about this spectacular event than the casual reader of Scripture might discern.

There were 120 in attendance in the Upper Room; the number 120 is symbolic of transition. In the Old Testament, Pentecost was also known as the Festival of First Fruits. Traditionally, farmers would visit the Temple, bringing the first fruits of their crops, praying and asking God to bless their coming harvest. It was a "feast of hope and expectation." Also, Jewish tradition linked the Pentecost celebration with the giving of the Law of Moses on Mount Sinai. In similar fashion, when Pentecost occurred, the Church was birthed in revelation and power!

Notice the progression of events that occurred that day:

1. Suddenly they *heard* something different. What did they hear? They heard a sound from heaven like a mighty, rushing wind. The Holy Spirit could be felt and heard.

2. Suddenly they *saw* something different. What did they see? They saw tongues of fire, which is symbolic of illumination, purification and purging.

3. Suddenly they *spoke* something different. What did they speak? They spoke in tongues as the Spirit gave them ability. The tongues they spoke were the diverse languages represented by those from the different nations who were there to witness this event. The various tongues spoken were not understood by those who spoke them. That was a supernatural phenomena.

Whenever God does something sudden and extraordinary in a believer's life or within a body of believers, three types of reactions in people can be discerned.

1. "THEY WERE CONFUSED AND PERPLEXED"
The crowds will always try to reason away or argue with the supernatural, much like they did that morning. The confusion of the as-

sembled crowds was the result of hearing languages spoken by people who were not of their own nationalities. The crowd could not believe what they were hearing.

John's Gospel gives an account of Jesus healing a blind man on the Sabbath.

Patronizing the young man, the Pharisees refused to believe that he didn't know who healed him. The young man's response was classic: "One thing I know: that though I was blind, now I see" (John 9:25, *NKJV*). Before they walked away in a puff of religious smoke, the young man who was healed challenged them, "If this Man were not of God, he could do nothing." A person with a genuine experience is never at the mercy of a religious debate.

2. "THEY WERE AMAZED AND MARVELED"
Again, they reasoned within themselves regarding the unlearned Galileans and their ability to know all these languages. "Aren't they fishermen?" they wondered. In those days, the image of the Galileans was comparable in our culture to that of a hillbilly. How could God use such people? How could they be well versed in the languages of Africa, Persia, Asia and Greece, for example? They would have had to go to school to learn them. God takes pleasure in using the foolish things to confound the wise.

3. "OTHERS MOCKED THE EVENT"
Attempting to explain away the evidence, the religious said that the Galileans were drunk. Any supernatural experience will leave the skeptics scratching their heads, wondering and scrambling for a logical explanation. Imagine that—drunk at an early morning prayer meeting! Watch out for the scoffers and mockers. They are no more interested in a move of God than the Pharisees were in Jesus' day, or the day of Pentecost.

Many in the religious arena today deny the Pentecostal experience, saying that "speaking in tongues is of the Devil." Don't you believe it. "Is the Spirit of the LORD restricted? Are these His doings? Do not My words do good to him who walks uprightly?" (Mic. 2:7, *NKJV*).

Don't let anyone's ridicule steal from you the power of an authentic, supernatural experience.

A PRIVATE PENTECOSTAL INVITATION

I've always taught my church that Christianity is more than following a set of intellectual or religious beliefs about Jesus. And it's more than going to church.

The abundant life that Jesus promised us involves a personal relationship with God through the Holy Spirit. Because Jesus promised that the Spirit would guide us into all truth, it follows that the Holy Spirit will illuminate us to all the benefits of our covenant with God.

Jesus taught, "If you then, being evil, know how to give good gifts to your children, how much more will your heavenly Father give the Holy Spirit to those who ask Him?" (Luke 11:13, *NASB*).

Have you been baptized in the Holy Spirit? If not, and you want to receive this Holy Spirit baptism, or you know someone who does, it is important to have the assurance of salvation first. The Holy Spirit is powerful, yet He usually works through our choices and decisions. He will not force anyone to be baptized or speak in tongues, but He will freely give the gift to those who ask. (Paul was speaking under the inspiration of the Holy Spirit when he wrote, "eagerly desire spiritual gifts" in 1 Corinthians 14:1 and "I would like every one of you to speak in tongues" in 1 Corinthians 14:5.)

Set aside a time to be alone with God or to attend a cell-group meeting, Bible study or church where this experience is common. Then, in prayer, ask Jesus to baptize you in the Spirit.

John's Gospel captured Jesus' thoughts on the matter: "The one who believes in Me, as the Scripture has said, will have streams of living water flow from deep within him" (John 7:38, *CSB*).

Something supernatural happens within you that can often be sensed. This experience can occur suddenly at the time of salvation or at another time, perhaps decades after one's conversion. It is called a "baptism of the Holy Spirit" because it is a baptism, meaning a drenching, an overflowing, a saturating of your soul and body with the Holy Spirit's presence. But the Spirit's baptism is only God's initial salvation work in the believer.

I have had many folks come to me asking questions, trying to understand the Holy Spirit baptism. I simply tell them that this baptism requires that you come to God as a child in simple faith, asking, and receive the promise of the Spirit as the disciples did in the upper room so long ago. Incidentally, you don't have to beg God for the gift of speaking in other tongues.

Being a Spirit-filled believer, I have experienced not only my own private Pentecost, but I have also participated in mighty moves of God that were marked by a fresh baptism of the Holy Spirit—clear evidence of God's outpouring among men.

I have included a couple of testimonies from people who received the Spirit's power through baptism and were changed in unimaginable ways. Today, they are movers and shakers with a powerful gospel witness.

"What happened 2,000 years ago on the Day of Pentecost happened for me when I was a mere child. As I called on God in a church service, suddenly all heaven seemed to crowd into my small frame. Without realizing what I was doing, I began praising God in tongues I had never learned," recounted missionary evangelist Reinhard Bonnke of his Pentecost experience.

Bonnke adds, "I realized even at a young age that although the experience of Spirit baptism is unforgettable, imparting thrills is not God's purpose. The Holy Spirit enters human flesh and blood personally to confer divine potential on those who serve Him."

World-renowned worship leader from Sydney, Australia, Darlene Zschech states:

> Rather than being freaked out about it, even though it felt initially strange, I was overwhelmed by how easy and voluntarily this language came. It was as if I was speaking a language I had always known yet never used. I knew that when I received Christ by faith I had also received the Holy Spirit, but this was definitely an experience I could not deny. I use my gift of praying in the Spirit as a real weapon

of warfare, especially because as a lead worshiper, I face much spiritual opposition.

Reaching divine potential and prevailing in spiritual warfare is an aspect of our covenant with God. At times, signs of New Testament exuberance have been scorned as in the sense of frantic possession by a spiritual force. I must say that the baptism in the Spirit is physical as well as profoundly spiritual. Speaking in tongues, for example, is the best evidence and sign of God's physical indwelling.

Until recently, the Pentecostal experience was restricted to Pentecostal groups who remained outside mainline denominations. "Mr. Pentecost," David du Plessis, known as the father of the modern Charismatic movement, and a South African preacher, dedicated his life to building bridges between different denominations and brought Pentecostalism to the mainstream. Using his infectious charismatic fervor, he said, "Brought together in that bond of recognition, Christians can work toward common goals with deep and abiding senses of oneness in the Spirit, a oneness that transcends but does not negate individual heritages and doctrinal developments."[3]

This misunderstood spiritual gift has value far beyond the assurance of being baptized in the Holy Spirit. It truly is the seal of the blood covenant in the New Testament believer.

PRACTICAL GUIDANCE

As long as Jesus was physically present with the disciples, the Spirit's ability was limited. Jesus was there to strengthen, comfort and guide them, but it was to their advantage that Jesus left them.

The power of Jesus' ministry was attributed to the Holy Spirit. If you'll recall, Jesus put aside His deity to live with and relate to humanity; at His water baptism the Spirit came upon Him for service.

While the Spirit's primary role is to convict the world of sin, once a believer comes to Christ, living in the kingdom of God requires spiritual insight and instruction that only the Spirit can provide. In other words, without that divine partnership, it is impossible for us to access the covenant of that kingdom to live a healthy and prosperous life. Those who mentally agree with the biblical principles of that kingdom lack spiritual perception and end up struggling through life, trying to operate in those principles to be successful Christians. Religious efforts are bound to leave the believer empty and fruitless.

There are still others who think that to enter the kingdom of God is to go to heaven. In the Gospels, the disciples did not have insight to understand the kingdom of God. It wasn't until Pentecost, when the life-giving Spirit entered the upper room, that their understanding was opened. Nineteenth-century preacher Charles Spurgeon said:

> But of what use or of what avail is the covenant to us until the Holy Spirit brings the blessings of the covenant to us? The covenant is, as it were, a holy tree, laden with fruit. If the Spirit does not shake that tree and make the fruit fall from it so that it comes within our reach, how can we receive it?[4]

The Holy Spirit is the powder keg of our new life.

Living the Spirit-filled life doesn't just happen because you mentally accept the graces or gifts of the New Covenant. This divine life requires you to make a conscious effort to yield to the voice of the Holy Spirit within. After all, it is the Holy Spirit's job to assist the believer in having an abiding relationship with the Father who is the initiator of our Covenant. The Holy Spirit does this through teaching, reminding, testifying, guiding, correcting (not punishing) and demonstrating the Word of God, which are all normal functions of His Person (see John 16:13).

Since God is a Father who loves and desires to relate to His children, the Holy Spirit's practical classroom setting is the believer's everyday life.

Did you know that when you are weary or discouraged, praying in your heavenly language brings rest and refreshing? (See Isa. 28:11-12.)

Dr. Oral Roberts provides an interesting look at this mystery of praying in the Spirit: "Our rational faculties are bypassed and we are enabled to give expression to that which is too deep for ordinary words. The result is a kind of relaxing and purging of our minds so that, though the mind is not directly involved in the 'prayer language,' it benefits from it." After praying in the Spirit, Oral Roberts testifies, "Solutions to previously insoluble problems suddenly appear as the mind is cleared and made open to them."[5]

When you closely examine the book of Acts after Pentecost, you learn about the nature of the Early Church. The quickening of the Spirit produced spontaneity in their lives, providing the modern-day believer with examples that should be a part of how we live.

Missionary William Carey planned to go to Great Polynesia in the South Seas to work there. The Holy Spirit guided him to India instead. There he translated the Bible into nearly 40 different languages and dialects.

David Livingstone's ambition was to work in China. But the Holy Spirit led him to Africa. There he worked as a missionary, statesman and explorer.

Adoniram Judson's choice was India. The Holy Spirit urged him to go to Burma. There he translated the Bible into Burmese.

The apostle Paul was forbidden by the Holy Spirit to preach the Word of God in Asia, and later he was not permitted to go into Bithynia (see Acts 16:6-7). But the Holy Spirit led Paul to Macedonia, which launched the spread of the gospel in Europe.

When baptized with the Holy Spirit, we receive power to witness for Christ and work with greater effectiveness in the Church and in the world. We receive the same divine anointing that descended upon Jesus and upon His disciples that enabled them to preach God's Word and to work miracles. Any time we submit to the leading of the Spirit, we are in for surprises and are pushed to new frontiers of action!

Our covenant with God puts all the resources of heaven at our disposal. That is why God encourages us to rely on His Spirit to enable us to do mighty things to propagate God's gospel everywhere.

PENTECOST CONTINUES

Spiritual revivals are nothing new. Man has experienced them for millennia as God's Spirit continues to be poured out on earth. Spiritual renewal has been a critical element of revival in every era since Pentecost. Without question, God has used men and women in many denominations throughout the centuries to bring revival and renewal to their nations.

In the twentieth century, two prominent figures made their mark in Church history and are part of our American spiritual heritage. The late Kathryn Kuhlman and Reverend William "Daddy" Seymour are both gone, but their legacy continues.

Recently, Pentecostals from around the world converged in Los Angeles to commemorate the one-hundredth anniversary of the revival that launched their movement. They held special revival services to celebrate Pentecostal pioneer William "Daddy" Seymour's Azuza Street Revival, which occurred in 1906.

Azuza was truly a miracle worth celebrating. What began in a tiny building on Azuza Street has grown to be a movement of 500 million Christians who believe that the power of God is still working among people today. Although Seymour was a poor, one-eyed, discriminated-against black American, he started one of the twentieth century's greatest Protestant movements.

Kathryn Kuhlman was known as the famous faith healer with a flamboyant style. She held packed miracle services in New York's Carnegie Hall, and in Los Angeles, California, for over 20 years, in the 1950s, 1960s and 1970s. Countless lives were touched and healed (some who had been given up to die) through the anointing of the Holy Spirit that was on her life. The sick arrived in ambulances and left healed. "The presence of the Holy Spirit was so tangible that many of the sick were healed as they waited outside for the doors to open," an evangelist said of her ministry.

We have much to be grateful for in the pioneers who have gone before us to pave the way for the global harvest. Other giants in the faith hail from foreign shores and an earlier age, yet they have had a profound influence on Christendom. These include Jonathan

Edwards, Andrew Murray, Evan Roberts, Charles Spurgeon and John Wesley, to name a few. They can all be considered revivalists.

Like our founding fathers who established America's roots in biblical principles, these spiritual founders or pathfinders inspired the Christian world to live a life worthy of their calling, spreading the gospel to the ends of the earth.

The baptism of the Holy Spirit is a part of the believer's spiritual inheritance. There are debates ad infinitum about that historical Pentecost experience in the upper room. The important thing to know is that the Spirit was sent to empower the Church for service and that same Spirit is available to you today.

Dr. Deere concludes: "Because its ultimate author is God, the book of Acts is a perfect witness to the kind of life the early church experienced. It is also a witness meant to teach us about life in God."[6] Today, the cloud of God's presence continues to move. We are being prepared for the greatest move of God's Spirit in history, the one that will usher the Lord's return.

Life Lines

- The spiritual activity of the first-century church should be the norm for Christians today.

- The Holy Spirit was sent to be our constant Helper and Guide, and He abides in all who confess Jesus as Lord and Savior.

- The Holy Spirit's baptism continues to influence the world today, proving the initial experience wasn't some ancient, far-fetched story that many in the religious community continue to dispute.

- "The baptism of the Holy Spirit will do for you what a phone booth did for Clark Kent—it will change you into a different human being." —Rod Parsley

- Jesus' work did not end with His resurrection. Pentecost marked a new beginning for the fulfillment of Christ's mission—the power to win souls.

- "[He] has identified us as his own by placing the Holy Spirit in our hearts as the first installment of everything he will give us" (2 Cor. 1:22, *NLT*).

- "The Holy Spirit not only unites us, but also ensures our infinite diversity in the Church."[7]

CHAPTER 13

Covenant of Prayer

In this manner, therefore, pray: Our Father in heaven, Hallowed be Your name. Your kingdom come. Your will be done On earth as it is in heaven. Give us this day our daily bread. And forgive us our debts, As we forgive our debtors. And do not lead us into temptation, But deliver us from the evil one. For Yours is the kingdom and the power and the glory forever. Amen.
MATTHEW 6:9-13, *NKJV*

Because the human heart has an insatiable hunger for relationship with God, prayer is woven into the fabric of societies the world over. It is a part of daily life and ingrained in the public and private experiences of millions.

- A CEO whose company is in trouble and is in desperate need of heavenly assistance shuts his door for a brief moment of prayer.
- A holy man leads rebel soldiers in prayer as night falls on the desert in Chad.
- A pierced and tattooed man quietly bows his head at lunch amid the sounds of drilling and hammering in his auto shop.
- A child and her family say grace before a meal in thanks for the bounty they have received.
- An entire nation awakens to the sounds of chanted prayer over loud speakers in the Islamic nation of Pakistan.
- A graceful woman adorned in a silk woven sari, with covered head, approaches her temple to pay homage to a Hindu god.

- A man inserts a small petitionary note, called "kvitlakh," in a crack of the Wailing Wall in Jerusalem, which is credited with having special power to reach God due to the Wall's sanctity.
- A church congregation shouts in one voice, "Amen."
- An Internet-savvy church holds prayer meetings simultaneously with other churches; or better yet, they access Web-cast church services live from anywhere in the world.

For many, prayer is a desperate plea in crisis. For the Christian and the Jew, prayer is rooted in a biblical understanding of God as a personal Being who hears and responds to His people.

GOT PRAYER?

Prayer is indeed an intricate part of covenant. If we begin from the most basic approach, prayer is carrying on a conversation with God, who resides in a place called heaven. That idea might intrigue some and frighten others.

Without a proper understanding of prayer and its purpose, the believer is limited. I liken this to having a large-caliber rifle and not knowing how to use it against the grizzly bear that is headed your way. There are many attacks or uncontrollable circumstances that come our way, and if we're not equipped to handle them in prayer, we'll be defeated at every turn.

Jewish author David Wolpe, in his book *The Healer of Shattered Hearts*, a book about the Jewish view of God, says, "God is emphatically not a human being, but since we have only human descriptions at our disposal, and have learned to value certain human traits, the Bible delights in fashioning a God who exemplifies the best we can conceive—a God of compassion, of goodness, tenderness, and care."[1]

Because Scripture says that when we receive Jesus Christ as our Lord and Savior, we have become children of God, it is important to our heavenly Father that we communicate with Him in a father-child relationship. How do a father and a child connect for meaningful dialogue if the child is afraid of the father? How does a child grow to trust someone he cannot see? Could it be that we don't understand our Father's care and concern for our welfare?

Our heavenly Father loves us—that must be the foundational truth in our approach to God. "O LORD, You have searched me and known me. You know when I sit down and when I rise up; You understand my thought from afar. You scrutinize my path and my lying down, And are intimately acquainted with all my ways" (Ps. 139:1-3, *NASB*).

When you first begin praying to God, effective communication in prayer involves certain tools of the trade, so to speak. Those tools are: having faith in God, knowing God's Word, listening and talking.

Having faith in God to answer your prayers is one of the fundamental keys to unlock your prayer life. If you come to God and don't believe that He wants to answer your prayers, or that He might answer them, chances are, you won't get an answer. Prayer involves the expectation of receiving what you ask for. Building a track record with God regarding His faithfulness toward you is important too. If God met your needs last month when you prayed, it is likely that you will believe that God will meet them this month when you pray.

Knowing the Word of God is essential to prayer because it helps us connect with the will of God. It also gives us confidence that whatever we ask in His name, He will do it for us (because we know His will by reading His Word, and our prayers reflect His will). "So let us come boldly to the throne of our gracious God. There we will receive his mercy, and we will find grace to help us when we need it" (Heb. 4:16, *NLT*).

A new convert may not be able to adequately convey his needs, but as he studies and learns what already belongs to him in the Word of God, his prayers get answered more often than not.

Unfortunately, many Christians who aren't anchored in the Word of God pray for things that are entirely out of the will of God. When God doesn't answer them, they become disappointed and disillusioned. It is important to grow to maturity in your prayer life. You don't want to be as those who always pray, "Give me, give me, give me." They never get past seeking God's hand for things.

Listening. Hearing the voice of God isn't difficult to do. It is essential to effective prayer. When God answers our prayers, there are different ways He will do this. Here are the most common:

1. Your conscience
2. A sermon from your pastor
3. Christian television
4. A cassette tape or conference you may attend
5. A total stranger
6. Dreams and/or visions
7. The Word of God

There are rare cases where an angel may appear to give you a little help, or God may speak audibly to you. This happened to me at dawn's early light on October 9, 1978. An angel appeared in my truck and sat next to me while I was driving. The angel began to talk to me about my future and told me that I would go to Bible school. My hair stood on end—it was a terrifying experience.

Since God uses prayer as a vital means of communication with us, discovering some of the different kinds of prayer there are and how to effectively use them in your everyday life is a must. After a period of time, you will begin to notice that your prayers change as your relationship with God develops.

If you are just starting out, some forms of prayer noted in this chapter will require some practice. For example, you don't want to try to raise the dead when you haven't exercised your faith to believe God to heal someone's headache. God can do anything, but it is likely that, faced with an impossible situation, you will find yourself in fear.

When you don't know what to pray for or how to pray, recall the previous chapter discussion on praying in the Spirit. Even the most skilled prayer warrior has found this method to be a lifesaver. Scripture says, "In the same way, the Spirit also joins to help in our weakness, because we do not know what to pray for as we should, but the Spirit Himself intercedes for us with unspoken groanings. And He who searches the hearts knows the Spirit's mind-set, because He intercedes for the saints according to the will of God" (Rom. 8:26-27, *CSB*).

The last part of that verse says that Christ is making intercession (a form of prayer) so that His ministry will be released through us.

It isn't necessary for you to pray complicated, long prayers in order to be heard by God. Your prayer language is your greatest asset. Remember, practice brings perfection in Christ!

COVENANT PRAYER

When Jesus was on earth, there was one important aspect of His life that He couldn't live without—prayer. It was His life source. I like to put it this way: Prayer to my spirit is like water to my body.

While Jesus observed the traditional Jewish custom of praying in the Temple, He often prayed in other settings. The Gospels reveal a model prayer Jesus instructed His disciples to pray, a prayer we traditionally call "The Lord's Prayer." It is an important form of prayer, but it certainly is not the only way to pray.

Through their religious background, the disciples knew how to approach God, but this particular type of prayer was foreign to their religious tradition. Before He instructed them in this covenant prayer, He gave them some pointers:

1. *Covenant prayer was to be done in private.* The disciples were to pray to their heavenly Father in secret and He would reward them openly. This was a far cry from their former approach to God, because religious men were known for praying loudly and publicly with a wrong motive. "And when you pray, do not be like the hypocrites, for they love to pray standing in the synagogues and on the street corners to be seen by men" (Matt. 6:5, *NIV*).

2. *Prayer is a personal and intimate conversation with God.* Don't pray empty, systematic prayers "as the heathen

do." The "heathen" Jesus referred to were those who did not have an intimate relationship with God, and their outward actions were always suspect. They thought that God would be more likely to answer a long, babbling prayer. This kind of prayer showed a lack of trust in the Father. Religious-sounding prayers don't move God. Furthermore, God isn't into formulas. Jesus was getting to the core of what was really in their heart.

Then Jesus instructed the disciples to pray this way:

> Our Father in heaven, Hallowed be Your name. Your kingdom come, Your will be done On earth as it is in heaven. Give us this day our daily bread. And forgive us our debts, As we forgive our debtors. And do not lead us into temptation, But deliver us from the evil one. For Yours is the kingdom and the power and the glory forever. Amen (Matt. 6:9-15, *NKJV*).

Let's examine the important facets of this prayer.

1. *"Our father"*—Jesus knew God as His own Father and taught His disciples to have the same type of relationship with Him. This prayer personalizes God: a Father-child relationship. Your confidence and faith rest on this relationship.

2. *"Hallowed be Your name"*—Literally, the word "name" should be rendered "names." Of course, "God" is not really His name, is it? God is who He is. In Genesis, the very first name of God is Elohim, which means three-in-one—God in plural form—Father-Son-Holy Ghost. The three are considered the Godhead, sometimes referred to as the Trinity. God is known only as Elohim in the first chapter of Genesis. However, God progressively

revealed other covenant names through the Scriptures. For example:

Jehovah Jireh—"God who provides"
Jehovah Rapha—"God who heals"
Jehovah Tsidkenu—"God our righteousness"
Jehovah Shammah—"God who is our Shepherd"

All these wonderful names identify God's personal characteristics. What personal characteristics of Christ can be found in the name of Jesus, Jesu and Yeshua? We find healing, provision and right standing with God and our Good Shepherd.

3. *"Your kingdom come, Your will be done on earth as it is in heaven"*—The kingdom of God on earth is what God is looking for in us. Before asking for our daily bread, we must first ask for God's will. Sometimes we think that Jesus is like Santa Claus. We want to sit on His lap and recite our Christmas list. Before going to our Father with our needs, we need to ask that His will, not our own, be done in our life.

4. *"Give us this day our daily bread"*—Jesus addressed the personal aspects of our life. We can ask God for more than simply bread, but this also means to begin with the basic necessities. We should thank God for our basic provisions of food, shelter, clothing and transportation. But we don't stop there—we also take our desires and dreams to God. He is a Father who cares about our future.

5. *"Forgive us our debts, as we forgive our debtors"*—We must do this every day because we sin every day. We might have fears or doubts—don't forget, the Bible says that doubt is a sin. On a daily basis ask God for forgiveness

for personal sin as well as forgiveness for those who have sinned against us.

6. *"Lead us not into temptation, but deliver us from the evil one"*—Actually, this verse is declared in the positive: *God, You will not lead us into temptation.* Always remind God that He will deliver you from the snare of the evil one. Thank the Lord for His saving grace and delivering power.

Did you notice how concise, simple and brief this prayer is? Praying an hour or two is not necessary to live in God's will or to get His attention. The calling of intercessors—prayer warriors—requires special kinds of prayer, but that is a unique ministry.

Notice that the Lord's Prayer begins with God and it ends with God. We are sandwiched in between. God is the author and finisher of our faith. We begin by glorifying God and we end by glorifying God. In other words, we give Him glory for every good thing. Glorifying God is a form of worship. Worship is not the articulation of our need; it is the consummation and expression of our love toward Him. It is what we offer God regardless of the status of our needs.

CALLING ON THE COVENANT IN CRISIS

Here is a great example of deliverance in a life-threatening situation through prayer.

Judah was being attacked by the Ammonites, the Moabites and other "ites" who joined them. King Jehoshaphat and his people were filled with alarm and sought the Lord. The king proclaimed a fast throughout all Judah. Good tactical move! Then King Jehoshaphat stood in the assembly of Judah and Jerusalem, and they all gathered to seek the Lord. The king and the people of Judah prayed the following covenant prayers:

- They reaffirmed God's ability to help them, referring to their past victories and how God had given them their land.

- They claimed God's special promise of victory.
- They detailed their crisis, telling God they did not instigate the war they were in.
- They didn't know what to do and admitted their utter dependence on God to deliver them. They asked for God's plan of attack.

What happened next is downright amazing. The Spirit of the Lord God came upon Jehaziel, the Levite minister, to speak to Jehoshaphat and the people, saying, "Listen, King Jehoshaphat and all who live in Judah and Jerusalem! This is what the Lord says to you: 'Do not be afraid or discouraged because of this vast army. For the battle is not yours, but God's'" (2 Chron. 20:15, *NIV*).

The only thing the people were instructed to do was position themselves to observe the great victory God would give them. King Jehoshaphat and his people were instructed to bow in worship to God, and the Levites would stand up to praise Jehovah.

The next day, the king and the people obediently went out to assume their appointed positions and assigned those who would go before the army to sing praises to God. Imagine that! A multitude of people were poised in battle to sing praises to God. The natural mind would argue, Where are your weapons?

As they went out before the army, they were declaring: *Praise the Lord, for His mercy endures forever.* Praise was the precursor to victory. Anyone can thank God after the fact; covenant people praise God in advance.

The people of God started out exuberantly, jumping up and down in a childlike way. Then they thrust their hands into the air, praising and shouting to high heaven. As they were jumping and shouting, pretty soon they entered into the kind of worship that God inhabits.

In an almost mystical way, they were energized, and their whole beings were enveloped in God. It was a supernatural encounter with the living God through worship. Consumed in worship, they lost sight of their crisis. Only after they experienced worshiping God in this way did God appear!

While they were in this place of worship, the Lord ambushed and destroyed the invading armies. The Ammonites and Moabites became confused and began killing each other! God sent a spirit of confusion and delusion against Israel's enemies. All the Israelites did was march toward their enemies armed with praise in their mouths.

The king and the people beheld the greatness of their victory and spent the next three days collecting the spoils that resulted. Afterwards, the king and his people assembled to bless and thank the Lord for what He had done for them.

They returned in triumph to the house of God in Jerusalem with a victory celebration. As a result of the miraculous victory God gave His people, great fear came upon all of Judah's neighbors, and rest and peace came over Jehoshaphat and his people (see 2 Chron. 20:16-30).

Indeed, in covenant, God takes it personally when His people are under demonic attack. True to His promise, the Lord acted to give them a miraculous victory. This was a covenant answer to prayer.

Do you ever feel overwhelmed? Do you ever feel like all hell and the kitchen sink are coming at you?

That's how King Jehoshaphat felt. He began in fear. Fear can be a great motivating factor. If you discover that you have high blood pressure, you go to the gym, exercise and start eating better. When a crisis hits, you first seek the Lord and maybe declare a fast to clear your thoughts. Then you go to the house of God where you'll find corporate prayer and pastoral covering. Remember, our battle in prayer is spiritual, not physical.

> Finally, my brethren, be strong in the Lord, and in the power of His might. Put on the whole armor of God, that you may be able to stand against the wiles of the devil. Therefore take up the whole armor of God, that you may be able to withstand in the evil day, and having done all, to stand. Stand therefore, having girded your waist with truth, having put on the breastplate of righteousness, and having shod your feet with the preparation of the gospel of peace;

above all, taking the shield of faith with which you will be able to quench all the fiery darts of the wicked one. And take the helmet of salvation, and the sword of the Spirit, which is the word of God (Eph. 6:10-11,13-17, *NKJV*).

The battle is the Lord's. He'll take care of it, but it is important to understand that God responds to faith. Simply having good thoughts is only the beginning. You must then put feet to your faith and proceed, knowing that your battle is indeed in God's hands.

It's amazing how many Christians pray and there isn't an ounce of faith in their prayers. Their pleas are disheartening and remain unanswered: "Well, God, if it be Your will; I hope You're there; if You're busy I understand; I probably deserve what is happening to me . . ."

Faith is *strong*.

Faith knows the Word of God and stands on the Scriptures, reminding God of His covenant promises.

Faith is not moved.

Jesus gave you His robe of righteousness and right standing with God. He has become so totally one with you that He has given you the authority to use His name. If you're going to pray, pray in faith, pray believing. And if you doubt, then you'll do without! Believe that you'll receive. Don't feed your doubts and starve your faith. Starve your doubts and feed your faith.

The devil has no right to interfere in the affairs of your life. Receive your deliverance—Jesus paid an incredible price for it.

*L*IFE LINES

- "Prayer is not conquering God's reluctance, but taking hold of God's willingness."[2]

- "Beloved, it is not our long prayers but our believing God that gets the answer."[3]

- "Do not always scrupulously confine yourself to certain rules, or particular forms of devotion; but act with a general confidence in God, with love and devotion."[4]

- "None can believe how powerful prayer is, and what it is able to effect, but those who have learned it by experience." —Martin Luther, the great reformer

- "Some people think God does not like to be troubled with our constant coming and asking. The way to trouble God is not to come at all."[5]

- Prayer is not merely talking to God. Prayer is fellowship, communion and surrender to His lordship.

- "Don't worry about anything, but pray about every thing. With thankful hearts offer up your prayers and requests to God" (Phil. 4:6, *CEV*).

CHAPTER FOURTEEN

Covenant of Wealth

You shall remember the Lord your God, for it is he who gives you power to get wealth, that he may confirm his covenant that he swore to your fathers, as it is this day.
Deuteronomy 8:18, ESV

One of the most fascinating books I've read lately was Steven Scott's book *Lessons from the Richest Man Who Ever Lived*. It is a book outlining King Solomon's secrets to success, wealth and happiness. Solomon was one of King David's sons. There has never lived another man with the wealth that was his. Bill Gates, Donald Trump and the Sheikh of the United Arab Emirates are some of the wealthiest tycoons in the world today, yet their wealth doesn't compare to the wealth that King Solomon possessed.

Wealth and poverty alike can instruct us all. While poverty is not the financial problem most perceive it to be, it certainly can be a spiritually complex one that few really understand. And biblical prosperity is far more than having an abundance of money or possessions.

The Hebrew meaning for "prosperity" is: peace, wholeness, nothing missing. Prosperity is a part of covenant, but it doesn't automatically fall upon the lap of the believer because he belongs to God. If you examine the word "prosper," which is a derivative of "prosperity," it also means "to push forward, to break out, to break away."[1] The description used is of a violent, forceful nature. "The kingdom of heaven suffers violence, and the violent take it by force" (Matt. 11:12, *NKJV*). In other words, the believer has to contend for or to forcefully advance in his covenant right to wealth.

The Bible is our instruction manual for life and can teach us quite a bit about money. Many people are not comfortable with the idea of talking about becoming wealthy, because it violates their consciences. The Christian community has been traditionally taught that wealth is carnal and therefore unscriptural. In the Church, we then must give the impression that making money is not important to us.

Who knew better than our heavenly Father that His children would need instruction on not only the privileges and blessings of prosperity, but also on the dangers that lurk behind a greedy and covetous heart? Wealth is a powerful tool, but in the wrong hands it can destroy. As with other important subjects in the Bible, there have been many books written about wealth and prosperity; some are good; yet others, unfortunately, teach "get rich quick" schemes that many Christians pursue. These schemes of pseudo-success aren't biblically sound and will not provide lasting success. A healthy biblical look at prosperity is essential. There is no better place to begin to build a case for covenant wealth than where it first appears in the Bible.

THE GARDEN—A VALUABLE RESOURCE

"You were the perfection of wisdom and beauty. You were in Eden, the garden of God. Your clothing was adorned with every precious stone . . . the beryl, onyx, jasper, sapphire, turquoise, and emerald—all beautifully crafted for you and set in the finest gold" (Ezek. 28:12-13, *NLT*).

Satan was physically covered with the most perfect and precious stones from the Garden of Eden before Adam came along. It is interesting to note that the Hebrew meaning for "Eden" is to live voluptuously (in pleasure and enjoyment) and in abundance.

Because Satan is the god of this world, he believes the earth's resources belong to him. The prophet Ezekiel continues with his words about Satan: "You were blameless in all you did from the day you were created until the day evil was found in you" (Ezek. 28:15, *NLT*). We know that from the beginning, Adam enjoyed life to its fullest, having had perfect, unhindered fellowship with God, and dominion in the earth. There was nothing lacking in Eden.

In Satan's fallen state, even as he rules this world's system, he has attempted to thwart God's plan for wealth. How? Man has a corrupted worldview, a result of iniquitous patterns in the bloodline that continue from generation to generation. For believers, this has not only affected the way we see ourselves but also our view of the marketplace and ultimately our approach to the Great Commission with its intended purpose of establishing God's covenant in the earth.

Even though the Bible declares, "The earth is the LORD's, and all its fullness" (Ps. 24:1, *NKJV*), through ignorance Satan has deceived the Church into thinking that obtaining wealth is wrong or that poverty is next to godliness. Many do not know how to break free from this mindset.

The book of Revelation describes the New Jerusalem, the city of God, filled with the most precious stones, and gates made of pearl; in fact, each individual gate is one pearl. If God makes streets of gold and gates of pearl, then perhaps we should explore the meaning of these things.

CAIN AND ABEL

The concept of sacrifices and offerings was ingrained in mankind from the beginning. Pagans offered to their gods 10 percent of all their possessions. Before coins and money were invented, the standard of value for a system of exchange was the natural resources God created. Because of the great value represented in small precious stones, this was the most convenient way to carry large sums of wealth.

The first offering mentioned in the Bible occurred after the first brothers were old enough to make a living at their chosen occupations. Cain took after his father and became a farmer. Abel became a shepherd. Certainly throughout their young lives growing up, Adam and Eve taught their sons about the virtues of approaching God with sacrifices and offerings.

Recall that when Adam and Eve sinned in the Garden, Yahweh covered them with the skins of a sacrificial lamb long before Cain and Abel were born. As a result, they were only to approach God with blood, not the produce of the ground. The Levitical law, which had not yet been instituted, would later set guidelines for the many different types of offerings required. So the offerings that would have been most common for the first family would have included animals.

One day, the two sons decided to bring offerings to God—Cain from his agricultural produce and Abel from his herds. God received Abel's sacrifice with favor, but not Cain's.

Why was the one brother's sacrifice favored by God but the other's was not? Are not all offerings acceptable to God? Presumably both Cain and Abel had offered their sacrifices in good faith. What did Cain bring to God that was unacceptable?

Although it seems to have come as a complete surprise to Cain, the offering of produce he presented to God was already cursed. Unfortunately for him, a bloodless offering was useless, because without the shedding of blood there is no remission of sin. The fruit, or produce, Cain offered was symbolic of good works. This is how the ignorant attempt to approach God, thinking they can halfheartedly draw near to God in any way they please.

Cain's offering was rejected because he refused to offer God his best. Instead, he should have humbled himself and approached Abel to ask for the best lamb in exchange for his best produce. Cain would then have approached God with a fitting sacrifice. And God would have received Cain's offering, just as He did Abel's.

Abel brought the best animal in his flock and sacrificially offered it to God. He had a revelation that he was a sinner and that the only way to approach God was with a blood sacrifice. So it is perhaps not surprising that Abel's gift was from his heart.

Refusing to humble himself, a jealous Cain instead got so angry at the truth that he decided to kill the one whose offering was accepted: his brother. When God questioned Cain about Abel's disappearance, Cain angrily denied knowing his whereabouts and refused to accept responsibility for him.

Here, we have another first family tragedy. The first dysfunctional family produces the first murder. Cain's judgment handed down by God for the murder of his brother was banishment from the settled land, and he was relegated to a life of wandering. Because Cain feared for his life, God mercifully placed a significant mark upon him; this provided the protection he needed.

Cain was the original "man without a country."

> Because Abel had faith, he gave a better gift in worship to God than Cain. His gift pleased God. Abel was right with God. Abel died, but by faith he is still speaking to us (Heb. 11:4, *NLV*).

This earliest offering scenario established a precedent with regard to giving. Cain's careless approach to God is a great lesson on how we should present our offerings to God. An innocent life was taken as a result of this offering. The motive of the heart is critical to the quality of the offering. Luke's Gospel aptly records Jesus' words concerning the matter: "For your heart will always be where your riches are" (Luke 12:34, *GNB*).

THE ABRAM–MELCHIZEDEK ALLIANCE

We learned that Abram was instructed by Yahweh to leave his country, his family and his father's house and go to an unknown land. Yahweh promised Abram that He would make Abram a great nation and bless him and his descendants (see Gen. 14:18). Abram became very rich in livestock, silver and gold.

Taking his nephew Lot with him, he journeyed to his final destination—Canaan. Lot, too, experienced the overflow of Abram's covenant blessings to the point that he had accumulated great flocks, herds and tents. As a result, the land was not able to support both of them, for their possessions were so great that they could not dwell together. What was the solution?

To eliminate the strife amongst their herdsmen, Abram made the amicable decision that they part ways. So he generously split in half the vast land he owned and allowed Lot to choose the part he wanted. Lot gravitated toward Sodom and Gomorrah, so Abram took the land that remained. Sometime thereafter, Lot was among those taken captive by the king of Chedorlaomer and three other kings. When Abram got wind of Lot's capture, he and his private army went out to rescue his nephew, attacking and slaughtering all four kings and their armies in battle. Abram and his army returned safely with his nephew and the spoils of their victory.

A mysterious priest named Melchizedek, who was also king of Salem, heard about Abram and his victory. Melchizedek met Abram after returning from war and prepared a priestly ceremony with bread and wine—sounds just like Communion. This "heavenly" priest was a type of Christ, offering Abram the symbolic Communion elements.

As this story illustrates, Abram would partake of his first Communion with God.

The Bible states that Melchizedek was the "priest of God Most High" (Gen. 14:18, *CEV*). How could this be? The priesthood had not yet been established. Melchizedek was without father or mother or genealogy, and had neither beginning of days nor end of life, but was made like the Son of God, and remains a priest continually (see Heb. 7:3). Mysteriously, Melchizedek had no known line of succession. He had to be a priest by divine appointment and not through priestly pedigree.

Melchizedek pronounced a blessing over Abram, declaring, "I bless you in the name of God Most High, Creator of heaven and earth. All praise belongs to God Most High for helping you defeat your enemies" (Gen. 14:19-20, *CEV*). Abram was promoted and now had real influence and power. The deal was sealed!

Did you know that God's people are possessors of heaven and earth? Are you satisfied simply to come to church to worship God and be blessed? God not only wants us to pay our bills and own property, but to have real influence in the earth.

Receiving a blessing of this magnitude comes out of fellowship and communion with God. There is fellowship at the Lord's table. God does most good things through an intimate relationship with His children. Life-changing anointing comes through intimacy with God.

After Melchizedek blessed Abram, the Bible says that Abram gave a tithe of all (see Gen. 14:20). And God received Abram's 10 percent as a covenant tithe through Melchizekdek. Shortly thereafter, God changed Abram's name to Abraham, meaning "a father of multitudes."

Although tithing was a part of the Old Covenant, it didn't originate with the Law. Abraham was a tither 400 years before the Law was ever given to Moses. The Law later served to give it form and procedure. Old Testament tithing was a shadow of what was to come. Old Testament saints were blessed through their tithing, but we enjoy even greater blessings through our tithing today, because we bring our tithes to a High Priest who is greater than Melchizedek or any other Old Covenant priest!

> Bring the whole tithe into the storehouse . . . and see if I will not throw open the floodgates of heaven and pour out so much blessing that you will not have room enough for it (Mal. 3:10, *NIV*).

Tithing does not buy God's blessings. Rather, simple obedience to this divine principle opens heaven's windows to pour out blessings in such abundance that you are unable to contain them. Today not everyone who attends church tithes; in fact, only approximately 14 percent do. Therefore, 85 percent or more of the Body of Christ do not walk in Abraham's blessings. Abraham's blessings include: promotion, possession and dominion.

From a Jewish perspective, tithing was an expression of covenant fidelity with God and was practiced throughout the Bible.

SOLOMON'S EXCEPTIONALISM

When God granted Solomon a request on the eve of his succession to the throne, Solomon asked for wisdom to discern between right and wrong. Solomon didn't ask for wealth, but for wisdom. God was well pleased with him and gave Solomon more than what he asked for. "I give you also what you have not asked, both riches and honor, so that no other king shall compare with you, all your days" (1 Kings 3:13, *RSV*).

What does this Scripture illustrate? God is the source of prosperity. Solomon not only gained spiritual wealth but was blessed by Abraham's covenant through his father David. When the Queen of Sheba heard about Solomon's wisdom and wealth, her curiosity led her to visit the king. She wanted to know just how wise this king was. She intended to test his knowledge and insight but was overwhelmed. Not only did Solomon have wisdom unlike any other, but she was also drawn to the magnificence of the Temple he built unto the Lord. The Bible describes her impression of her visit: "There was no more spirit in her." The Queen of Sheba concluded, "Your wisdom and prosperity exceed the fame of which I heard" (1 Kings 10:5,7, *NKJV*).

Much of the reason for Solomon's wealth could be attributed to his father, David. Solomon's Temple was built from David's wealth. History revealed that David's military conquests reached to the Euphrates River, which brought him the booty of these campaigns. On the other hand, King Solomon was known as a savvy businessman. He would buy horses, chariots and fine linens in Egypt and sell them for profit to heathen kings. The king certainly walked in the power to gain wealth, influence and blessings beyond his wildest dreams.

AN UNFATHOMABLE LESSON ON GIVING

When Jesus said, "The thief comes only in order to steal and kill and destroy. I came that they may have and enjoy life, and have it in abundance (to the full, till it overflows)" (John 10:10, *AMP*), He didn't mean that you would experience this abundance when you get to heaven, but now, in this life.

Much of Jesus' teachings about money and wealth were not focused on the accumulation of "things," but on the condition of the heart. Jesus amassed few possessions. Yet there was never a need that wasn't met. Money wasn't a problem for Jesus. He had no lack in life.

The disciples were with Jesus when they observed an offering being given in the Temple court. Jesus saw the rich dressed in their finery strutting through the court putting their gifts into the treasury. What He witnessed next was much more than your typical convert placing a buck in the bucket at offering time. Distracted by the rich in their display of piety, the disciples were quickly nudged by the Master to pay attention to a poor widow woman dressed in threadbare clothes, who inconspicuously made her way to the treasury to place her two mites in the offering. Embarrassed, trying not to draw attention to herself, she quietly bowed her head in reverence to God and returned to where she was seated.

Jesus used this incident to illustrate two attitudes of giving that were as different as night and day. The rich were highly regarded, while the widow in their society was in a class with the orphans and was a subject of pity. The disciples were about to learn a lesson that would challenge their religious mindsets on giving. Surely the offerings of the rich were more valuable. Or were they?

Jesus said of the widow's offering, "This poor widow has put in more than all of them. For all these people have put in gifts out of their surplus, but she out of her poverty has put in all she had to live on" (Luke 21:3-4, *CSB*). In the days of Jesus, giving was a public event; people would clap when a person would go to the Temple and give a huge offering. Yet, according to Jesus, this widow put in more than the rich folks. Baffled, the disciples asked how this could be?

The difference was in what was left over from each giver after the gifts were given. The rich gave an offering out of their abundance; they still had plenty of money left over when they left the Temple. It didn't take much faith for them to offer something they had in abundance. By contrast, the widow gave all she had. She had nothing left over. That was pretty extreme on her part, but that activated her faith for God to provide a return on her giving.

Your money is attached to your heart in giving and reveals the level of commitment you have toward God. Giving is just as important as receiving. If faith is not activated in your giving, how does the return come? Expecting to receive is a part of faith. You plant the seed and expect a harvest. It is easy to become rote in your giving and lose sight of its intended purpose.

Nowhere in the Bible is wealth depicted as being sinful per se. Indeed, Israel was commanded to honor the Lord with her substance and the tithe was an integral part of worship (see Prov. 3:9). Wealth, however, can become a temptation when one focuses on "things" rather than God. The psalmist David wisely advised, "Even if you gain more riches, don't put your trust in them" (Ps. 62:10, *NCV*).

GETTING TO THE HEART OF THE MATTER—WALKING IT OUT!

Let's face it, there are far too many Christians today reading their Bibles and confessing prosperity over their lives, yet they continue to live in poverty and defeat.

Ignorant Christians are frustrated in their poverty and don't know what to believe anymore but resolve one day to be prosperous. Some go to church and put their bucks in the bucket, desperately trying to give their way out of poverty. God will not drop abundance out of heaven. That only happened in the wilderness exodus, and it was never for more than the day's needs.

Credit card debt is growing in epidemic proportions in the Body of Christ. Is filing bankruptcy the answer for the lack of integrity and discipline some have with their money? It is certain that spending habits and financial practices need to be drastically altered.

The sting of an ungovernable appetite makes the undisciplined feel as though they will suffer great loss if they don't have the object of their affection. The self-control needed to regulate this negative force is lacking. Spiritual values are not yet a priority in one who is controlled by an unholy appetite.

Satan hates prosperity and dominion. He doesn't want God's children to prosper, because prosperity in the hands of the righteous who understand the principles of covenant wealth is the greatest threat to Satan's kingdom. When we don't understand that conformity to the world's system results in a shallow Christian life, pursuing wealth from that standpoint is futile.

Responsible stewardship is developed and refined through making wise choices when tempted, tested and tried. God is concerned about what motivates the heart. A believer with selfish motives cannot possibly understand wealth from God's perspective. He is looking for what he can get without taking into consideration the critical part of sowing seed for a harvest.

How do we distinguish between faith, foolishness or presumption in the arena of prosperity? When one's focus is on material blessings, there is a temptation to go after the god of wealth. Jesus warned that we cannot serve two masters—our focus must be on the giver of the blessing rather than on the blessing.

The subject of responsible stewardship isn't exactly what zealous jetsetters determined to prosper expect to hear when sitting in conferences listening to their favorite heroes in the faith who have forged a path to prosperity and success. There is a mistaken focus on wealth rather than on righteous living. Climbing to the top without a foundation of integrity and uprightness is foolishness. When fueled by carnal compulsions, you will do anything to get there, even if it means taking advantage of others.

ROADBLOCKS TO SERIOUSLY CONSIDER

Satan rules this world's system, and in his attempt to thwart God's plan for wealth in the earth, he continues to negatively influence how the believer views his life. He doesn't have to work up an elaborate scheme to do this; the iniquitous patterns that are resident in each family's bloodline are what he accesses to do his greatest damage. Hence, the need to renew your mind to what the Word of God says about covenant wealth and not the strongholds that were produced from your "family's roots," unless, of course, they are filled with promise and prosperity.

Since faith comes by hearing and hearing by the Word of God, let's review a few points covered in earlier chapters as we relate them to the subject of wealth.

ROADBLOCK #1—YOUR BELIEF SYSTEM

An honest inquiry of the Lord concerning your root system is the first step to recognize the problem areas that need to be dismantled. Since we happen to be discussing wealth, here are a few questions to consider first:

1. Do you really trust God?
2. If given a million dollars, what would you do with it?
3. What do you believe about poverty?
4. What do you believe about tithing?
5. What do you believe about wealth?

These questions appear to provide obvious answers, but don't be too quick to answer them. If you honestly examine your heart in these matters, the answers might provide some insight as to why you may be stuck in this area of your life.

For your covenant of wealth to be effective in your life, changes must first occur inside you.

ROADBLOCK #2—FEAR

Fear is a powerful emotional response to a lack of trust and confidence in God. For example, fear destroys faith in tithing because fear says you can't afford to tithe. Fear will cause you to covet money; and the love of money becomes the root of all evil. All you will think about is what you don't have.

Fear is one of the biggest hindrances to embracing prosperity and practicing tithing and giving. Fear can incapacitate the believer, preventing him from even trying to reach beyond his present circumstances. Fear of the unknown is the problem, but faith is the remedy to the unknown. Are you willing to take the risk or do what is required in order to possess your covenant inheritance?

A word of caution! In God's economy, covenant wealth must have a divine purpose; otherwise it will be consumed on the lusts of the flesh. It is certain that you cannot be delivered from a lack of trust. Neither does God dismantle your mental strongholds, because that would violate your soul's attempt to guard itself; it is a self-preservation mechanism. Through your willing surrender and conscious effort to pursue God, those strongholds will begin to give way to your freedom.

In his book *Rich Dad, Poor Dad,* Robert Kiyosaki says, "Most people never win because they're afraid of losing. Winners are not afraid of losing. But losers are. Failure is part of the process of success. People who avoid failure also avoid success."[2]

Remember, faith isn't faith if it isn't conquering fear.

ROADBLOCK #3—A GENERATIONAL CURSE OF POVERTY
"The wealth of the rich is his fortified city; the ruin of the poor is their poverty" (Prov. 10:15, *CJB*). My friend Ken Eldred describes poverty this way:

> Poverty is a disease that afflicts millions around the world. Perhaps most damaging is the attitude that poverty often brings. Hopelessness and lack of confidence lead to depression and desperation. There are no perceptions of opportunity, no visions and dreams for the future. These attitudes often permeate a community. They are passed on to successive generations. A cycle of despair is formed, and those caught in the cycle face great challenges in extricating themselves from the generational curse of poverty. People become limited by their own view. They see themselves resigned to their plight due to fate and a lack of opportunity. When coupled with a view that creating wealth is wrong, the problem is compounded, and people are kept in poverty.[3]

Fear is what keeps poverty alive.

Some spiritual truths are more difficult to grasp than others, especially when you consider how deeply rooted strongholds can be—some go to the very fabric of our being. Lack, defeat, unbelief and discouragement all crowd the mind when you don't know the truth concerning poverty. If you have been raised in poverty, poverty will control your thinking. These enemies of faith live in the natural realm of one's un-renewed mind. Contrary to the way poverty would argue, God does not withhold anything from you. Robert Kiyosaki further says:

> One of the reasons the rich get richer, the poor get poorer, and the middle class struggles in debt is because the subject of money is taught at home, not school. Most of us learn about money from our parents. So what can poor parents tell their children about money? They simply say, "Stay in school and study hard." The child may graduate with excellent grades, but with a poor person's financial programming and mindset. It was learned while the child was young.[4]

Your prosperity has nothing to do with the economy or your current situation. "There is a difference between being poor and being broke. Broke is temporary and poor is eternal," Kiyosaki explains of his rich dad's optimism in a financial crisis.[5]

You will be taken advantage of if you don't know your covenant rights as the prophet Hosea warns: "My people are destroyed for lack of knowledge" (Hos. 4:6, *NRSV*), which brings us to the fourth roadblock.

ROADBLOCK #4—IGNORANCE

The great reformer Martin Luther said, "Every Christian must undergo three conversions: heart, mind and pocketbook."

The paradigm of poverty will resist change. That is why I mentioned at the outset that the word "prosper" carries with it a violent and forceful approach to wealth. The fact that we have been given the power to obtain wealth that we might establish God's covenant on the earth can be mind-boggling. Frustration and impatience often fuel a heart that is shallow and without understanding of covenant. Through faith and patience we inherit the promises of God; so cultivating a mindset of abundance will take persistence. The Enemy's greatest deception is to try to convince you to dismiss your faulty belief system as being the root cause of your financial woes.

Often, Christians mentally agree with the Word of God but have no faith that it has the power to deliver what it says. They are so "knowledgeable" but have not applied what they have learned to combat their strongholds. Godly wisdom is the ability to apply what you learn.

Going to church and being a good citizen isn't enough to combat the stronghold of ignorance. Furthermore, a good-paying job will pay the bills, but your paycheck isn't an indication of the kind of wealth I am talking about. Many are entirely satisfied living with the pseudo-wealth of their paychecks. But my message is about living the higher life in a covenant of wealth that far exceeds anything your mind can imagine. It is the difference between eating the crumbs that fall from the Master's table and feasting at His table and fellowshipping with Him to boot.

Many of God's children cannot receive from God—they don't know how to because of their ignorance or wrong teaching. Tithers can also falter because they give based on their religious duty and obligation, not faith. They have not gone astray; they just haven't received the wealth of God. Guilt and an embarrassment of riches prevent some from enjoying what God has given them. The Pharisees didn't understand Jesus' mission on earth. Therefore, they remained outside of the reality of their "living" covenant because they religiously prided themselves in the knowledge of its content. Their religious paradigm reduced the covenant to works, which totally obliterated the purpose of Jesus' death on the cross.

I want to share an interesting story to bring home the point.

Long ago there was a maid who worked for the Queen of England. When the Queen passed away, she was found to have been so appreciative of her maid that the Queen included her in her Last Will and Testament. The Queen's lawyers sent the maid a certificate guaranteeing her income for the rest of her life.

Proud of this official piece of paper, but unable to read, the maid had it specially framed and it hung in her living room for years. One day, she had a visitor, and he recognized the legal document and took a closer look. Perplexed, the visitor inquired of this poverty-stricken woman concerning the document and asked why she hadn't cashed it in. In her ignorance, this woman was unable to access what belonged to her. You see, as long as she made no demand on that document, the blessing was kept from her.

COVENANT FAITH

As we have seen thus far, covenant living requires faith; and faith without corresponding actions is dead. The Bible is a faith-filled book that must be embraced with the Holy Spirit's guidance.

The more the Word of God has been quickened or made alive in you by the Holy Spirit, the more it is possible to walk in the revelation of the kind of wealth that covenant provides. Knowledge about your covenant won't fix the problem. Revelation of your covenant releases you to walk in it.

By the time the children of Israel took hold of the promises of God, entered into the Promised Land and drove out the giants that lived there, they were no longer slaves. They were conquerors. Why? Because they finally thought differently about God's covenant with them.

Faith works in the heart, not in the head. Faith acts and talks as though it has already come to pass. You have to picture it on the inside before you see it come to pass. This is covenant lingo, taking God's Word as an expression of your faith.

Without faith, we, just like many in the world, are bound to live from paycheck to paycheck. That is not God's will. The eye of faith sees beyond obvious limitations. Faith transfers what is already done in the spirit world into the natural world where we need it. God may use the money we operate with here on earth, but God is not limited to our economy. God's economy runs on unlimited resources and is not fickle or risky. So invest in His business!

THE POWER OF GOD'S WORD SPOKEN

The law of faith declares, "You shall have whatsoever you say . . ." (see Mark 11:23). This does not mean that you can confess whatever you want. Faith requires a strong belief in what the Word of

God says, because that is what we are supposed to confess or "say." If you don't know what the Word of God says about your particular need, you are already defeated. Grab hold of the Word of God and speak life into your lack and poverty. *The law of faith is the law of change.* You will have to speak differently from the way things are. Don't deny that lack exists, but call forth abundance in its place, and the power of the creative Word will begin to change your circumstances.

By the way, it is possible to confess failure and defeat while at the same time confessing the Word of God. But "faith's" confession and "doubt and unbelief's" confession won't work together. Negative words will resist your confession of faith. The one that you believe the strongest—your belief or your doubt—is the one you will have faith in the most. If you don't know which one that is, when you are under pressure in life's unpredictable crisis, you will speak out whatever is in your heart. It has to do with your "belief" and not God.

This appears obvious to most people, and they would agree with me about this principle of confession; but you may not be aware that you are doing this, and therefore can't adjust your thinking or your confession. The questions I asked you to ponder earlier were hopefully not an exercise in futility. Reflecting on what is in your heart is critical to changing your confession.

"Death and life are in the power of the tongue" (Prov. 18:21, *NKJV*). Change the way you think so that what you speak will be life-giving, not death-giving. Positive change will not happen until faith is released. So be persistent. Faith puts you in the supernatural realm of the impossible. You have a choice in the matter—so choose life!

A man who was leaving on a journey gave money to three of his servants: one talent to one, two talents to another, and five talents to the third. The servants with five and two talents invested their money and doubled their return. The servant with one talent simply buried it for safe-keeping and waited for his master to return.

When the master returned, he praised the first two servants for their faithfulness and their fruitfulness in multiplying what he had given them. He punished the third servant, however, and took away the talent he had given him and gave it to the servant who now had 10 talents. To the two faithful servants, he said, "Well done, good and faithful servant; you were faithful over a few things, I will make you ruler over many things. Enter into the joy of your lord" (Matt. 25:14-21, *NKJV*).

With the wealth of experience that Ken Eldred has had in the area of finance, he encourages, "We are stewards of the material possessions entrusted to us. The parable of the talents makes it clear that God holds us accountable for wise deployment of these resources. God commands us to grow the resources He gives. Wealth comes with huge responsibility, and proper management of it is an act of worship to God."[6]

A GODSEND

Two of the most important events in my life occurred because of my wife: Carla led me to the Lord, and she convinced me to become a tither.

The day that I was born again, my life wasn't radically changed. I possessed heaven but not earth! Some of my habits changed. I stopped smoking after Carla prayed for me; I kind of quit cussing; and I sort of quit drinking. I threw away all my *Black Sabbath* music albums and went to church on Sunday. I had the same job, the same paycheck, the same problems; I was still struggling. I was a believer, but I wasn't a committed Christian.

I remember the Sunday I brought 10 percent of my income to church for the first time. My life drastically changed after that. I went to Oklahoma to study the Bible and our income was drastically reduced; that was normal; it was my desert experience. Shortly thereafter, God called me into the ministry full-time.

When we built our new church, we didn't have the astronomical sum on hand to pay for the land and build a sanctuary in Silicon Valley, California. Our tithes and offerings were paying our bills and we had just a small amount left over. During those early years, a man wrote a check for $100,000, and another man wrote a check for $25,000.

Many years later, I was prompted to make contact with evangelist Jimmy Swaggart, who had fallen into sin in the early 1990s. God told me to pray with him. So I did. Then I invited him to our church. He flew out to California, and Carla and I took him to dinner in San Francisco. While we were enjoying crab legs, I asked Jimmy if he wanted to preach the Sunday morning service. He agreed and preached a great message.

There was a little white-haired gentleman seated at the back of the church. Jimmy said this man was saved under his ministry and gave $1 million a year to his ministry. "Since he lives in Silicon Valley, maybe he will join your church and help build your new sanctuary," Jimmy suggested.

Well, I didn't see this gentleman again until six months later. He came to visit us at Jubilee one Sunday. After the service, he came up to me and we arranged to have lunch the next day. We became friends. Not six months later, he told me, "God told me to give you $5 million." He helped us build our new sanctuary. You see, although Jimmy Swaggart and I were not close friends, nevertheless, it was because of Jimmy Swaggart that this man joined our church.

God declares that if you're a tither, He'll open the windows of heaven and pour you out a blessing that you cannot contain. That sounds like a bounty of a blessing. God also says that once you've received those blessings, the devil won't have any right to steal them from you. But that doesn't mean he won't try. You must remind him of your covenant rights—he has to back off!

When you give your tithes and offerings to a church, you are not donating to or supporting the church—that should not be the reason you give. You shouldn't give for a tax write-off either. You shouldn't give to acquire influence or gain the pastor's favor. There are people at Jubilee who give out of convenience and give inconsistently. The Bible says that the Philippian church gave more than any other church; they gave even when they had no more to give. It is not how big your offering is, but it is how big your heart is in your giving.

"Give, and it will be given to you, good measure, pressed down, shaken together, and running over, will they give into your bosom.

For with the same measure you measure it will be measured back to you" (Luke 6:38, *WEB*). It takes a covenant with Almighty God to attain your wealthy place in life!

CONCLUSION

By now you are aware that the kingdom of God and this earthly kingdom clash. Like oil and water, they do not mix. Understanding the principles of covenant wealth is key to prospering where you live. Your lasting commitment to obey those principles is essential if you hope to preserve your convenant and pass it on to successive generations.

God has a plan for the transference of goods and the wealth of this world. When our hearts are right, not perfect, there is nothing wrong with acquiring that wealth. We are supposed to be the administrators of God's wealth. And as we have learned, covenant goes beyond "me and mine" and extends to the ends of the earth.

God's covenant wealth defies the world's system of economy. In other words, the world's system has to bow to this supernatural covenant. "All the silver and gold is mine," says El Shaddai, the God of more than enough!

Covenant is a deal backed by a promise and sealed in blood. God's sole purpose for wealth is for us to establish His covenant on earth. Every child of God has a right to access all that belongs to God.

Wealth is necessary because of the millions who still don't know Christ's gospel and the unfinished work yet to be done to advance God's kingdom. You can preach the gospel without money, but you can't establish God's covenant in the earth without it.

Life Lines

- Cain's careless attitude caused God to reject his offering. Can God trust you with your giving?

- "A good man leaves an inheritance to his children's children, But the wealth of the sinner is stored up for the righteous" (Prov. 13:22, *NKJV*).

- What are you confessing over your life today: God's blessings, or are you cursing yourself and your circumstances?

- Poverty says, "I can't afford to tithe." You can't afford not to. No deposit, no return!

- Poverty is a mindset that must be confronted with the truth of the Word of God; otherwise covenant wealth can never be realized.

- You can never operate successfully in the kingdom of God without understanding the principles that govern that world—including wealth.

- Tithing is the most fundamental truth that a believer must learn and apply to daily living. If you desire to live in the overflowing abundant life of wealth, learn the principles that begin with tithing. Unlocking God's wealth won't come just by believing. You must put action to your faith.

- According to Jewish tradition, tithing was stressed as an expression of covenant fidelity.

Chapter Fifteen

Covenant Calling

To Him who loved us and washed us from our sins in His own blood, and has made us kings and priests to His God and Father, to Him be glory and dominion forever and ever. Amen.

REVELATION 1:5-6, *NKJV*

There is an insatiable yearning in the heart of man to find his purpose in life. Statistics show that the average American will work at 3 careers and 18 different jobs over a lifetime. Our society tells us that we can be whatever we want to be, make a lot of money and live the American dream. That is, until we become Christians.

When the believer surrenders his life to Christ, all of a sudden he is faced with a dilemma that I call a "career crisis." Well-meaning, religious veterans of the faith surround the impressionable new believer with ideas such as, "You are called to the ministry. Sell everything you have and follow Jesus." However, God might not be calling the newcomer into full-time ministry in the traditional sense; but the ol' veteran of the faith continues making the newcomer feel guilty as he continues to pursue his career outside of the church.

Confused, the new convert seeks God for further direction and is encouraged by God that he is on the right track in his profession. Do you suppose there are fellow employees within the new convert's sphere of influence who might be in the valley of decision as to their future? Perhaps the person sitting right next to him is contemplating suicide because of a failed marriage. Yet, when the newcomer goes to church, he is still affected by clamoring voices that tell him to leave his "worldly" job. So he vacillates between opinions.

Have you been there?

The "crisis" I've just mentioned is all too common among our ranks. Clearly defined roles are difficult to establish when guilt, shame and ignorance abound in the Church. One's God-given purpose or calling in life is important to discover, otherwise there is no way to fulfill that destiny. Going to Bible school is good, but it may not necessarily change a career path. However, being well versed in the Bible helps in reaching the lost regardless of one's occupation.

I must admit that I was a reluctant recruit in responding to the call of God on my life. Leaving the comforts of a predictable and comfortable life to step out into full-time ministry and learn how to trust God, when I was self-sufficient in the world, was a daunting task. Bible college didn't teach me how to walk out the practical aspects of my faith, so I learned by trial and error, especially during those first years of ministry. I'd like to think all that's behind me now, but the longer that I am in God's business, the more I value and draw from the lessons learned during those lean years.

I hope this chapter will help define your role in God's kingdom so that you, too, can become fruitful, productive and well pleasing to your Lord.

KINGS AND PRIESTS: GOD AT WORK IN CHURCH AND AT HOME

"To Him who loved us and washed us from our sins in His own blood, and has made us kings and priests to His God and Father, to Him be glory and dominion forever and ever. Amen" (Rev. 1:5-6, *NKJV*).

The book of Revelation is probably the most difficult book to understand in the Bible. It is apocalyptic literature rich with symbolism, prophetic insight and foresight. But one thing that particularly fascinates me is where John speaks of us being made "kings" and "priests" to God the Father. Now that is an interesting concept.

Why would John go back to Old Testament titles to describe New Testament people?

Jesus and the apostle Paul, in giving names and titles to the Church, came up with disciples, apostles, pastors, elders, evangelists, even saints; but John uses kings (small "k") and priests (small "p").

Most are familiar with our Lord's title:

King of kings and Lord of lords; Great High Priest

But when church people are referred to as kings and priests, well, this raised my eyebrows. Allow me some liberty as I discuss what I believe this means. In other words, there is wiggle room for alternative ideas.

I interpret John's reference to "kings" as business people (in secular fields), and "priests" to be pastors and all manner of church workers. People like me, full-time pastors, are not special or unique—only different. Just because a person falls in love with Jesus and loves sharing the Bible doesn't necessarily mean he or she should quit work, go to seminary and then move to Africa in order to minister to the lost.

I believe this passage in Revelation is John's original mandate for us to evangelize the world through marketplace evangelism as well as from church pulpits. The world doesn't go to church, but we're told to go to the world. What better way to reach business people or people working in secular fields than from their fellow workmates! Many outside the Church are bound by the powers of darkness and need the ministry of the Body of Christ right where they are. Work is not identified as the curse that came when Adam and Eve sinned, as some ignorantly believe. God wants to bless you in your workplace!

A paradigm shift in the believer's thinking about faith and work is necessary, otherwise many will remain frustrated, thinking that because they are not in "full-time ministry," they are useless to God and others. With that defeated approach, many don't attempt to reach out to their coworkers.

It is far reaching for some to imagine that God could perform miracles just as easily in the marketplace as in church. "More than 90 percent of all Christians know that their purpose and their vision from God lie outside the pulpit of the local church. Unfortunately, few know how to release the vision and walk in it successfully," says Richard Fleming in his book *The Glory Returns to the Workplace*.[1] He, too, understands the marketplace strategy to reach the unreached.

God greatly uses people who do not have "priestly" callings. Being used by God is a role for everyone, not just for professional clerics. Notice this verse: "And has made us kings and priests to His God and Father, to Him be glory and dominion forever and ever. Amen."

Let me add to "glory" *vision*; and to "dominion" *provision*. When God's people gather, God's glory descends, which is God's presence. I believe, and again I speak by suggestion, that we pastors, i.e., Levites and priests, are in the *glory/vision* business. Our church services should welcome God's presence. God's "kings," or anointed business people, are in the *dominion/provision* business. God wants believers to dominate the marketplace: government, sports and entertainment, Wall Street, academia, Silicon Valley—everywhere! If God is everywhere, we should be everywhere, and be as salt and light to everyone.

Have you ever stopped to think that, for the most part, the Bible was written by businessmen? Moses, King David, King Solomon, Peter, John and Paul—all had backgrounds in business. Furthermore, Abraham, Isaac, Jacob, Esther and Job are other examples of God's call and favor on the very wealthy!

A CASE OF MISTAKEN IDENTITY

A few years ago, my wife, Carla, and I were visiting a friend's church in Pensacola, Florida, that was experiencing quite a spiritual revival. During the worship service, a lady standing next to us was weeping profusely. Carla asked her if she was okay.

"It's my husband," she blurted out, "I think he might be suicidal." She went on to share that her husband was a very successful doctor who loved the Lord and shared Christ with all his patients. At their church, a so-called "prophetess" told him in very strong terms that he was out of God's will and was making too much money. The doctor quit his practice and started a church because he was told that he was "called."

After four years of struggling with very few people in the church and a meager income, he became depressed. He was convinced God had deserted him. I opened my Bible and showed her our subject Scripture. "See, we're not all called to be priests or full-time church workers (modern Levites). Most of us are called to the marketplace as New Testament kings. You tell your husband that he's called by God to be a doctor in the Kingdom. That's his full-time ministry."

Her eyes opened wide and the lights came on. "O my God," she whispered, "I see it! Thank you so much." She hurried toward the sanctuary exit like a woman on a mission. This dear lady came to the revival for answers—and she got one! For four years this doctor lived with a case of mistaken identity.

In 1995, I was speaking to a large church congregation in Denver, Colorado. My subject for two days and evenings was "Kings and Priests." A very successful businessman, whose company handled over a billion dollars in business, took me golfing in the afternoon. He asked me to pray for his business partner who believed in God and the Lord Jesus but wouldn't come to church or even to a home Bible study group. His business partner feared that if he did he would turn into a fanatic or Jesus freak, then quit the business and become a minister. I challenged my friend to give his business partner my tape sermon from this two-day conference.

One year later, I was invited back to Denver and was met at the airport by my pal. The first thing out of his mouth was a praise report. "Dick, guess what?! My business partner is in church. He loves it. Your tapes last year set him free; he now knows that he can serve God through business just as our pastor serves God in his ministry calling full-time."

ANOINTED FOR BUSINESS

Author John Beckett has recaptured the biblical understanding of work and ministry in his recent book *Mastering Monday*. He, too, struggled with his calling in the marketplace. "I made an important discovery about faith and work. It was the day I realized that these two seemingly opposite worlds didn't need to be separate; that I didn't have to be one person on Sunday, another on Monday. That I could be called to the workplace with the same intensity and purpose as ministry."

His discovery regarding the marketplace led him to explore certain assumptions that were hindering him from embracing his calling: "My impression was that real significance occurs only when we are engaged in some kind of church-related work." This type of mindset is limited because the believer is unable to explore his giftings or spiritual potential while in the workplace: "I realize that my desire to serve God had been based on a romantic notion, not a personal relationship." Consequently, Beckett said, "I was nagged by the notion that work was a second-class pursuit."[2] His journey was arduous, but finally he realized the value and purpose of his high calling in the marketplace.

When I speak to young pastors just getting started, I warn them not to put too much pressure on business people to come to every activity the church is having. At my church, Jubilee Christian Center, we have five or six meetings or activities going on every week. I don't expect people to live at church. They have jobs, hobbies, kids in Little League baseball or soccer, and the like. If pastors use guilt or shame to motivate, business people will quit going to church!

I love our corporate worship services, but my goal is to see people on most Sundays and hope they gravitate toward one of our small cell groups for fellowship and to cross-pollinate. We call our small cell groups ACTS 2:46: "They worshiped together at the Temple each day, met in homes for the Lord's Supper, and shared their meals with great joy and generosity" (Acts 2:46, *NLT*).

In relation to calling and ministry, the question I've heard most often is, "Pastor Dick, how will I know what I'm called to?" It's really quite easy. What do you love to do? What are you gifted in? What comes natural, even easy, to you? If you're called to be a millionaire, then support your local church and other missionaries. Go for it! Be a king!

While working on a construction site back in 1979, when I closed my eyes and saw myself behind a pulpit, that excited me; I went for it! I became a priest. Remember, kings do more than support the church, yet that is a key role of their calling. Further, you may be a king for a while until perhaps God transitions you into becoming a priest. Don't let others "call you," and pay no attention to those who try intimidation, shame or guilt to get you to do what they feel is right for you.

A healthy church is one in which its members know their purpose in serving their Lord. I've seen the extremes, where businessmen sit on church boards and ride the pastor or hire a hireling to do their bidding. On the other end of the spectrum, there are pastors who are dictators and listen to no one's counsel. I believe that God's design is that kings and priests work hand in hand with a kind of divine synergy to advance the kingdom of God on earth.

"We thought God was just for Sunday church or mid-week study. But, God is showing up in small businesses and on construction sites, in schools and in politics. God is showing up everywhere outside of where we expect Him to be," says *God @ Work* author and my friend Rich Marshall.[3] Which brings me to my next point.

HOLLYWOOD, SPORTS AND POLITICIANS

I recall the apostle Paul's beginnings. When Paul was brought to a saving knowledge of Christ on the road to Damascus, like anyone else, one might have thought his calling would be to preach to the Jews, his own people. But God had other plans. The apostle Paul's primary calling was to the Gentiles! His colleagues weren't exactly supportive of his calling, because they didn't understand what God was doing with this renegade Pharisee.

And although the apostle Peter had a hard time believing Paul was called to be a missionary to the Gentiles, under a heavenly trance he saw a clue of God's plan. All kinds of four-footed animals of the earth, creeping things, and birds of the air were in Peter's vision. A voice came to Peter and said, "Rise Peter; kill and eat." But Peter said, "Not so, Lord! For I have never eaten anything common or unclean." And a voice spoke to him again the second time, "What God has cleansed you must not call common" (Acts 10:11-16, *NKJV*).

Traditionally, a pastor-preacher's ministry calling is to the poor, the despised and the rejected. This religious view is limited through ignorance, because it doesn't include the rest of the world. Often, the Church is comfortable with that limited paradigm of the Great Commission. After all, while He was on earth, much of Jesus' ministry affected society's outcasts. But He died for the world.

God loves the sinner and saint alike. The mission field that you and I are called to may be something that not everyone will agree with.

AN UNTRADITIONAL MINISTRY CALLING

In spite of criticism and controversy, another aspect of my priestly calling is to the entertainment and political world. This has proven to be an unusual and provocative mission field, one that I had never set my sights on. Yet, I am not afraid to sail into uncharted waters or cross the line between the secular and sacred.

Although in the past, wholesome movies and TV shows were commonplace, today, the airwaves are littered with illicit daytime soap operas, and sitcoms that anesthesize the viewing audience with messages encouraging same-sex marriage and sexual immorality. But with the recent success of Mel Gibson's masterpiece movie *The Passion of the Christ*, and Disney's *The Chronicles of Narnia: The Lion, the Witch, and the Wardrobe*, Hollywood was awakened to the fact that we Christians are hungry for good, wholesome, spiritual entertainment.

When *People* magazine published its cover story about *The Passion of the Christ* in April 2004, it posed the question "Does Hollywood Have Faith?" According to the popular publication, Hollywood had some believers, but they were few and far between—

or very hard to find. Those Hollywood stars for some reason didn't reflect their spiritual light to mainstream America.

After the 9/11 disaster in New York, in 2001, talk regarding the things of God intensified in the media. Every time a major calamity hits somewhere in the world, news anchors always scramble to interview someone from the church world to get their angle on the subject matter.

Sure, there is a nucleus of people in the entertainment industry with godless philosophies and lifestyles they pedal through their platforms. Yet most of the elite, with all their fame and fortune, are like the rest of us; they think deeply about the issues of life, death and eternity.

It's easy for Christians to throw up their hands and dismiss Hollywood, San Francisco, and other places, like Berkeley, labeling them "unsavable," but I disagree. Genesis 1:2 tells me that God's Spirit, His presence, is always hovering over dark places. God enjoys being unconventional.

A SHIFT IN THE HEAVENLIES

Celebrity and the media are the world's most influential mission field. If you don't believe it, just take a few minutes to check out prime-time television programming and see what is holding the interest of the world.

I invited legendary recording artist Smokey Robinson to minister at Jubilee, and he has returned many times. When I first met Smokey, he asked me if I would help him do a Bible study at his home, which I did once a month for three years. That opportunity opened doors for Carla and me to minister to a whole host of celebrities, including Gary Busey, Judge Reinhold, Natalie Cole, Barry Gordy, and others. Smokey's my golfing buddy, but more than that, he considers me one of his pastors.

Christians behind the scenes of today's movie industry say that God is working to redeem Hollywood. Twentieth Century Fox has opened up Fox Faith, a division of Fox designed to go after church people. As a guest of Judge and Amy Reinhold, Carla and I went to the premier of *Akeelah and the Bee* in Hollywood. At the party given after the premier, one executive from Lions Gate Films told me they are opening up a division for "spiritual movies." There is a shift in the heavenlies over the media capital of the world.

Actress Dyan Cannon, a messianic Jew, is also impacting Hollywood with her "God Parties," which are an expression of her faith and where she ministers divine healing to packed audiences.

One day, I was on a Hollywood set with former NFL great Merton Hanks. We were fellowshiping with actress Halle Berry on the set of *X-Men 2*. The assistant producer approached me and asked, "Dick, what does it mean to be born again? I think I'm a Christian, but I was working on that movie *Left Behind*, and I don't want to be left behind." I began to share my testimony, planting seeds of the truth of salvation into this young man, and now the seeds are being watered with prayer.

"We are praying for a revival like never before," said Lou Engle, who is cofounder of The Cause, a prayer initiative to mobilize nationwide prayer and fasting for America. "We believe that God wants to influence Hollywood for His kingdom," Lou says.

Controversy follows me whenever I reach out to touch someone that the Church world labels an "outcast." If I have been accused by my brethren, I'm guilty as charged. Befriending Jimmy Swaggart at a time in his life when he needed a friend gave many something to talk about. God blessed us when we reached out to Jimmy and his family. We had no idea what was on the other side of our obedience.

Unlike the average churchman or local pastor who would be handicapped with prejudice against the people who host secular radio programs, I accepted an opportunity to interact with Northern California's former number-one radio show, *The Dog House*. This program was aired on FM 94.9 and had well over 400,000 listeners tuning in each morning. Although I was a guest on *The Dog House*, which pushed the broadcast envelope with dubious language and lewd conduct, I saw this as an opportunity to reach the youth who weren't in church.

For two years we had an opportunity to reach hundreds of thousands of Silicon Valley's listening youth. This opened up an opportunity for me and M. C. Hammer to host *The God House* on Sunday mornings. We fielded callers' questions about God, the Bible and other spiritual matters. We often had a variety of well-known celebrity guest appearances to encourage, exhort and bring the listeners into the knowledge of Jesus Christ.

When I met Jim Brown, Hall of Fame football star and movie actor, he was actively involved in a variety of community and national causes, namely the Amer-I-Can program he founded back in 1988. I was curious.

Looking to better our communities and make a positive impact for God, Jim explained the heart of his vision: "The beauty of Amer-I-Can is that it transcends race, age, gender, religion and socioeconomic status. The teaching and sharing of the program concepts related to individual self-esteem can significantly impact the problems our society disregards. It's never too late to attain a full, meaningful life. The objective of the program is to cause an individual to examine his past conditioned behavior patterns that have negatively influenced his life, and to systematically apply proven methods to overcome that behavior."

We soon joined forces to implement this program in our community and it has opened doors of opportunity to reach some of the most difficult and dangerous areas of the inner city.

My dear friend, the late Reggie White, nicknamed "Minister of Defense," was an ordained minister and humanitarian. "Reggie was one of the best defensive players the NFL has ever seen—if not the best ever," said *New Man* magazine editor Robert Andrescik. "He lived an exemplary life. All of the scandals you hear about with pro athletes . . . Reggie rose above all that. He made us proud because he played hard and lived godly, both on and off the field."[4] I was also blessed to have former Coach Fitz Hill and his San Jose State University football team visit Jubilee during our Sunday church services.

Other acquaintances I have had the pleasure of spending time with include Presidents of the United States Bill Clinton and

George W. Bush, Jerry Rice, other Hollywood luminaries, football players, politicians, and powerful people like King Abdul of Jordan.

Rubbing elbows with the rich and famous showed me that they are really no different from you and me. Many of them have some of the same struggles and problems that we have. They may live in a world that we cannot relate to, but they need a savior. Even though many in the church world despise the celebrity elite for their excesses, Christ died for them. Indeed, recognizing this universal need has broadened my sphere of gospel influence to some of the most unusual places and diverse people on this planet.

I've been told that the life of faith is an odyssey. An odyssey is an adventure full of surprises. Once I got hold of covenant truth, by the Holy Spirit, I began to understand that God is a God of love, truth, principle and goodness. Every day is a wonderful experience for me. This is what God wants for your life too—an odyssey of faith-filled adventures as your covenant destiny is fulfilled. The question is, Do you want it too?

Your covenant destiny to live your life for Christ does not mean that you need to become a pastor or missionary. You are called to let Christ live through you and reach people right where you are, smack dab in the middle of your current sphere of influence. On the other hand, God may be calling you to a new place. He calls each of us to a unique ministry for Him, and He will empower us to accomplish it. But do not look for so-called "greener grass" unless you are convinced that God is calling you to a place to which you've not yet been. Chances are good, however, that you're right where God wants you to be, right now!

Life Lines

- Be open to your mission field of God's choosing. Hollywood was the last place I thought about when I began ministry; yet this opportunity to reach the elite has touched those who probably considered church the last place they wanted to visit.

- "I make an active effort to remain a positive role model to kids. They need people to show them there is another way." —M. C. Hammer

- "He took my mess and gave me a message. He took those tests and gave me a testimony." —Gary Busey

- "I think for most hardheaded people, it is not easy when you put your faith and your trust and your destiny in the hands of God. You have to go on faith, but I have learned over the years to turn my life over to God." —Natalie Cole

- When George W. Bush was asked to name the philosopher that had the greatest influence on his life, he said, "Christ, because he changed my heart."

- "One thing about God that is so beautiful, He is omnipotent and He is Almighty, but He is not a dictator." —Smokey Robinson

- "Once I got saved, I thought I had to give up business to pursue missions, but God soon showed me I could do both." —Ken Eldred, author of *God Is at Work* and CEO of Living Stones Foundation

Acknowledgments

I can hardly believe this book is finished! It's been nearly two years in the making, but I am elated for the finished product. No book of this magnitude is ever put together by just one individual. For this, I am grateful to my good friends at Regal who believe in me and recognize that this simple and uncomplicated message of covenant is both noteworthy and timely. I am indebted to Steve Lawson for his tireless enthusiasm over this book. A special thanks to my dear friend Dr. Paul Kim, who was instrumental in connecting me with Regal.

Thank you to my assistant editor and former secretary, Virginia Obregon, who dug up every lecture and sermon I ever preached, along with notes of my early attempts to put my thoughts in writing concerning this subject. She and her husband, George, when they are not home writing, travel to the regions beyond our borders to continue developing their role in God's Great Commission. Thanks for your untiring dedication to this major undertaking.

And then there are my friends and colleagues with whom I am privileged to be in covenant. As I acknowledge these unnamed but much appreciated "partners" for their value in my life and their contribution to my writing, I could not be more grateful.

Finally, I wish to acknowledge my pastoral staff—your support and constant input have done more to make my job easier and to lighten the load than anything else. You're the best!

ENDNOTES

Chapter 1: Covenant Introduced
1. Larry Richards, *Every Man in the Bible* (Nashville, TN: Thomas Nelson, 1999), p. 105.
2. James Boswell, quoted in *The New Encyclopedia of Christian Quotations,* compiled by Mark Water (Grand Rapids, MI: Baker Books, 2000), p. 231.

Chapter 2: Covenant with Adam: The First Family
1. Larry Ambrose, quoted in *The New Encyclopedia of Christian Quotations,* compiled by Mark Water (Grand Rapids, MI: Baker Books, 2000), p. 824.
2. Larry Richards, *Every Man in the Bible* (Nashville, TN: Thomas Nelson, 1999), p. 9.
3. John Tauler, quoted in *The New Encyclopedia of Christian Quotations*, p. 1036.

Chapter 3: Covenant with Noah
1. Encarta Online World English Dictionary, s.v. "favor." http://encarta.msn.com/dictionary_/favor.html (accessed June 2008).

Chapter 4: Covenant with Abraham
1. Gordon Dalby, "When Your Father Wasn't There," *Charisma*, October 2000, p. 90.
2. Ibid.
3. Larry Richards, *Every Man in the Bible* (Nashville, TN: Thomas Nelson, 1999), p. 13.

Chapter 5: Covenant with Jacob
1. Matthew G. Easton, Web Bible Encyclopedia, Christian Answers Network Website, www.christiananswers.net, Eden Communications, Gilbert, Arizona, 1996.
2. Larry Richards, *Every Man in the Bible* (Nashville, TN: Thomas Nelson, 1999), p. 69.
3. Francis Frangipane, *The Three Battlegrounds* (Cedar Rapids, IA: Arrow Publications, 1989), p. 29.
4. John C. Maxwell, *Winning with People* (Nashville, TN: Thomas Nelson, 2004), p. 15.
5. Jim Sheard and Wally Armstrong, *Playing the Game, Inspiration for Life and Golf* (Nashville, TN: Thomas Nelson, 1998), p. 121.

Chapter 6: Covenant with Joseph
1. Larry Richards, *Every Man in the Bible* (Nashville, TN: Thomas Nelson, 1999), p. 77.

Chapter 7: Covenant with Moses
1. Larry Richards, *Every Man in the Bible* (Nashville, TN: Thomas Nelson, 1999), p. 33.
2. Jim Sheard and Wally Armstrong, *Playing the Game, Inspiration for Life and Golf* (Nashville, TN: Thomas Nelson, 1998), p. 18.
3. Walter C. Kaiser, Jr., *The Old Testament in Contemporary Preaching* (Grand Rapids, MI: Baker Books), pp. 43-44.

Chapter 8: Covenant with David—Part 1: Inward Development
1. Christian Classics Ethereal Library website, Matthew Henry's Complete Commentary on the Whole Bible, 1 Samuel 17, public domain. http://www.studylight.org.

Chapter 9: Covenant with David—Part 2: A Time of Transition
1. Christian Classics Ethereal Library website, Matthew Henry's Complete Commentary on the Whole Bible, 2 Samuel 11, public domain. http://www.studylight.org.
2. Larry Richards, *Every Man in the Bible* (Nashville, TN: Thomas Nelson, 1999), p. 49.

Chapter 10: Covenant with Isaiah
1. *Life Application Bible, The Living Bible* (Wheaton, IL: Tyndale House Publishers, 1988), p. 993.

Chapter 11: Covenant of Redemption
1. *Life Application Bible, The Living Bible* (Wheaton, IL: Tyndale House Publishers, 1988), p. 1475.
2. Dr. Jack Deere, *Surprised by the Voice of God* (Grand Rapids, MI: Zondervan Publishers, 1996), p. 28.
3. Dr. Harold G. Koenig, *The Healing Connection* (West Conshohocken, PA: Templeton Foundation Press, 2004).

Chapter 12: Covenant Sealed with the Spirit
1. *Life Application Bible, The Living Bible* (Wheaton, IL: Tyndale House Publishers, 1988), p. 1619.
2. Dr. Jack Deere, *Surprised by the Voice of God* (Grand Rapids, MI: Zondervan Publishers, 1996), p. 52.
3. Theodore Runyon, ed., *What the Spirit Is Saying to the Churches* (New York: Hawthorn Books, Inc. 1975), p. 10.
4. Charles Spurgeon, *Spurgeon on the Holy Spirit* (New Kensington, PA: Whitaker House, 2000), p. 39.
5. Runyon, *What the Spirit Is Saying to the Churches*, p. 7.
6. Deere, *Surprised by the Voice of God*, p. 62.
7. Kallistos Ware, quoted in *The New Encyclopedia of Christian Quotations*, compiled by Mark Water (Grand Rapids, MI: Baker Books, 2000), p. 490.

Chapter 13: Covenant of Prayer
1. David J. Wolpe, *The Healer of Shattered Hearts, A Jewish View of God* (New York: Penguin Books, 1991), p. 59.
2. Phillip Brooks, quoted in *The New Encyclopedia of Christian Quotations*, compiled by Mark Water (Grand Rapids, MI: Baker Books, 2000), p. 757.
3. John G. Lake, quoted in *The New Encyclopedia of Christian Quotations*, p. 763.
4. Brother Lawrence, quoted in *The New Encyclopedia of Christian Quotations*, p. 763.
5. Dwight L. Moody, quoted in *The New Encyclopedia of Christian Quotations*, p. 765.

Chapter 14: Covenant of Wealth
1. James Strong, *The New Strong's Exhaustive Concordance of the Bible* (Nashville, TN: Thomas Nelson, 1990), p. 848.
2. Robert Kiyosaki, *Rich Dad, Poor Dad* (New York: Warner Books, 1997), p. 125.
3. Ken Eldred, *God Is at Work* (Ventura, CA: Regal Books, 2005), p. 319.
4. Kiyosaki, *Rich Dad, Poor Dad*, p. 14.
5. Ibid., p. 16.
6. Eldred, *God Is at Work*, p. 315.

Chapter 15: Covenant Calling
1. Richard Fleming, *The Glory Returns to the Workplace* (Italy: Destiny Image Europe, 2004).
2. John Beckett, *Pray Magazine*, July/August 2006 issue, p. 16.
3. Rich Marshall, *God @ Work* (Shippensburg, PA: Destiny Image Publishers, Inc., 2000).
4. Jarrod Gollihare, "Reggie White Remembered," *Charisma Magazine*, Lake Mary, Florida, March 2005, p. 23.

ABOUT THE AUTHOR

Dick Bernal has been in ministry for over 40 years. He and his wife Carla were Youth Leaders in the late 70's then pioneered Jubilee Christian Center in San Jose, Calif. in 1980. Jubilee became a MegaChurch and in 2018 they turned Jubilee over to Ron and Hope Carpenter and is now Redemption Church. Dick continues to travel and release his unique anointing on and over Churches, Ministries, Pastors, business leaders, and God's people.

You may contact Pastor Dick at Dickbernal44@gmail.com
Jubilee Legacy Int'l
3941 Park Dr. Ste 20743
El Dorado Hills, CA 95762-4549

THE REAL YOU – *The Real You* is written to help with the discovery, understanding and walking in the fullness of who we are in Christ. Dick Bernal and Larry Huggins share the secret they discovered early on that set them apart from the crowd. They join forces to walk us through the Bible discovering the IN HIM scriptures that identify who we are, what we have and what we can do through our divine union with Christ.

I HEAR A SOUND – Your coming abundance has a sound. Everything in existence started with the sound of God's voice. Are you listening? Do you believe God wants you to prosper and be successful? *I Can Hear a Sound* was written to help you have your breakthrough and will give you pleasure beyond measure! The anointing on the message of this book is prophetic and is addressed to you! Dick Bernal shares his amazing story of divine promotion, breakthrough, abundance and dreams coming true. It can change lives dramatically for God's glory and kingdom advancement.